CW00944056

The People and the State

Protest has proliferated in the early part of the twenty-first century, forcing change in political systems and challenging established patterns of behaviour. The factors driving these protests range from religion and inequality through to the effectiveness of the state and its role in protecting the rights of citizens. The growth in discontent represented by these protests potentially threatens the stability of the state by raising questions about the right of governments to govern. Anger and frustration embodied in many of these actions has resulted in the growth of support for populist political actors promising simplified solutions to the complex underlying issues. In this way, the inability of the state to address the claims of its population potentially places its continued viability at risk. The cases in this collection examine a range of protest movements from around the world, in both democratic and authoritarian political systems, to provide an overview of contemporary issues and protest forms. Addressing contemporary protest in this manner is an important task in supporting our understanding of the root causes of the current tensions and their possible future effects.

This book is a compilation of articles from a special issue of *Contemporary Social Science* with additional papers selected from *Contemporary Politics, Journal of Contemporary China* and *Democratization*.

Thomas O'Brien is a Lecturer in the Centre for International Security and Resilience, Cranfield University, at the Defence Academy of the United Kingdom, UK. His research interests include leadership during democratisation, environmental politics and social movements.

Contemporary Issues in Social Science
Series editor: David Canter, *University of Huddersfield, UK*

Contemporary Social Science, the journal of the **Academy of Social Sciences**, is an inter-disciplinary, cross-national journal which provides a forum for disseminating and enhancing theoretical, empirical and/or pragmatic research across the social sciences and related disciplines. Reflecting the objectives of the Academy of Social Sciences, it emphasises the publication of work that engages with issues of major public interest and concern across the world, and highlights the implications of that work for policy and professional practice.

The *Contemporary Issues in Social Science* book series contains the journal's most cutting-edge special issues. Leading scholars compile thematic collections of articles that are linked to the broad intellectual concerns of *Contemporary Social Science,* and as such these special issues are an important contribution to the work of the journal. The series editor works closely with the guest editor(s) of each special issue to ensure they meet the journal's high standards. The main aim of publishing these special issues as a series of books is to allow a wider audience of both scholars and students from across multiple disciplines to engage with the work of *Contemporary Social Science* and the Academy of Social Sciences.

The People and the State

Twenty-First Century Protest Movement

Edited by
Thomas O'Brien

Routledge
Taylor & Francis Group

LONDON AND NEW YORK

First published 2018
by Routledge
2 Park Square, Milton Park, Abingdon, Oxon, OX14 4RN, UK

and by Routledge
711 Third Avenue, New York, NY 10017, USA

Routledge is an imprint of the Taylor & Francis Group, an informa business

Chapters 1, 2, 4, 5, 7, 9 and 11 © 2018 Academy of Social Science
Chapters 3, 6, 8, and 10 © 2018 Taylor and Francis

All rights reserved. No part of this book may be reprinted or reproduced
or utilised in any form or by any electronic, mechanical, or other means,
now known or hereafter invented, including photocopying and recording,
or in any information storage or retrieval system, without permission in
writing from the publishers.

Trademark notice: Product or corporate names may be trademarks or
registered trademarks, and are used only for identification and
explanation without intent to infringe.

British Library Cataloguing in Publication Data
A catalogue record for this book is available from the British Library

ISBN13: 978-1-138-03808-0

Typeset in Times New Roman
by RefineCatch Limited, Bungay, Suffolk

Publisher's Note
The publisher accepts responsibility for any inconsistencies that may have
arisen during the conversion of this book from journal articles to book chapters,
namely the possible inclusion of journal terminology.

Disclaimer
Every effort has been made to contact copyright holders for their permission to
reprint material in this book. The publishers would be grateful to hear from any
copyright holder who is not here acknowledged and will undertake to rectify
any errors or omissions in future editions of this book.

Contents

CONTENTS

Citation Information

The chapters in this book were originally published in a variety of Taylor and Francis journals. When citing this material, please use the original page numbering for each article, as follows:

Chapter 1
Populism, protest and democracy in the twenty-first century
Thomas O'Brien
Contemporary Social Science, volume 10, issue 4 (December 2015) pp. 337–348

Chapter 2
The origins of labour autonomy in authoritarian Tunisia
Keenan Wilder
Contemporary Social Science, volume 10, issue 4 (December 2015) pp. 349–363

Chapter 3
The legacy of compliant activism in autocracies: post-Communist experience
Alexander Libman and Vladimir Kozlov
Contemporary Politics, volume 23, issue 2 (June 2017) pp. 195–213

Chapter 4
Context, image and the case of the Shahbag movement
Sanchari De
Contemporary Social Science, volume 10, issue 4 (December 2015) pp. 364–374

Chapter 5
Social movements and constitutional politics in Latin America: reconfiguring alliances, framings and legal opportunities in the judicialisation of abortion rights in Brazil
Alba Ruibal
Contemporary Social Science, volume 10, issue 4 (December 2015) pp. 375–385

Chapter 6
Pollution, Institutions and Street Protests in Urban China
Yang Zhong and Wonjae Hwang
Journal of Contemporary China, volume 25, issue 98 (March 2016) pp. 216–232

Chapter 7

Political activists' frames in times of post-politics: evidence from Kirchnerism in Argentina and Podemos in Spain
Iban Diaz-Parra, Beltran Roca and Silvina Romano
Contemporary Social Science, volume 10, issue 4 (December 2015) pp. 386–400

Chapter 8

Protest in South Africa: motives and meanings
Tom Lodge and Shauna Mottiar
Democratization, volume 23, issue 5 (August 2016) pp. 819–837

Chapter 9

Intellectual radicals challenging the state: the case of Hizb ut-Tahrir in the west
Elisa Orofino
Contemporary Social Science, volume 10, issue 4 (December 2015) pp. 401–412

Chapter 10

When actions speak louder than words: examining collective political protests in Central Asia
Dilshod Achilov
Democratization, volume 23, issue 4 (June 2016) pp. 699–722

Chapter 11

Political religion and the rise of transnational right and left-wing social movements since 9/11
David Martin Jones
Contemporary Social Science, volume 10, issue 4 (December 2015) pp. 413–426

For any permission-related enquiries please visit:
http://www.tandfonline.com/page/help/permissions

Notes on Contributors

Dilshod Achilov is an Assistant Professor of Political Science at East Tennessee State University, USA. His research focuses on the dynamics of contentious politics, comparative democratization, civil society and politics in the Islamic world; and his work has appeared in journals such as the *Journal of Civil Society*, *Problems of Post Communism*, and *Asia Policy*.

Sanchari De is a Doctoral Student in Film Studies at Jadavpur University, India, and an Erasmus Mundus fellow in Communication and Media at Lund University, Sweden. Her research interests include digital media, memory and political mobilization, in addition to films, specifically New Iranian Cinema.

Iban Diaz-Parra is a Postdoctoral Fellow in the Department of Human Geography at the Universidad de Seville, Spain. His research focuses on urban social geography and social movements, and he has been published in journals such as the *International Journal of Urban Sciences* and *Scripta Nova*.

Wonjae Hwang is an Associate Professor in the Department of Political Science at the University of Tennessee, USA. His research interests focus on globalization, compensation politics and Korean politics.

David Martin Jones is an Honorary Reader in Politics at the University of Queensland, Brisbane, Australia, and a Visiting Professor in the War Studies Department at Kings College, University of London, UK.

Vladimir Kozlov is an Associate Professor and Researcher at the Higher School of Economics in the Institute of Demography, Moscow, Russia. His research interests lie in population and migration studies, problems of ageing and institutional and new political economics.

Alexander Libman is an Associate at the German Institute for International and Security Affairs in Berlin, Germany. His research focuses on the Russian sub-national politics, regional cooperation and integration in Eurasia and the role of historical legacies in post-Communist transition.

Tom Lodge is Professor of Peace and Conflict Studies and Dean of the Faculty of Arts, Humanities and Social Sciences, University of Limerick, Ireland. His most recent book is *Sharpeville: An Apartheid Massacre and Its Consequences* (2011).

Shauna Mottiar is Senior Lecturer in Development Studies in the School of Built Environment and Development Studies, University of KwaZulu-Natal, South Africa. Her research is centred on social movements and social protest in South Africa, and her work has appeared in *Development and Change*, the *Journal of Contemporary African Studies*, and *Politikon*.

NOTES ON CONTRIBUTORS

Thomas O'Brien is a Lecturer in the Centre for International Security and Resilience, Cranfield University, at the Defence Academy of the United Kingdom, UK. His research interests include leadership during democratisation, environmental politics and social movements.

Elisa Orofino is a PhD student based at the Asia Institute, University of Melbourne, Australia. Her research project is focused on the radicalisation of young Muslims in the West, taking the group Hizb ut-Tahrir (HT) as a case study. Her main research interests are radicalization in the West, social protest movements, Islamist groups and Hizb ut-Tahrir.

Beltran Roca is Lecturer in Sociology at the Universidad de Cádiz, Spain. His research interests are social movements, trade unions and third sector, and he has published articles in journals such as *Labor History*, *Anthropology of Work Review*, *Anthropological Quarterly* and *Voluntas*.

Silvina Romano is a Researcher at CONICET in the Institute for the Study of Latin America and Caribe, University of Buenos Aires, Argentina. Her research focuses on the relationship between the USA and Latin America, critique of development aid, integration, underdevelopment and dependency, and democracy and security in the USA.

Alba Ruibal is a Full-Time Researcher at CONICET (National Research Council, Argentina) and the Center for Legal and Social Research, UNC, Argentina. Her current research focuses on legal mobilisation, judicial politics in Latin America, women's rights and the impact of federalism on legal strategies.

Keenan Wilder is an Independent Researcher, who received his MA in Near Eastern Studies from New York University, USA. His research focuses on the political economy of the Middle East and North Africa with a special interest in Tunisia.

Yang Zhong is a Changjiang Scholar in the School of International and Public Affairs at Shanghai Jiao Tong University, China, and a Professor in the Department of Political Science at the University of Tennessee, USA. His main research interests include Chinese political culture and local government and politics in China.

Foreword

The win for Donald Trump in the US presidential election raises many questions about democracy and the ways in which populist movements and protest against the state are emerging in the twenty-first century. His success reflects a trend in mass protests against existing regimes that have been endemic in both democratic and non-democratic states over the last twenty years. The review of these matters in this volume is therefore very timely.

A central point made in the introduction by Thomas O'Brien is that democracy can take many forms and operate in many different ways. Consequently, it does not always contribute to the well-being of all citizens. When there are perceived to be great inequalities that the existing government does not address, there is a tendency for conventional political processes to be undermined and protest against the established political order to emerge. In Western democracies, populist movements and politicians capitalise on this natural expression of discontent, but the results are not always good for democracy. They can undermine the possibility of the state providing effective governance to deal with the concerns that underpin the protests.

An interesting illustration of how protests can emerge as a response to democratic inadequacies is given by Tom Lodge and Shauna Mottiar in their examination of the record levels of protest in present-day South Africa. They argue that, in a country still developing as a democracy after so many years of autocratic rule, these protests are best seen as a form of engagement with the political process. New social movements can emerge from these communal activities, providing opportunities for political re-engagement.

The aftermath of autocratic governance may leave its mark on emerging democracies in a number of different ways. Alexander Libman and Vladimir Kozlov demonstrate, when considering contemporary Russia, that one way is the maintenance of the habit of what they call 'compliant activism'. People continue to support an implicit autocracy because of internalised norms that become self-enforcing.

A broader examination of post-Soviet, collective political action is provided by Dilshod Achilov in his consideration of attitudes in Central Asian states towards elite-challenging protests. He argues that there are complex processes at work, but that, as elsewhere, economic grievances and limits over access to other resources fuel both low-risk and high-risk challenges to the hegemony of the elite. Furthermore, the likelihood of participation in these protests can be predicted from membership of Islamic religious groups and social networks.

The consideration of protests in a number of different countries throws into high relief the many different agencies that need to be considered if these protests are to be understood. One interesting example is provided by Keenan Wilder in this volume. He examines the 2011 Tunisian revolution in relation to the waxing and waning powers of Tunisia's national trade union. He shows that the strength or weakness of labour organisation was an integral part of the political process in Tunisia. The disruptive role of labour unrest both before and after 2011 influenced the nature of the revolution and its resultant politics. But although organised labour is less influential, in most countries these days it was once very important. Perhaps the resurgence of right-wing politicians will reawaken the labour movement?

In contrast to the role of the trade union movement in Tunisia, Alba Ruibal from Argentina draws attention to the significance of the judiciary in Brazil in bringing about social change. In particular she shows how feminist organisations framed the abortion issue as a rights matter in the constitutional courts. The Brazilian Supreme Federal Tribunal, as Ruibal points out, was gaining constitutional powers in the early part of the twenty-first century. These were harnessed by campaigners to liberalise the abortion law. This, then, is a powerful illustration of the role of an independent judiciary as a bulwark of democracy. A role that is all too often undervalued.

The redirection of political action to the courts in Brazil is one illustration of what Iban Diaz-Parra and his colleagues from the University of Seville call the 'post-political situation'. This is when there is such a mistrust of the possibility of large scale political change that formal partici-pation in politics and state institutions is regarded as pointless. Diaz-Parra argues that, both in the social protests in Argentina in 2001 and the mobilisation of the *indignados* in Spain in 2011, one primary, motivating narrative was that 'professional politicians are burglars'. One important consequence of this endemic distrust in earlier forms of politics is an acceptance of existing economic structures and a focus on short-term, pragmatic issues rather than grand ideological movements.

An extreme example of the open rejection of political democracy as the foundation of a protest movement is explored by Elisa Orofino from the University of Melbourne. She describes the rhetoric of Hizb ut-Tahrir, an Islamic protest movement that has a presence in 45 countries. It's most fundamental argument is that nation states have no legitimacy and that a cross-national caliphate is more reliable, accountable and effective. This radical movement can therefore be recognised as drawing on similar disgust with existing political processes to many other protest movements. It may be taken as a warning of how extremists can hijack public concerns if conven-tional politics does not address them.

Besides these pragmatic influences on the nature of the political process, seen in Tunisia and Brazil, attention also needs to be paid to symbolic issues. Sanchari De from Lund University explores the role of symbolic images in the formation and support of protest movements. She takes as her example the image of Kader Molla flashing a V for victory sign after being sentenced to life imprisonment. This photograph of an accused war criminal became a dominant memory that supported the Shahbag movement in Bangladesh. It became what she calls 'a material codification of the tension and struggle' that the movement enshrined. This is one of many exam-ples of how populist leaders create and manipulate symbols to great effect. Trump's campaign was a prime example of turning reality into simplified images, such as a 'wall' and 'banning Muslims' that were very influential.

A more optimistic note is struck by David Jones from the University of Queensland. For although he reviews the widespread growth of anti-democratic right-wing parties, and leaderless networks right across Western Europe, the Middle-East, the US, Australia and New Zealand, he comes to the conclusion that 'democracies have a way of stumbling through crises'. He sees the various populist protests as being energised by a fervour that is analogous to religious belief systems, promulgating aspirations for a 'harmonious new order', with or without an all-powerful God to encourage it happening. In the end, the pragmatism of democratic politics tends to over-ride existing belief systems, even though that may take some time.

The contributions to this special issue from around the world show that Trump's success can be seen as part of a global antagonism towards conventional governance. The limitations of the predominant neoliberal democracies, which have increased inequalities, have led many to despair of influencing political outcomes. This has encouraged the growth of alternative movements seeking different routes for social change. As Trump himself indicated in his acceptance speech, he did not lead a political party but a protest movement. That blurring of the boundaries between social movements and political parties can possibly be seen as a return to the routes of radical politics. But taking it in an unpredictable direction.

David Canter

Populism, protest and democracy in the twenty-first century

Thomas O'Brien

Protest is an important measure of discontent within society and can be seen as a form of politics by other means. In periods of uncertainty and instability, protest can harm incumbent regimes by heightening and amplifying tensions, potentially leading to crisis and collapse in extreme cases. The wave of democratisation that characterised the last quarter of the twentieth century saw a number of weak democracies emerge and struggle, whereas other regime changes saw new forms of authoritarianism emerge. Crises in the early twenty-first century have shaken both democratic and non-democratic states, leading to large-scale 'occupy' movements and uprisings that have brought down regimes in the former Soviet Union and across the Middle East and North Africa (MENA)[1] region. Common to these diverse protests is a feeling of antipolitics that draws on populist and religious motivations to challenge the state. The aim of this paper is to consider the significance of this apparent wave of protest and identify the driving factors. In order to do this, the paper examines arguments around the quality of democracy (and autocracy), state–social movement interactions and the rise of populist and religious movements.

Introduction

The early part of the twenty-first century has been characterised by an apparent proliferation of protest. Recent actions around Occupy and its manifestations echoed and appeared in some senses to resurrect the anti/alter-globalisation movement of the 1990s (Tarrow, 2013; Wood, 2012). However, protest has not been confined solely to Europe and North America; the Colour Revolutions and the Arab Spring demonstrated the way in which large-scale contentious events were able to diffuse to different geographical regions (Bunce & Wolchik, 2011; della Porta, 2014). The food riots that captured the world's attention in 2007–2008 fit within this wave of protest, reinforcing the effects of globalisation on dispersed groups (O'Brien, 2012). The spread of technology has also facilitated the spread of information and resources in these protests and enabled the targets to respond more quickly (Bennett & Segerberg, 2013). Protests in other parts of the world were not unique; they echoed and were reminiscent of protests in the 1980s that contributed to the fall of communism and challenged the hegemony of global organisations such as the IMF and World Bank (della Porta, 2014; Walton & Seddon, 1994).

In the majority of the recent protests, the state has been the target of claims, as people seek remedies for perceived injustices and problems. These claims are also being presented in a very different context, as the wave of democratisation that characterised the last quarter of the twentieth century has slowed and arguably began to recede (Diamond, 2015; Huntington, 1991). The promise of prosperity and freedom following the end of the Cold War has been challenged by events that highlight the relative weakness of the state in the face of non-state actors and global trends. Just as the Occupy movement sought to challenge the power of big business and corporate greed, new (and old) nationalist movements have emerged to question the underlying premise of globalisation.

Disillusionment with politics and a rising populist tide has seen far right groups such as Golden Dawn (GD) and the *Alternative für Deutschland* (AfD) perform well across Europe and enabled Donald Trump to secure the nomination of the Republican Party for the 2016 presidential elections (Allin, 2016; Berbuir, Lewandowsky, & Siri, 2015; Ellinas, 2015). The reaction of the state to these challenges has varied, depending on the nature of the claim and the resources available to deal with it. Uncertainty over the role and function of the state coupled with the rise of extreme ideologies has led to a search for scapegoats and targets for the rage that has resulted. The manifestation of religious terrorism has provided one such focus and enabled some states to find a target for the frustrations of their populations.

In contrast to the late-twentieth century when globalisation was on the march and increased openness was seen as the future, the twenty-first century appears to favour retrenchment and a closure of opportunities. The reaction against established politics has been widespread and led to the emergence of oppositional movements in a variety of forms. The aim of this paper is to consider the significance of this apparent wave of protest and identify the driving factors. The remainder of the paper is divided into three sections that reflect the core themes. The first section considers the arguments around quality of democracy, considering the extent to which weak democracies are able to resist the authoritarian temptation. In the second section, the characteristics of civil society are outlined, examining the nature of the interaction between social movements and the state. Finally, the focus shifts to the rise of populist and religious movements in response to the crises underpinning the contemporary environment of antipolitics to determine the extent of the threat they pose to practice of democracy.

Weak democracies and authoritarian challenges

The last quarter of the twentieth century saw a widespread pattern of democratisation as authoritarian regimes were overthrown or collapsed. Huntington (1991) defined this period as the third wave of democratisation, as it followed two earlier periods of democratic advance and subsequent recession. This was a period of optimism, as it was argued that in a wide range of cases, removing authoritarian regimes would open the space for democratic regimes to flourish, exemplified by the negotiated transition in Spain following the death of Francisco Franco (Linz & Stepan, 1996). Despite the early optimism, it soon became apparent that moving towards fully fledged democracy was not a simple or linear process. A central challenge in this regard was the legacies of the prior regime that continue to cast a shadow in the form of 'behavioural patterns, rules, relationships, social and political situations, norms, procedures, and institutions' (Hite & Morlino, 2004, p. 26).

As Lagerspetz (2001) noted, attitudes of distrust in the former Soviet countries hindered the development of generalised forms of trust that would facilitate effective institutions of governance (see also Morris & Polese, 2015). Managing legacies that have solidified over time and become part of the cultural landscape presents a significant challenge, as it requires changes to established behaviours and also threatens the position of powerholders. During periods of democratisation, choices are limited by non-democratic legacies, as the culture of democracy and associated norms are still being embedded within society (see Weßels, 2015). However, more established democracies may also face challenges to their legitimacy where they are unable to meet expectations as a result of external or internal crises.

When considering processes of democratisation and the strength of commitment, it is important to examine the prior regime type and mode of transition. Non-democratic regimes that exercised a greater degree of control, such as the Soviet Union, leave a stronger imprint than those like Ben Ali's Tunisia, where the regime focused more narrowly on enriching the elite (see O'Brien, 2015a). Establishing a democratic political system in such an environment requires the construction of mechanisms for representation, accountability and rule of law (see Morlino, 2004a). Additionally, the way in which the old regime is replaced determines the options available and the path it follows. Outlining the key features shaping the mode of transition, Munck and Leff (1997, p. 345) pointed to the level of 'elite competition ... institutional rules ... [and the] key actors' acceptance or rejection of the rules of the game.' Transitions involving a negotiated resolution like those in South Africa and South Korea arguably have the potential to be more durable, as they give both incumbents and challengers a stake in the outcome (see O'Brien, 2016). By contrast, regime changes driven by mass mobilisation threaten to permanently displace incumbent elites and therefore increase the chances that they will reject the new democratic procedures. The events in Egypt following the removal of President Mubarak in 2011 show the risks, as the military intervention that overthrew President Morsi in 2013 (Pinfari, 2013) ushered in a harder form of authoritarianism than had existed previously (Springborg, 2016). While removal of a non-democratic regime by either means is not a guarantee that a strong democracy will result, events during the initial transition will influence who participates and the options open to them.

Escaping from the grasp of the authoritarian political system is only part of the transformation required to achieve democratic stability. Considering the features of democracy, Tilly (2007, p. 189) argued that 'a regime is democratic to the extent that political relations between the state and its citizens feature broad, equal, protected and mutually binding consultation.' Central to this definition is the idea that democracy exists on a spectrum. As a state democratises, it moves along this spectrum, developing new tools and mechanisms such as a free press, term limits and effective forms of participation necessary to reach the ideal end point. Such progress is not guaranteed, as regimes face pressures to maintain the status quo and not threaten power holders within society, which may lead to progress stalling or reversing over time. In this context, In this context, Hui (2015) considered the shift in the response of the Hong Kong government to the 2014 Umbrella movement. Facing challenges from below, the government moved away from earlier promises of democratic reform towards a more pro-Beijing, authoritarian form of governance. The recognition of the difficulties of democratisation initially led to the emergence of classifications of semi-authoritarian/semi-democratic regime types that were stranded partially along the spectrum between authoritarianism and democracy (see Bogaards, 2009). These classifications point to the messiness and reality of political regimes and the need to consider their distinctive characteristics in order to assess the extent to which they reach the ideal Tilly identified.

In an attempt to assess the risk of authoritarian reversion or de-democratisation, attention has turned to measures of quality of democracy. At the most basic level, Högström (2014, p. 405) argues 'that if democracies have a low level of legitimacy and ... low effectiveness' they can be classified as weak. Addressing the factors that determine the quality of a democratic regime and therefore its strength, Morlino (2004a, pp. 12–13) points to rule of law, accountability, responsiveness, freedom and equality. These interconnected factors shape the extent to which the regime is seen as legitimate, as well as its ability to address the concerns of its population. Rule of law and accountability are arguably most significant in a democratic regime, as they provide the space and mechanisms by which democratic participation can be facilitated and managed. The extent to which a particular regime can meet these dimensions is in turn 'driven by various combinations of [contingent] choices and concrete opportunities.' (Morlino, 2004b, p. 21) Identifying manifestations of weak or lower quality democracies, Morlino (2004a, p. 28) identifies features such as an absence of electoral alternatives, suppression of opposition voices and restrictions on the media. This highlights the fact that weak democratic regimes may serve the interests of the ruling elite, as currently illustrated by states such as Hungary (Kornai, 2015) and Turkey (Öniş, 2015) that have seen dominant parties introduce reforms to undermine the rule of law and accountability.

In a recent critique of the literature on quality of democracy, Munck (2016) has advanced a number of challenges. An important element of his argument is that the concept of quality of democracy should not be used solely for assessing democratic regimes (Munck, 2016, pp. 9–10), as applying:

> the concept of quality of democracy to cases deemed to be democracies removes from consideration a key implication of this new line of research: the possibility that the conventional description of a country as a democracy should be revised.

The risk is that countries that are labelled democratic in this perspective will be more likely to retain the label, regardless of their actual practices and behaviour. This is a particular concern in so-called weak democracies where periods of de-democratisation as observed in Turkey may not be recognised as such. Such recognition allows for critical assessment of states identified as established democracies, as well as more firmly authoritarian regimes, enabling their legitimacy and effectiveness to be opened to discretion on the terms such as those identified by Morlino (2004a). In bringing the issue of assessment of quality of democracy to the fore, Munck (2016) argues that it is essential to bring government decision-making into the equation, moving beyond simple measures of democracy, to determine where power lies.

The challenge facing democracies ranges from authoritarian reversion in the case of weak democracies to questions around governability in more established political systems. Identifying the source of the threat, Weßels (2015, p. 95) reminds us of the important point that:

> Democracy is the only regime that allows for contestation of its own rules. Thus, it can be questioned, its legitimacy can vanish, and the acceptance that the majority will create binding decisions for all can disappear. If this happens, democracy is in question.

The emergence of strong and arguably successful authoritarian regimes, such as China, present a model that groups within democratic states may seek to emulate if existing practices are deemed to be failing. Recent analyses of 'black knights' point to the way in which such regimes may seek to influence practices in neighbouring states (see Bader, 2015; Way, 2015). With the democratic recession that has characterised the past decade (Diamond, 2015) and the increasing recognition of the challenge posed by subnational authoritarian regimes (Behrend & Whitehead, 2016), domestic challenges to democracy must increasingly be taken seriously to guard against a crisis of democracy. While such a crisis will be felt more acutely in weakly democratised states, established democracies are also vulnerable to democratic regression (as suggested by Munck, 2016).

Social movements, civil society and protest

Within the literature on the quality of democracy, civil society features as an important element, providing both legitimacy and ensuring accountability (Morlino, 2004a). Defining the outlines of civil society, Linz and Stepan (1996, p. 7) have argued that it is:

an arena of the polity where self-organizing groups, movements and individuals, relatively autonomous from the state, attempt to articulate values, create associations and solidarities, and advance
their interests.

The breadth of this arena will be determined by the nature of the state, with authoritarian systems
reducing and in some cases controlling organisations outside the formal state apparatus (Johnston,
2011). Where civil society activity is constrained in this way, associational activity declines, as
individuals become isolated, demoralised and focused on individualistic needs (Galston, 2000).
Even in contexts where civil society has freedom to operate, Chandhoke (2001, p. 8) argues
that it is not possible to 'assume civil society is emancipated or abstracted from the ethos that
permeates' the economic and political spheres. Wilder (2015) notes the embedded nature of
civil society in his analysis of the labour movement in Tunisia prior to 2011. This is reflected
in the way in which the labour movement was able to exercise its influence at moments of
crisis and instability, advancing and withdrawing, as the pattern of opportunities and threats
shifted. This clearly illustrates the way the civil society environment in a particular state is
bound up in the interaction between social, political and economic constraints and interests.

Associational activity is at the core of civil society, as individuals interact and groups form to
pursue particular interests. The state sets the terms on which this activity takes place, ensuring that
it is not harmful to the wider interests of the population. In a more direct manner, the state undertakes activities that range from providing a legal and political setting through to supporting and
influencing the shape and activities of civil society itself (Chandhoke, 2001). Civil society actors
in turn place demands on the state, seeking to bring about changes that serve perceived priorities
(Whittington, 1998). While civil society is generally viewed in a positive light, Berman (1997,
p. 427) notes that it can present risks where:

> political institutions are weak and/or the existing political regime is perceived to be ineffectual and
> illegitimate, then civil society activity may become an alternative to politics, increasingly absorbing
> citizens' energies and satisfying their basic needs ... civil society activity in these circumstances
> signals governmental and party failure and may bode ill for the regime's future.

In states that are weakly democratised, civil society organising may therefore present a threat to
the stability of the state. Considering how civil society asserts its claims, Kopecký and Mudde
(2003) argue that civil society is a sphere in which various groups mobilise at various times
and that non-violent protest provides the voice with which citizens communicate with the political
elite.

Contentious politics in the form of protest and direct action provides an important tool with
which civil society actors can present their claims (see Travaglino, 2014). Tilly (2008, p. 5)
defined contentious politics as 'interactions in which actors make claims bearing on someone
else's interests, in which governments appear either as targets, initiators of claims, or third
parties.' The breadth of the concept means that it is able to capture a full range of activities undertaken by civil society actors, ranging from meetings and demonstrations to actions that threaten
the stability of the state. Further teasing out these understandings, Sewell (2001, p. 55) makes the
case that it 'might also be defined as concerted social action that has the goal of overcoming deep
rooted structural disadvantage.' Dealing with these claims, the state determines and conveys
which actions are prescribed, tolerated and forbidden, with repercussions associated with each
(Tilly & Tarrow, 2007). As De (2015) notes, competing interpretations of events often serve as
triggers for protest, revealing submerged tensions. Examining the Shahbag movement in Bangladesh, she argues that a single photograph activated feelings of historical injustice and contemporary inequalities, leading to large-scale mobilisation. This case reinforces the fact that the limits of

what the state permits are shaped by what is deemed socially acceptable by society, as well as by the level of democracy and capacity within a particular state.

Protest is an important tool for civil society actors, as it disrupts and challenges these settled understandings and practices. Categorising the forms of protest open to such actors, Tarrow (2011, p. 99) argues that the 'repertoire of contention offers movements three broad types of collective action – disruption, violence and contained behavior.' The disruptive form of protest is the most effective in generating attention, as it 'incorporates claims, selects objects of claims, includes collective self-representations, and/or adopts means that are either unprecedented or forbidden within the regime in question.' (see also Drury & Stott, 2011; McAdam, Tarrow, & Tilly, 2001, p. 8) Contained behaviour represents a form of action that uses formal channels to pursue claims and may be seen as more legitimate, given the particular context or the issue (see Doherty & Hayes, 2014).

Ruibal (2015; see also Abers & Tatagiba, 2015) argues that in Brazil, the courts have served as a key venue for abortion activists to achieve change in social and political context where other channels are closed. Where such formal mechanisms are weak or absent, the possibilities of less contentious forms of civil society activity are also reduced and violence may be seen as a legitimate option (see O'Brien & Podder, 2012). This is particularly significant in regimes with limited histories of democratic engagement or during periods of crisis when normal politics may be weakened.

By challenging the state in this way, civil society actors are able to test the limits of what is tolerated and force the state to take action. When responding to claims from civil society actors, states in turn can respond with 'a mix of concessions and repression' (Goldstone & Tilly, 2001, p. 185). While democratic regimes may be more likely to make concessions in the face of protest mobilisations, they will also likely make use of subtle forms of social control, generally falling short of repression, due to the costs involved. In addition to formal mechanisms for channelling and governing civil society behaviour, the state may also encourage and support countermovements (Gale, 1986) or seek to directly subvert organisations through the deployment of agents to infiltrate and undermine (Marx, 1974; O'Brien, 2015b).

In the relationship between the state and civil society, the nature of the regime is key in determining what civil society actors will deem to be acceptable. As Tilly and Tarrow (2007, p. 161) argue:

> In mainly democratic regimes, the repertoire of contention leans towards peaceful forms of contention that intersect regularly with representative institutions and produce social movement campaigns; in mainly authoritarian regimes, the repertoire leans towards lethal conflicts and tends to produce religious and ethnic strife, civil wars and revolutions.

As noted above, states that are weakly democratised or where the quality of democracy is in question may have less capacity to deal with demands from civil society, particularly where their legitimacy is in question. This weakness may in turn lead to radicalisation of civil society actions, as noted by Tilly and Tarrow (2007), or it may lead to an acceptance of oppressive measures to deal with perceived threats to the existing order (Galston, 2000).

Populism and religion in times of crisis

Alongside the apparent increase in the breadth and scale of protest in the early twenty-first century has been a resurgence of populism. This presents a difficult challenge to democratic regimes, in particular those that are weakly institutionalised. Populist challengers base their appeal on a 'claim to represent the rightful source of legitimate power – the people, whose interests and wishes have been ignored by self-interested politicians and politically-correct individuals.'

(Canovan, 2004, p. 242) Mudde and Kaltwasser (2013, p. 153) further note that 'populism has a "chameleonic" character: populism can be left-wing or right-wing, organized in top-down or bottom-up fashion, rely on strong leaders or even be leaderless.' Claims made by populist challengers can have resonance in democratic regimes, as they point to the mismatch between what is promised and what is delivered by a democratic regime, fostering feelings of disillusionment and cynicism (Högström, 2014). As democratic regimes rely on generating legitimacy among the population, such a challenge can threaten the viability and stability of the regime.

Populist appeals speak to a people in such a way that they place themselves outside the standard political arena, performing a type of antipolitics (Rosanvallon, 2008). Although the populist claims are impractical in modern politics, as the demands cannot realistically be satisfied, they do appeal to elements of the population who feel left out. In order to bolster what is ultimately a thin claim, Stanley (2008, p. 107) argues that populists must link their claims to existing ideological bases, in the sense that 'it does not so much overlap with as diffuse itself throughout full ideologies.' The result is that populists will 'take on the colour of their surroundings' (Canovan, 2004, p. 242) attaching themselves to issues that are relevant and significant for the particular time and place. In their definition of the will of the people, Plattner (2010, p. 88) argues that:

> populist movements tend to be antagonistic to cultural, linguistic, religious, and racial minorities ... Those who differ from the majority in basic cultural traits are more typically viewed as enemies of the people rather than as potential allies.

In defining who constitutes the people, populist challengers 'may pursue problematic goals such as the exclusion of ethnic minorities and the erosion of horizontal accountability.' (Mudde and Kaltwasser, 2013, p. 149) The result is that populists potentially undermine and disrupt the current political order and create discord within society in order to achieve their aims.

The threat posed by populist actors is greater in weak democracies, as the institutions to manage such demands and address claims from the population are less well developed. Democratic political systems are in constant fluctuation, as they adjust to demands from below, with the resilience of the particular regime determined by its ability to manage this fluidity. Periods of crisis and uncertainty provide ample opportunity for populist actors to emerge and present their claims. In such situations, populists conceive of a zero sum game, where the opposition has to be delegitimised and removed from power permanently (Kaltwasser, 2012). This tendency provides a clear indication of the way in which populism can slide over into non-democratic regime forms, as 'the preservation [of democratic arrangements] also essentially requires the active support of citizens' (Abts & Rummens, 2007, p. 421).

Considering the situation in the Andes, Levitsky and Loxton (2013, p. 108) make the case 'that the primary catalyst behind competitive authoritarian emergence ... is populism, or the election of personalistic outsiders who mobilize mass constituencies via anti-establishment appeals.' The ability of populists to mobilise support is key to their success to the extent that Jansen (2011, p. 77) argues that it should be 'understood as a flexible way of animating political support' rather than an ideology in itself.

Populism in the twenty-first century has taken on a variety of forms that echo the specific socio-political and cultural context. The rise of groups such as Podemos in Spain (Kioupkiolis, 2016) and the Five Star Movement in Italy (Bordignon & Ceccarini, 2013) draw on anger with the political class following the 2008 economic crisis and its ongoing impact. Developing the ability of populist movements to gain purchase in the political sphere, Diaz-Parra, Roca, and Romano (2015) examine the rise of Podemos and Kirchnerism in Argentina to determine how such movements can make the transition and the challenges they face in doing so. As suggested by the emergence of abundant parties in recent years, they argue that crises provide an opportunity for movement parties to challenge post-political technical management that had prevailed previously.

Meanwhile in Greece and Germany, GD and the AfD have played on fears of refugees and religion to compound the uncertainty felt following the economic crisis (Berbuir et al., 2015; Ellinas, 2015). All of these groups explicitly claim to challenge the corrupt elite and emerge from a more bottom-up form of populist mobilisation. This contrasts with the situation in Hungary and Russia, where incumbent leaders have played on fears of outsiders and promises to protect the integrity of the state (Bozóki, 2011; Smyth, Sobolev, & Soboleva, 2013). Comparing the situation in Europe with that in Latin America, Kaltwasser (2012, p. 199; also Mudde and Kaltwasser, 2013) argues that while the populists in the latter are more inclusive, both 'show little respect for the rules of political competition … [as they] foster a moralization of politics'. The diversity of populist actors suggests that the feeling of antipolitics may indeed threaten the quality of democracy unless a way can be found to bring them inside the forum of 'normal politics'.

An important mobilising factor of populism in Europe has been the issue of religion. Debates around the representation of Islam in European society have been important since the early parts of the current century (El Hamel, 2002; Larsson & Lindekilde, 2009). However, the recent flows of refugees entering Europe coupled with the lasting effects of the economic crisis have heightened such tensions. Minkenberg (2007, p. 900) points to the challenge in that:

> established institutional and political arrangements to regulate the relationship between religion and politics in the framework of liberal democracies, long seen to have been solved once and for all, are challenged fundamentally and require new justifications.

As with the pattern of populism, the conflicts over religion point to the apparent inability of state institutions to regulate social order. Considering the nature of 'Islamism' from a social movement perspective, Bayat (2005) argues that it contributes to an imagined solidarity that is shaped by the context, rather than being a unified movement (see Yates, 2007). Orofino (2015) examines the role of Hizb ut-Tahrir as a social organisation working to advance its interests through non-traditional means. Drawing on research in Australia and the UK, she argues that the ultimate goal of the organisation presents a direct challenge to the state. Reaction against this perceived movement has animated the European right (see Bhatt, 2012), with the established church supporting and legitimising such views in some cases (on GD and the Greek Orthodox Church, see Papasthathis, 2015). Jones (2015) considers the broad spectrum of social movements of the right and left in the early twenty-first century and takes a more positive stance. Treating these emergent movements as political religions, he argues that although they present a threat to the continued viability of democracy, it has a way of stumbling through and will weather the current storm.

Conclusion

The early part of the twenty-first century has seen a number of significant, large-scale protests across the globe. Uprisings in the countries of the former Soviet Union and the MENA region have brought down non-democratic regimes and forced concessions. In contrast with the regime changes of the late twentieth century, the result has not been an apparent flourishing of democracy as was initially predicted. At the same time, protests in the established democracies of Western Europe and the Americas have targeted levels of inequality and forms of governance. These events are generally viewed positively, as they appear to represent the expression of the popular will and greater participation. However, the underlying drivers and outcome of such large-scale mobilisations are not necessarily positive. The collapse or loss of control in countries such as Libya and Syria has led to eruptions of sustained violence and radicalisation. In Western Europe and the United States, populist movements and politicians have capitalised on the discontent expressed and the antipolitical feeling to challenge the established political order.

Protest is a natural expression of discontent in society, enabling participants to present claims that are not being satisfied or addressed. In situations where the democracy is weak or the state lacks capacity to mediate between competing demands, the threat of democratic collapse or reversion is ever present. Where the state feels threatened by social protest, it may choose to adopt more authoritarian practices in order to safeguard the existing order, potentially amplifying grievances. For their part, civil society actors and social movements have a range of tactics and strategies available to press their claims on the state, ranging from large-scale protests to legal challenges and the formation of political parties. Motivations for the mobilisation of civil society actors are key. The contemporary antipolitical, populist mood presents a particular challenge, as it risks dismissing the role of the state in effective governance. In such a situation, social movements can therefore present a direct threat to the viability of the state in presenting an alternative vision of society. Ultimately, the ability of the state to cope with these threats will depend on its flexibility and adaptability. Democracy as a form of governance is most able to address the competing and conflictual demands entailed.

Acknowledgements

The author would like to thank David Canter and Petra Mäkelä for comments made on the earlier versions of this paper.

Disclosure statement

No potential conflict of interest was reported by the author.

Note

1. The MENA region stretches from Morocco to Iran.

References

Abers, R., & Tatagiba, L. (2015). Institutional activism: Mobilizing for women's health from inside the Brazilian bureaucracy. In F. Rossi & M. von Bülow (Eds.), *Social movement dynamics: New perspectives on theory and research from Latin America* (pp. 73–101). Farnham: Ashgate.

Abts, K., & Rummens, S. (2007). Populism versus democracy. *Political Studies, 55*, 405–424.

Allin, D. (2016). Donald Trump's America. *Survival, 58*, 221–228.

Bader, J. (2015). *China's foreign relations and the survival of autocracies*. London: Routledge.

Bayat, A. (2005). Islamism and social movement theory. *Third World Quarterly, 26*, 891–908.

Behrend, J., & Whitehead, L. (2016). The struggle for subnational democracy. *Journal of Democracy, 27*, 155–169.

Bennett, L., & Segerberg, A. (2013). *The logic of connective action: Digital media and the personalization of contentious politics*. Cambridge: Cambridge University Press.

Berbuir, N., Lewandowsky, M., & Siri, J. (2015). The AfD and its sympathisers: Finally a right-wing populist movement in Germany? *German Politics, 24*, 154–178.

Berman, S. (1997). Civil society and the collapse of the Weimar Republic. *World Politics, 49*, 401–429.

Bhatt, C. (2012). The new xenologies of Europe: Civil tensions and mythic pasts. *Journal of Civil Society, 8*, 307–326.

Bogaards, M. (2009). How to classify hybrid regimes? Defective democracy and electoral authoritarianism. *Democratization, 16*, 399–423.

Bordignon, F., & Ceccarini, L. (2013). Five stars and a cricket: Beppe Grillo shakes Italian politics. *South European Society and Politics, 18*, 427–449.

Bozóki, A. (2011). Occupy the state: The Orbán regime in Hungary. *Debatte: Journal of Contemporary Central and Eastern Europe, 19*, 649–663.

Bunce, V., & Wolchik, S. (2011). *Defeating authoritarian leaders in postcommunist countries*. Cambridge: Cambridge University Press.

Canovan, M. (2004). Populism for political theorists? *Journal of Political Ideologies, 9*, 241–252.

Chandhoke, N. (2001). The 'civil' and the 'political' in civil society. *Democratization, 8*, 1–24.

De, S. (2015). Context, image and the case of the Shahbag movement. *Contemporary Social Science, 10*(4), 364–374.

della Porta, D. (2014). *Mobilizing for democracy: Comparing 1989 and 2011*. Oxford: Oxford University Press.

Diamond, L. (2015). Facing up to the democratic recession. *Journal of Democracy, 26*, 141–155.

Diaz-Parra, I., Roca, B., & Romano, S. (2015). Political activists' frames in times of post-politics: Evidence from Kirchnerism in Argentina and Podemos in Spain. *Contemporary Social Science, 10*(4), 386–400.

Doherty, B., & Hayes, G. (2014). Having your day in court: Judicial opportunity and tactical choice in anti-GMO campaigns in France and the United Kingdom. *Contemporary Political Science, 47*, 3–29.

Drury, J., & Stott, C. (2011). Contextualising the crowd in contemporary social science. *Contemporary Social Science, 6*, 275–288.

El Hamel, C. (2002). Muslim diaspora in Western Europe: The Islamic headscarf (Hijab), the media and Muslim's integration in France. *Citizenship Studies, 6*, 293–308.

Ellinas, A. (2015). Neo-nazism in an established democracy: The persistence of Golden Dawn in Greece. *South European Society and Politics, 20*, 1–20.

Gale, R. (1986). Social movements and the state: The environmental movement, countermovement, and government agencies. *Sociological Perspectives, 29*, 202–240.

Galston, W. (2000). Civil society and the "art of association". *Journal of Democracy, 11*, 64–70.

Goldstone, J., & Tilly, C. (2001). Threat (and opportunity): Popular action and state response in the dynamics of contentious action. In R. Aminzade, J. Goldstone, D. McAdam, E. Perry, W. Sewell, Jr., S. Tarrow, & C. Tilly (Eds.), *Silence and voice in the study of contentious politics* (pp. 179–194). Cambridge: Cambridge University Press.

Hite, K., & Morlino, L. (2004). Problematizing the links between authoritarian legacies and 'good' democracy'. In K. Hite & P. Cesarini (Eds.), *Authoritarian legacies and democracy in Latin America and Southern Europe* (pp. 25–83). Notre Dame, IN: University of Notre Dame Press.

Högström, J. (2014). Democracies in crisis. *Contemporary Politics, 20*, 402–420.

Hui, V. (2015). The protests and beyond. *Journal of Democracy, 26*, 111–121.

Huntington, S. (1991). *The third wave: Democratization in the late 20th century*. Norman: University of Oklahoma Press.

Jansen, R. (2011). Populist mobilization: A new theoretical approach to populism. *Sociological Theory, 29*, 75–96.

Johnston, H. (2011). *States and social movements*. Cambridge: Polity Press.

Jones, D. (2015). Political religion and the rise of transnational right and left-wing social movements since 9/11. *Contemporary Social Science, 10*(4), 413–426.

Kaltwasser, C. (2012). The ambivalence of populism: Threat and corrective for democracy. *Democratization, 19*, 184–208.

Kioupkiolis, A. (2016). Podemos: The ambiguous promises of left-wing populism in contemporary Spain. *Journal of Political Ideologies, 21*, 99–120.

Kopecký, P., & Mudde, C. (2003). Rethinking civil society. *Democratization, 10*, 1–14.

Kornai, J. (2015). Hungary's u-turn: Retreating from democracy. *Journal of Democracy, 26*, 34–48.

Lagerspetz, M. (2001). From 'parallel polis' to 'the time of tribes': Post-socialism, social self-organization and post-modernity. *Journal of Communist Studies and Transition Politics, 17*, 1–18.

Larsson, G., & Lindekilde, L. (2009). Muslim claims-making in context: Comparing the Danish and Swedish Muhammad cartoons controversies. *Ethnicities, 9*, 361–382.

Levitsky, S., & Loxton, J. (2013). Populism and competitive authoritarianism in the Andes. *Democratization, 20*, 107–136.

Linz, J., & Stepan, A. (1996). *Problems of democratic transition and consolidation: Southern Europe, South America, and post-communist Europe*. Baltimore, MD: Johns Hopkins University Press.

Marx, G. (1974). Thoughts on a neglected category of social movement participant: The agent provocateur and the informant. *American Journal of Sociology, 80*, 402–442.

McAdam, D., Tarrow, S., & Tilly, C. (2001). *Dynamics of contention*. Cambridge: Cambridge University Press.

Minkenberg, P. (2007). Democracy and religion: Theoretical and empirical observations on the relationship between Christianity, Islam and liberal democracy. *Journal of Ethnic and Migration Studies, 33*, 887–909.

Morlino, L. (2004a). What is 'good' democracy? *Democratization, 11*, 10–32.

Morlino, L. (2004b). 'Good' and 'bad' democracies: How to conduct research into the quality of democracy. *Journal of Communist Studies and Transition Politics, 20*, 5–27.

Morris, J., & Polese, A. (Ed.). (2015). *Informal economies in post-socialist spaces: Practices, institutions and networks*. Basingstoke: Palgrave.

Mudde, C., & Kaltwasser, C. (2013). Exclusionary vs. inclusionary populism: Comparing contemporary Europe and Latin America. *Government and Opposition, 48*, 147–174.

Munck, G. (2016). What is democracy? A reconceptualization of the quality of democracy. *Democratization, 23*, 1–26.

Munck, G., & Leff, C. (1997). Modes of transition and democratization: South America and Eastern Europe in comparative perspective. *Comparative Politics, 29*, 343–362.

O'Brien, T. (2012). Food riots as representations of insecurity: Examining the relationship between contentious politics and human security. *Conflict, Security and Development, 12*, 31–49.

O'Brien, T. (2015a). The primacy of political security: Contentious politics and insecurity in the Tunisian revolution. *Democratization, 22*, 1209–1229.

O'Brien, T. (2015b). Social control and the New Zealand environmental movement. *Journal of Sociology, 51*, 785–798.

O'Brien, T. (2016). Unbuilding from the inside: Leadership and democratization in South Africa and South Korea. *Government and Opposition*. Advance online publication. doi:10.1017/gov.2015.41.

O'Brien, T., & Podder, S. (2012). Introduction. *Politics, Religion and Ideology, 13*, 429–437.

Öniş, Z. (2015). Monopolising the centre: The AKP and the uncertain path of Turkish democracy. *The International Spectator, 50*, 22–41.

Orofino, E. (2015). Intellectual radicals challenging the state: The case of Hizb ut-Tahrir in the West. *Contemporary Social Science, 10*(4), 401–412.

Papasthathis, K. (2015). Religious discourse and radical right politics in contemporary Greece, 2010–2014. *Politics, Religion and Ideology, 16*, 218–247.

Pinfari, M. (2013). The EU, Egypt and Morsi's rise and fall: 'Strategic patience' and its discontents. *Mediterranean Politics, 18*, 460–466.

Plattner, M. (2010). Populism, pluralism, and liberal democracy. *Journal of Democracy, 21*, 81–92.

Rosanvallon, P. (2008). *Counter-democracy: Politics in an age of distrust*. Cambridge: Cambridge University Press.

Ruibal, A. (2015). Social movements and constitutional politics in Latin America: Reconfiguring alliances, framings and legal opportunities in the judicialisation of abortion rights case in Brazil. *Contemporary Social Science, 10*(4), 375–385.

Sewell, Jr., W. (2001). Space in contentious politics. In R. Aminzade, J. Goldstone, D. McAdam, E. Perry, W. Sewell, Jr., S. Tarrow, & C. Tilly (Eds.), *Silence and voice in the study of contentious politics* (pp. 51–88). Cambridge: Cambridge University Press.

Smyth, R., Sobolev, A., & Soboleva, I. (2013). A well-organized party: Symbolic politics and the effect of pro-Putin rallies. *Problems of Post-Communism, 60*, 24–39.

Springborg, R. (2016). Caudillismo along the Nile. *The International Spectator, 51*, 74–85.

Stanley, B. (2008). The thin ideology of populism. *Journal of Political Ideologies, 13*, 95–110.

Tarrow, S. (2011). *Power in movement: Social movements and contentious politics* (3rd ed.). Cambridge: Cambridge University Press.

Tarrow, S. (2013). *The language of contention: Revolutions in words, 1688–2012*. Cambridge: Cambridge University Press.

Tilly, C. (2007). *Democracy*. Cambridge: Cambridge University Press.

Tilly, C. (2008). *Contentious performances*. Cambridge: Cambridge University Press.

Tilly, C., & Tarrow, S. (2007). *Contentious politics*. Boulder, CO: Paradigm.

Travaglino, G. (2014). Social sciences and social movements: The theoretical context. *Contemporary Social Science*, *9*, 1–14.

Walton, J., & Seddon, D. (1994). *Free markets and food riots: The politics of global adjustment*. London: Blackwell.

Way, L. (2015). The limits of autocracy promotion: The case of Russia in the "Near Abroad". *European Journal of Political Research*, *54*, 691–706.

Weßels, B. (2015). Political culture, political satisfaction and the rollback of democracy. *Global Policy*, *6*, 93–105.

Whittington, K. (1998). Revisiting Toqueville's America: Society, politics, and association in the nineteenth century. *American Behavioural Scientist*, *42*, 21–32.

Wilder, K. (2015). The origins of labour autonomy in authoritarian Tunisia. *Contemporary Social Science*, *10*(4), 349–363.

Wood, L. (2012). *Direct action, deliberation, and diffusion*. Cambridge: Cambridge University Press.

Yates, J. (2007). The resurgence of jihad and the specter of religious populism. *SAIS Review*, *27*, 127–144.

The origins of labour autonomy in authoritarian Tunisia

Keenan Wilder

Among the most remarkable things about the Tunisian revolution of 2011 was the role of the national trade union (UGTT). Joel Beinin has shown the critical importance this institutional power gave Tunisian workers in comparison to Egypt. I argue that its pre independence history is inadequate to understand this phenomenon given the weakness of Tunisian labour in the 1950s and 1960s. Instead, it can be traced to elite political crises of the 1970s, relatively continuous base militancy from 1970 to 2011 and the collapse of state military relations in the early 1990s. I use State Department archives combined with data from the International Labor Organization and the Tunisian Ministry of Social Affairs to make this case. These results support the idea that co-optation of Tunisian unions was far less extensive than pre 2011 studies suggested, but that labour unrest was less widespread and less disruptive to strategic industries in comparison to 2011 and after.

Introduction

The discussion of the 2011 Arab revolts too often revolves around a simplistic analysis of the people and the state that obscures the role of social class, and of working class politics in particular. Recently, a number of authors have begun to correct this, highlighting the central role of working class movements to these events. Authors such as Beinin (2015), Bishara (2012) and Zemni (2013) have shown how central working class movements were to the overthrow of authoritarian regimes in Egypt and Tunisia. Buehler (2015) further illustrates the major role of trade unions even when governments were able to survive, and shows how Moroccan public sector unions extracted material concessions the government had previously ruled out.

If labour protests were indeed a universal factor in the Arab revolutions, this might suggest that they cannot account for the enormous variance in their outcomes. Recent work by Beinin however suggests a different possibility. He argues that while workers' movements were central to the overthrow of authoritarian governments in both Tunisia and Egypt, the ability of Tunisian workers to force the national labour union, the UGTT (*Union General Tunisien du Travaile*) into confrontation with the regime has given them critical institutional and organisational capacity that Egyptian workers lacked. This ability stemmed from the fact that the UGTT was never fully subjugated to state authority, giving it a degree of relative autonomy that is highly unusual for the Arab world.

This paper tries to answer the question of how the UGTT was able to achieve and maintain a degree of autonomy from the state.[1] In particular, why the state allowed, or was forced to allow, an autonomous and often militant labour movement to both form and reproduce itself. While the UGTT was able to develop as an autonomous and powerful organisation prior to independence, it was very easily co-opted to state interests in the 1950s and 1960s. Despite falling real wages, strikes were all but unheard of between 1955 and 1969. The ideological pluralism, militancy and size of the current UGTT only emerged in the early 1970s.

Explaining how the UGTT's autonomy re-emerged so suddenly requires understanding the source of worker's influence generally. Bellin identifies two structural sources of workers' influence, the political power of numbers and the ability to disrupt economic activity (Bellin, 2002, pp. 123–124). Even when unionised workers have relatively small numbers they can still be powerful politically, since they can galvanise much broader social instability by providing the critical mass needed to give collective action credibility, as Buehler argued was the case for Moroccan unions in 2011. The essential commonality between worker's political and economic influence is that both require collective action, making labour's influence highly dependent on external political and economic factors.

When workers were able to exercise collective action independently, state officials faced a dilemma; if the UGTT supported the state against workers in the short run, it would undermine the credibility it needed to help the state in the long run. However, in circumstances where workers were unable to organise independently, the state faced no such trade-off between long-term and short-term stability and would have every reason to tightly control the UGTT, as it did from 1955 to 1969. While the political factors that initially allowed for the revitalisation of the UGTT in the early 1970s were highly contingent; the fact that UGTT leaders used this window of opportunity for a massive expansion drive laid the foundations for a more permanent shift in labour's structural influence.

Even more puzzling than the initial emergence of a relatively independent labour movement was its continuation under Tunisia's second president Zine Elabidine Ben Ali, whose rule combined increasing authoritarianism with economic liberalism; projects that were both antagonistic to labour and weakened its capacity to resist. While many of the factors that pushed the state towards collaboration with the UGTT since the 1970s continued to apply, this decision cannot be fully understood without considering the limits imposed by civil military relations. This is not to say that the Tunisian military has always stood against the use of violence in domestic politics, the army was used against protestors on several occasions under Bourguiba. Ironically, however, the arrival of a former army officer to power actually coincided with a total loss of confidence in the army's political loyalty, limiting the possible range of state responses to labour militancy. This insured Ben Ali could not more fundamentally alter the balance of power between the state and labour.

Labour and the state 1955–1969

The UGTT played a pivotal role in supporting Bourguiba and the nationalist movement prior to independence and secured generous promises both for workers' rights and the socialist development of the economy (Beinin, 2015, p. 19). While Bourguiba's financial backers had never been happy with his populism or his close ties to labour, the ability of the UGTT to deliver numbers and organisation was essential for both the Neo Destour and Bourguiba's political survival. However, after independence the importance of these two sources of pressure reversed themselves. Command of an authoritarian state made labour's political backing much less important, while at the same time he became much more dependent on the good will of Tunisian and French investors to maintain the national economy (Alexander, 1996, p. 117).

Bourguiba's removal of the UGTT's post-independence leader Ahmed Ben Salah has often been portrayed as an attempt to stop the rise of a dynamic political rival or to pre-empt his radical proposals for economic planning (Bellin, 2002, pp. 93–94; Moore, 1965, p. 83). This focus on Ben Saleh, however, cannot explain the much broader shift in labour relations that followed his removal. This shift consisted of three components: a close alliance with UGTT leaders and some white-collar unions, the incorporation of high-level UGTT bureaucrats into the government and a consistent campaign to demobilise workers and limit the UGTT's political independence.

In this light, the removal of Ben Saleh and restructuring of the UGTT is best explained not by the UGTT's call for statist development, but rather the escalation of strikes. In 1955, Tunisia experienced a then unprecedented wave of wildcat strikes; in a single day during the summer of 1955 the ministry of social affairs counted more than 100 incidents (Alexander, 1996, p. 87). That same year, the UGTT demanded a 30% increase in wages and was days away from launching a general strike. While the UGTT ultimately caved to government pressure and accepted a 10% increase, even threatening this kind of action was far more than they would ever do after Ben Salah's removal, and the 10% increase was the only one they would win for the better part of a decade (Bellin, 2002, p. 97; American Consulate General Tunis, 1959).

Ben Saleh's removal signalled that any UGTT leader could only survive by Bourguiba's good graces. UGTT leaders adapted to this new world by trading demobilisation for a role in the new government. Of course, by doing so they fundamentally undercut the original source of their influence. Without a source of structural influence, labour was limited to operating as an ordinary interest group, which could never overcome the structural pressure for wage restraint, whether to stem capital flight in the 1950s or to increase national investment in the 1960s.[2] The credibility and capacity of UGTT leaders to demobilise their base was a valuable commodity in 1955, but by the mid-1960s their own success made them an increasingly marginal force. When Bourguiba removed Ben Saleh in 1956 and his successor Ahmed Tlili in 1963, he was careful to do so indirectly and through the UGTT's parliamentary procedures. By 1965 such legal niceties were no longer needed and the UGTT's chairman Habib Achour was simply arrested.

The consequences of the UGTT's co-optation were fully realised with the removal of Habib Achour in 1965. The UGTT's role in policing labour unrest had been largely replaced by ruling party industrial cells and the organisation itself was reduced to an 'educational arm of the ruling party' (American Embassy Tunis, 1968; Bin Hasan, 2014). Internally, Ahmed Ben Saleh's supporters in the civil service unions fully consolidated control of the UGTT bureaucracy. This was nominally the UGGT's left wing, but their role at this point was solely defined by a state building project that relied on suppressing consumption to boost the rate of investment. The role of civil service workers as the primary base of the pacified UGTT is also strikingly similar to the role played by Egypt's government workers in Beinin's account of the Egyptian Trade Union Federation (Beinin, 2015, p. 4). Despite their very different histories, the two organisations were forced into a remarkably similar shape.

The origins of relative autonomy

In 1969, Ben Saleh's decision to expand of collective farms to include large commercial properties put him in direct conflict with large landowners, among the party's most powerful supporters, and soon led to his downfall (Alexander, 1996, p. 137; American Embassy Tunis, 1969). Opponents of Ben Saleh exploited, and probably encouraged, a 1969 wildcat railway strike and a subsequent revolt of local federations against the UGTT central. The organisers chose their targets strategically to put maximum pressure on the government, these relatively brief strikes caused the loss of 5.5 million dinars in export earnings and phosphate production

dropped by 22% that year (Alexander, 1996, p. 138). While only 400 workers participated in officially recorded strikes that year the threat to Tunisia's largest export industry seriously shook state
officials (International Labor Organization [ILO], n.d.).

At the same time, Ben Saleh was removed from his political position, his allies in the UGTT
were replaced by supporters of the recently rehabilitated Habib Achour. Party elites who feared
Ben Saleh's threat to landed property presumably had no desire to disrupt the system of labour
discipline, but in attacking his political base in the UGTT bureaucracy they inadvertently dis-
mantled the main apparatus of top down control. Similarly, the party closed all but a few of
the ruling party industrial cells, seen as dangerously close to Ben Salah, despite being the
party's most important tool in controlling the UGTT base (American Embassy Tunis, 1970).

The events of 1969 are however insufficient to explain the scale of the shift that the UGTT
underwent in the following decade. Between 1970 and 1972 membership rolls more than
doubled from around 90,000 to 200,000 (American American Embassy Tunis, 1972) and by
1978 they had reached half a million (Disney, 1978). This fivefold expansion is in notable contrast
to the late 1950s when the UGTT had avoided any expansion so as not to be accused of 'seeking
to increase its political power' (American Embassy Tunis, 1959). The other element of the
UGTT's expansion was the organisation of a number of new white-collar unions including secondary school teachers, university professors and bank workers, which to this day have been
among the most political and independent federations (Alexander, 1996, p. 180; American
Embassy Tunis, 1972). Both teachers and bank workers had previously been known to contain
contingents of communist activists in the 1950s (American Embassy Tunis, 1958a, 1958b).
Given this, it is hard to imagine Achour was unaware of the consequences of increasing these federations' representation, especially since at this same time he quietly dropped the UGTT's long-
standing policy of excluding communists from union offices. This newfound pluralism is
particularly notable since the UGTT chairman continued to have the rather dictatorial power to
summarily expel members, a power Achour made regular use of to remove his personal rivals
(Alexander, 1996, p. 268; Americian Embassy Tunis, 1976). If the UGTT had desired to maintain
its anti-communism (which dated back to its founding), it would have seemingly been easy to do
so (American Consulate General, 1956).

Whereas in the late 1960s American observers had largely written off the UGTT as an independent actor in 1974 they rated it as the third political force in the country, second only to the
army and the ruling party. While the ruling party claimed a larger membership, the UGTT was
considered better organised, more cohesive and even *financially* stronger (American Embassy
Tunis, 1974). Such a significant shift in the balance of power could not go unnoticed by the political and economic elite, and the party's response to the growing strength of the UGTT was very
much up for debate in the early 1970s (American Embassy Tunis, 1972).

In October 1971, UTICA (*Union tunisienne de l'industrie, du commerce et de l'artisanat*),
representing private sector employers, and the director of the ruling party tried to bring down
Achour over recent wage increases and his sudden tolerance for communists in the secondary teachers' union. They probably would have succeeded were it not for the Monastir crisis, in which a
self-described liberal faction openly challenged Bourguiba and nearly took control of the party
convention (American Embassy Tunis, 1972).

This political crisis was not really about the liberal identification of the party rebels, but the
widespread belief that Bourguiba's health would soon force a succession crisis. In early 1970
Bourguiba spent several months in a French hospital and already showed signs of weakened
cognitive function and changing personality (American Embassy Paris, 1970). The next year,
while he was in Walter Reed for more than six months, the White House was told that a political
transition was imminent and Bourguiba himself openly reflected on the end of his life
(Memorandum for the President, 1971). In this context, it is easy to explain the sudden breakdown

of party discipline, which had little to do with ideology but very much to do with the scramble for power (Alexander, 1997).

At the end of the Monastir congress, Achour and another trade unionist were re-elected to the 14-person ruling council while the vice president of UTICA that had first raised concerns about the UGTT was removed (American Embassy Tunis, 1972). In return, Achour (who had publically questioned Bourguiba's fitness to rule only a few months prior) and the UGTT enthusiastically applauded when the leaders of the liberal revolt were subsequently purged. Whatever concerns the government and UTICA had with the radicalisation of the UGTT were quietly dropped. It is to this point very specifically that we can date the government's willingness to accept a much larger and more autonomous labour federation than it ever had previously (American Embassy Tunis, 1973a). It is important to note that this top-level alliance between the head of the UGTT and Bourguiba did not necessarily imply a reversal of fortune of the labour movement as a whole. After all, this could have simply meant a second incorporation of trade union bureaucrats into the state and party as in the 1950s. What gave this moment its singular importance was Bourguiba's agreement, tacit or otherwise, to ignore the expansion and radicalisation of the UGTT base.

Despite the demise of the liberal faction, the succession crisis remained fundamentally unresolved. Because Bourguiba could no longer rule alone he increasingly relied on the prime minster, then Heidi Nouira, to both govern and succeed him. Yet he also insured no single individual or faction, very much including the prime minster, could ever consolidate enough power in the party to remove him from the presidency (Alexander, 1997). This in turn sharply limited the possibilities for rebuilding the old labour regime. With more than half of the party's membership willing to openly challenge even Bourguiba, these same members could hardly be relied on to administer a full takeover of the UGTT or to staff new industrial cells. Party members hoping to see the current prime minister embarrassed or brought down would have every incentive to ignore if not encourage labour militancy at politically sensitive moments, just as enemies of Ben Saleh had done in 1969.[3] As Alexander has argued, this 'intermingling of elite and popular politics' continued to be a staple of Tunisian politics until the issue of succession was finally resolved by the coup in 1987 (Alexander, 1997). This left Nouira with two options; either he could further strengthen the UGTTs peak level leadership in the hopes that they could manage their own members, or he could turn labour surveillance and discipline over to the state's coercive apparatus, at the cost of risking a much greater escalation of social conflict.

At least in the short run he adopted the first strategy, and this offers an interesting new understanding of two policy shifts in 1972. The first was the restoration of collective bargaining at the peak level. As Alexander has shown, this system of bargaining bypassed sectorial and regional leadership, giving the central organisation massive power to press or refuse wage demands (Alexander, 1996, p. 170). Second, the government passed a new strike law with harsher penalties but which also made UGTT leaders the de facto arbiter of a strike's legality, another source of leverage over locals (American Embassy Tunis, 1973b). Finally, the government granted a significant minimum wage increase to prop up the central leadership's legitimacy (American Embassy Tunis, 1973c).

Initially, this strategy seemed to pay off; whereas there were more than 150 strikes in 1972, there were less than 50 in 1973. However, in subsequent years, strikes would rise to even higher levels, peaking at 452 in 1977 (ILO, n.d.) (Figure 1). Centralisation may have given new power to top-level leaders, but as Alexander shows, it also created very strong incentives for cross class solidarity in regional federations. White and blue-collar workers would sink or swim together in a single set of annual negotiations over which they had no direct input. Not only was the UGTT opening itself to more radical cadres, but its newly centralised structure also gave these same white-collar workers a very strong incentive to organise industrial action on as broad a base as possible (Alexander, 1996, pp. 187–189).

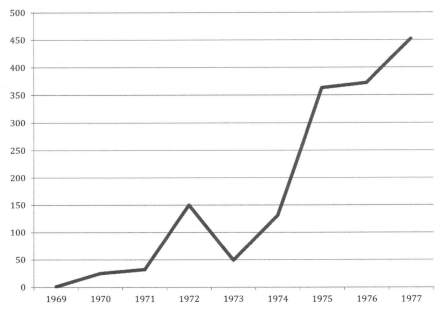

Figure 1.   Annual strikes 1969–1977.

Indeed, there were some in both the ruling elite and the UGTT who correctly foresaw how centralised bargaining and a more powerful UGTT could actually lead to increased strikes.[4] Even after 1971, powerful voices continued to warn of the danger of a rapidly growing labour movement. However, even as late as early 1977 these hardliners represented a minority view (Amembassy Tunis, 1977a). The UGTT alliance was far from perfect, but it did provide a useful tool in containing, if not preventing, labour instability in addition to serving as an important political ally against both elite and popular challengers. Against these political benefits were the relatively light costs imposed. Even a 35% increase in the real minimum wage between 1970 and 1978 (Bellin, 2002, p. 103) could be born relatively easily when GDP per capita more than tripled over the same period and petroleum products provided 50% of exports (The World Bank, 2014).[5] The increasing power of the UGTT also had a self-reinforcing logic to it; the more it expanded the more costly it became to confront. Whereas demobilising the UGTT might have been relatively easy in the early seventies, by 1977 it was increasingly seen as a flawed reality that could only be changed at a prohibitive cost (Amembassy Tunis, 1977a).

Confronting the state

The year 1977 marked a clear turning point in relations between the state and the UGTT. The year started with the signing of a social pact that gave workers inflation indexed wages, but also meant the end of real wage increases in the following years (Amembassy Tunis, 1978b). In addition, an economic slowdown caused employers to try to evade agreements on wages and work conditions that now posed a greater threat to profitability (Alexander, 1996, p. 173). These factors led to a sudden surge in strikes and in turn to a new policy of increased repression by the end of the year, starting with a strike by textile workers in Ksar Hellal. The strike soon turned into a popular revolt by the towns 10,000 residents, similar to the dynamic described by Beuhler, and was only broken by the deployment of elite riot police and 5000 soldiers, a full quarter of the army's strength (Amembassy Tunis, 1977b). However, even at this point the interior ministry was unwilling to condone a general crackdown. Nouira was only able to proceed after bringing in a new ministerial team of hardliners in December 1977, which for the first time included Zine El Abedine Ben Ali. The replacements at the interior ministry caused the resignation of six other ministers and most senior party officials pointedly declined to replace them when asked, showing the extent of elite reluctance to risking an all out assault on labour (Amembassy Tunis, 1977c).

In late 1977, party militias began attacking UGTT offices and picket lines, then in early 1978 the government demanded new union elections and control of UGTT finances. In response, the UGTT called a general strike for 24 hours (Amembassy Tunis, 1978b; Bellin, 2002, p. 106). The general strike provoked a massive groundswell of opposition far beyond the UGTT's own membership and led to several days of riots in all of Tunisia's major cities. However, it was not striking workers who led the turn to violence but party militias, providing a context for military intervention and a general crackdown (Amembassy Tunis, 1978a; Disney, 1978). While the party surely never intended to provoke such a large reaction, it is clear that it was the main driver of escalation. After two days of street fighting, in which as many as 300 people died, the army restored order and the union's leadership was replaced by more pliant alternatives (Bellin, 2002, pp. 106–107). This defeat and direct subordination could have led to the total co-optation of the UGTT; however, the policy of direct party control was reversed within three years.

While this sharp reversal might at first seem unusual, it is much less so in light of how strong the cabinet opposition to the crackdown had been in December 1977. Moreover, Bellin shows that during periods when the union was controlled directly by the party many firms turned to underground organisers to resolve disputes, showing that it was not only political leaders that found it in their interest to negotiate (Bellin, 2002, p. 209). Finally, the massive increase in strikes starting in 1980 showed the industrial peace produced by the repression of 1978 was clearly not a sustainable solution (Figure 2). In 1983, Achour himself was released from prison and allowed to return to the leadership of the UGTT (Bellin, 2002, p. 111). He again tried to accommodate the government's interests alongside union autonomy, but was again unable to do so (Zemni, 2013). Strikes in the first

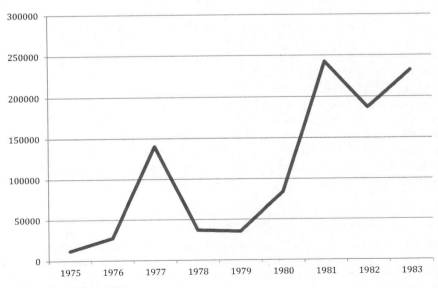

Figure 2. Days lost 1975–1983.

half of the 1980s were not only more numerous, but far more intense than at any point in the previous decade. Strikes in 1977 had resulted in 140,000 days not worked whereas those in 1981 and 1983 resulted in 242,000 and 231,000, respectively (ILO, n.d.). In 1984, the announcement of an International Monetary Fund backed subsidies cut that would have doubled the cost of bread and other staples led to several days of major riots across the country. This, combined with an increasing number of UGTT backed strikes, soon led to a new wave of repression (Bellin, 2002, pp. 111–112). In addition to re-arresting the UGTT leaders, trade union meetings were banned in the workplace, the automatic deduction of dues was ended and large numbers of activists were arrested or fired from the civil service. For the first time, the new leadership was appointed from outside of the union and the arrests extended deep into the base (Bellin, 2002, pp. 111–112). Yet again, at its moment of greatest weakness the organisation was revived under its old leadership (albeit without Achour).

The paradox of reconciliation under Ben Ali

The combination of economic liberalism and political repression pursued by Ben Ali is hardly unusual, Pinochet in Chile being an obvious example. What is much harder to explain is why this should also come with an effort to revive and court trade unions (corporatist or otherwise). Ben Ali's concessions were limited, but they were certainly real. All trade unionists were released from prison and all public sector workers who were fired for union involvement were reinstated (Bellin, 2002, pp. 116–117). Elections for union offices again returned most of the same leaders to power. The state may have hoped this would buy social peace, but this effort can only be described as a limited success. In the first eight years of Ben Ali's rule, there were 3623 strikes (525,380 days lost) whereas there had only been 1574 (365,802 days lost) in the eight years leading to 1978.[6] Most remarkably, the reconstituted UGTT continued to endorse strikes, as many as 118 in 1990, not far from the 142 endorsed in 1984 (Bellin, 2002, p. 205). Yet this time, there was no return to overt oppression. Despite the structural imperative for wage restraint and labour quiescence, the new regime decided it could live with a labour organisation that was unable or unwilling to control its base (Figure 3).

While the UGTT was unable to truly demobilise its base, it nevertheless played a significant role in limiting the scope of labour militancy. While the total number of strikes was similar, the number of workers involved (with the exception of 1990) and days lost was significantly lower than in the early 1980s. In the late 1970s and 1980s, UGTT regional federations coordinated waves of strikes to maximise disruption to public sector firms during bargaining sessions, whereas in the 1990s, they were forbidden to do so and when a strike was approved it was often only for a day (Alexander, 1996, p. 266) (Figure 4).

The containment of labour militancy is even clearer in comparison to the post-revolutionary period; from 2011 to 2014 there were nearly as many days lost to strikes as in the *entirety* of Ben Ali's rule.[7] Ben Ali's approach to labour is thus better understood not as a reinvention, but an adjustment of the model first established by Nouira and Bourguiba in the early 1970s. To fully explain why he did not attempt a more fundamental revision requires understanding Ben Ali's relation with the armed forces.

Ben Ali and the military

While Bourguiba famously kept the military at a distance, it would have been easy to imagine that Ben Ali's military background might have given him a closer relationship with it and allowed him to compensate for his political weakness with some version of the praetorianism that is so common in the Middle East (e.g. Egypt or Syria). Indeed, when Ben Ali came to power there

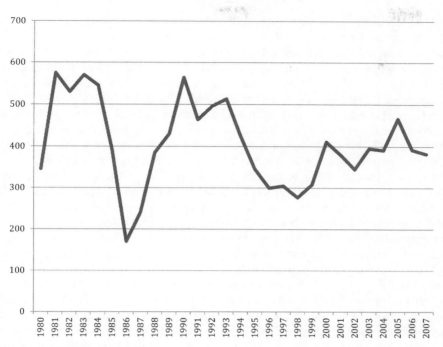

Figure 3.   Annual strikes 1980–2007.

were many both within and outside of the military that thought the army's time in the sun had finally arrived (Bou Nassif, 2015). However, as Jebnoun argues, the opposite was ultimately the case. While Bourguiba always funded the military slightly more than the interior ministry,

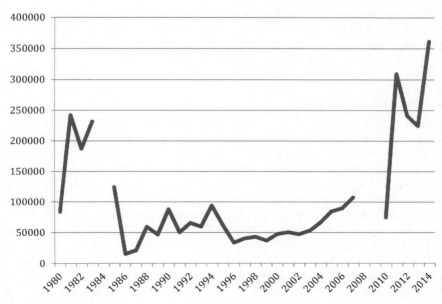

Figure 4.   Days lost 1980–2014.

under Ben Ali the interior ministry's share of the budget was increased sharply while the military's share was slowly eroded (Jebnoun, 2014).

Whatever weak relation Ben Ali had with the army in his early years was destroyed by the announcement in 1991 that 244 military personnel had been arrested for plotting an Islamist coup. In reality, there was no plot and the officers allegedly involved had confessed under torture (Bou Nassif, 2015). Even if Ben Ali had suspected the authenticity of this plot, whose fabrication originated in the interior ministry, it would have changed little. So long as he was unwilling to confront the interior ministry in public, the damage with the officer corps had already been done. After this, officers were placed under much tighter surveillance, army units were rebased as far as possible from major cities and military units were only allowed to move with permission from the Interior Ministry (Bou Nassif, 2015; Jebnoun, 2014). Perhaps the best indicator of Ben Ali's fear of the armed forces was his reaction to the events of 2011. As late as January 11, less than 72 hours before he fled the country, Ben Ali was preoccupied more with the possibility of a coup than a revolution. It was only on January 13 that he allowed the military to build up strength in the capital greater than the interior ministry's forces. Further, the elite presidential guard was deployed in Carthage throughout the crisis, protecting the presidential palace from the army rather than moving against protestors (Bou Nassif, 2015).

While Ben Ali's rule marked a notable increase in reliance on rule by force, the strained relation with the military foreclosed the possibility of taking this system to its logical conclusion. Without the support of the officer corps any coercive strategy could only operate under the shadow of limited escalation. Social uprisings on the scale of 1978 and 1984 could only be defeated by the large scale deployment of the army in the capital city; given Ben Ali's fear of a military coup in 2011 this would have posed an unacceptable risk.

The peak level UGTT leadership had never been the government's real problem, but in 1990 and 1991 this was more so than ever before. In 1990, more workers participated in strikes than in any other year prior to 2011, and in June 1991 sympathy strikes peaked at a quarter of the total (Alexander, 1996, p. 276). The number of sympathy strikes was particularly concerning because it implied that one firm taking a hard line with its workers could disrupt the production of others that could not afford to do so. Threatening union leaders would do little to realise the government and private capital's objectives. Either the government would have to make concessions or they would have to steel themselves for a new level of violence. Once the regime was resigned to granting concessions, fighting for a less autonomous UGTT leadership would have served little point. It would only have undermined the effort to sell the bargain to workers.

From co-optation to revolution

In many ways, the beginning of Tunisia's 2011 revolution can be traced to the 2008 Gafsa rebellion, started by phosphate workers striking over local corruption. The original protest rapidly spread to other towns throughout the Gafsa Basin and lasted more than six months (Gobe, 2010). Similar to the 1977 strike in Ksar Hellal, the Gafsa rebellion started as a protest over a specific economic grievance, but rapidly escalated into a highly politicised local rebellion. Also similar to Ksar Hellal, the regime felt the need to respond with both interior ministry and army resources. However, unlike in 1977 the army remained strictly in reserve and the rebellion was crushed not in a matter of days but of several *months* (Zemni, 2013). Unsurprisingly, the Gafsa rebellion was in no way supported by the UGTT's national leaders, who did their best to ignore the events altogether (Gobe, 2010). The top-level UGTT made every effort to do the same in 2011. However, very early in December 2010, local syndicates and activists, ignoring their hapless leaders, organised and spread nationally a very similar movement in the aftermath of Mohamed Bouazizi's immolation. By January 11, protests had reached such a massive scale so that even the top-level leadership was forced into offering tentative support, officially permitting regional federations to organise protests (Zemni, 2013, pp. 129–132). Finally on the 13th, by which point the regimes fate had probably been sealed, the national office threw its full weight behind the revolution, calling a general strike for the following day, January 14. Ben Ali was forced to flee the country by the end of the day (Figure 5).

This wave of working class social movements has continued largely unabated since 2011. While the total number of strikes in 2011 was only marginally higher than in 1990, the 309,343 days lost was nearly four times greater. The post-revolutionary period also marks the first time in which a majority of strikes have been legal (Ministry of Social Affairs, 2014). Aside from the larger scale, strikes since 2011 have had a much greater effect on key sectors of the economy. For example, in 2011 the chemical and transportation sectors accounted for around half of the decrease in GDP but only 12% of strikes (Ministry of Social Affairs, 2014; The World Bank, 2014).

The impact of protests and strikes has been greatest in the phosphates sector, where output had fallen by more than 80% by 2012. Even in 2014 output was only half of it what it had been in 2010.[8] This collapse is explained by a wave of strikes and protests by mineworkers and the unemployed, blocking railroad lines used to transport phosphate rock (Gall, 2014; US Geological Survey, n.d.). Oil refining is another sector that has been greatly effected by strikes since 2011. In the beginning of 2010, the Tunisian government announced a planned 33% reduction in output for maintenance and retooling at the country's only refinery in Bizerte, often a prelude to privatisation (Webmanagercenter.com, 2010). This resulted in a wave of strikes and demonstrations, the exact scale of which can only be inferred given the press controls of the time (Tunisian Observatory, 2010). In 2010, output of refined petroleum products fell not by the planned third, but by more than 80%.[9] In 2011, production was up from the previous year, but still only 50% of the 2009 level. The fact that strikes can threaten economic interests in this way has given Tunisian labour a critical source of enduring leverage beyond the extraordinary, yet ultimately ephemeral, events of 2011.

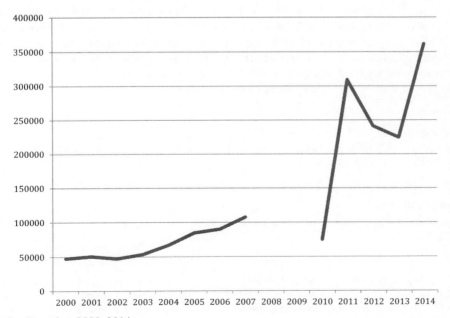

Figure 5.   Days lost 2000–2014.

So far, both economic and political elites have responded by making concessions and deepening their alliance with the UGTT bureaucracy, most famously through the national quartet that received the 2015 Nobel Peace Prize. Economic concessions have primarily come from the public sector; hiring and pay increases have doubled total public wages since 2011 (Trouble in Tunisia, 2016). Concessions have not been exclusive to the public sector though. In 2011, UTICA agreed to phase out temporary contracts and to 6% wage increases in 2012 and 2016 (Beinin, 2015; Reuters, 2016).

Conclusions

While it has never had the strength to dominate Tunisian politics outright, the UGTT was one of the strongest and most independent political forces in both Bourguiba and Ben Ali's iterations of one party rule. Accounts of the UGTT written prior to 2011 tended to draw a very sharp line between its heroic role in the 1970s and 1980s and its near total subordination to the state under Ben Ali. However, this view was based on a misunderstanding of both periods. The fact that the UGTT took such a visible political role in the 1970s and 1980s owed a great deal to the unique circumstances created by a succession crisis of perhaps unparalleled length. What is remarkable is not that UGTT ceased to be political in the 1990s, an entirely typical feature of authoritarianism, but that it ever took such a visible role at all.

Tunisia's colonial history may have given labour important organisational advantages, but this political leverage evaporated almost immediately after independence. Instead, the organisational features that allowed for UGTT autonomy re-emerged only after Achour's return to power in 1970, and that their reproduction in the 1990s depended, at least in part, on the collapse of civil–military relations. In both cases, one can easily imagine a counterfactual in which either the UGTT's initial subordination persisted into the 1970s, or in which Ben Ali continued the hard-line policies he had inherited. This suggests that, rather than anything innate about its political culture or national legitimacy, the strength of working class organisation in Tunisia can be traced to the balance of power at critical moments, which allowed for building the capacity for collective action. Whether or not similar factors can help to explain the weakness of organised labour in the rest of the Arab world will require much more extensive comparative research. Certainly, the fact that Tunisian Labour reached its nadir under import substituting industrialisation rather than neoliberalism seems to demand further investigation. However, I hope that this paper can serve to contribute to this broader project by illuminating the origins of the UGTT's autonomy, and perhaps the Tunisian exception more generally.

Acknowledgements

Many thanks to Arang Keshavarzian, John Entelis, Benoit Challand, Vivek Chibber and Jamil Choura for their invaluable advice and support.

Disclosure statement

No potential conflict of interest was reported by the author.

Notes

1. To make this argument I have drawn heavily on archives from the Department of State. These records are limited in the voices they represent, however, they do provide detailed accounts of how Tunisian and UGTT officials discussed events in private. Since these sources are primarily used to assess elite decision-making, this should not pose a serious issue for integrity of the argument. Readers wishing

to evaluate the nature of these sources can follow links to the records from 1975 to 1979, which are available online.
2. Chibber makes a similar argument to explain the weakening of Indian Unions after independence (2005).
3. Alexander shows how this same dynamic greatly facilitated the strike wave in Algeria between 1988 and 1990. Despite a high degree of ruling party control, resistance to liberalisation by the many in the FLN meant that orders to fire militant organisers were often ignored and some party officials actively encouraged militancy starting in 1988 (Alexander, 1996, pp. 336–339).
4. Achour himself expressed this to embassy officers (American Embassy Tunis, 1973b).
5. Authors calculation (The World Bank, 2014).
6. Authors calculation (ILO, n.d.).
7. Authors calculation (ILO, n.d.; Ministry of Social Affairs, 2014).
8. Authors calculation (US Geological Survey, n.d.).
9. Authors calculation (INS, 2015).

References

Alexander, C. (1996). *Between accommodation and confrontation: State, labor, and development in Algeria and Tunisia* (Doctoral dissertation). Duke University.

Alexander, C. (1997). *Back from the Democratic brink: Authoritarianism and civil society in Tunisia.* (Middle East Report). Retrieved from https://www.jstor.org/stable/3013093?seq=1#page_scan_tab_contents.

al-maʻhd al-watanī alihṣāʼ [National Institute of Statistics (INS)]. (2015). Retrieved from http://www.ins.tn/ar/themes/energie#sub-377|horizontalTab1

al-mrṣd al-tūnsī llḥqūq ū al-ḥryāt al-nqābīa [Tunisian Observatory For Trade Union Rights and Freedoms]. (2010, July 23). taḥarikk iḥtijājī bimuṣniʻ takrīr al-nuft bijarzūna - binzurt [Protest movement at the oil refinery in Jarzouna - Bizerte]. Retrieved from http://www.alhiwar.net/PrintNews.php?Tnd=8562

American Consulate General. (1956, April 4). *Annual labor report for Tunisia* (872.06/4-456, RG 59). Washington, DC: National Archives.

American Consulate General Tunis. (1959, August 13). *Labor problems in present economic situation* (872.06/8-1259, RG 59). Washington, DC: National Archives.

American Embassy Paris. (1970, April 20). *Call on President Bourguiba* (POL 15-1 TUN, RG 59). Washington, DC: National Archives.

American Embassy Tunis. (1958a, January 23). *Communist activity in the Tunisian Labor move* (872.06/1-2358, RG 59). Washington, DC: National Archives.

American Embassy Tunis. (1958b, April 15). *Communist penetration of secondary teachers union* (872.062/4-1558, RG 59). Washington, DC: National Archives.

American Embassy Tunis. (1959, October 22). *The UGTT: Its organization and control: The national apparatus* (872.062/10-2259, RG 59). Washington, DC: National Archives.

American Embassy Tunis. (1968, February 26). *Annual labor report* (LAB 2 TUN, RG 59). Washington, DC: National Archives.

American Embassy Tunis. (1969, October 21). *Ben Saleh and the almost revolution* (POL 23-9 TUN, RG 59). Washington, DC: National Archives.

American Embassy Tunis. (1970, October 03). *Spring Hourse cleaning at the PSD* (POL 12 TUN, RG 59). Washington, DC: National Archives.

American Embassy Tunis. (1972, April 17). *Annual labor report* (LAB 2 TUN, RG 59). Washington, DC: National Archives.

American Embassy Tunis. (1973a, April). (LAB 3-2 TUN, RG 59). Washington, DC: National Archives.

American Embassy Tunis. (1973b, December 18). *National assembly passes tougher strike law* (LAB 3-2 TUN, RG 59). Washington, DC: National Archives.

American Embassy Tunis. (1973c, December 25). *Tunisian workers get modified SMIG* (LAB 3-2 TUN, RG 59). Washington, DC: National Archives.

American Embassy Tunis. (1974, April 23). *Annual labor report* (LAB TUN, RG 59). Washington, DC: National Archives.

American Embassy Tunis. (1976, January). *UGTT holds national council meeting to demonstrate support for habib achour and expels his enemies*. Retrieved from https://aad.archives.gov/aad/createpdf?rid= 128417&dt=2082&dl=1345

American Embassy Tunis. (1977a, January). *UGTT celebrates anniversary, consolidates domestic position*. Retrieved from http://aad.archives.gov/aad/createpdf?rid=17677&dt=2532&dl=1629

American Embassy Tunis. (1977b, October). *Disorders in Ksar Hellal*. Retrieved from http://aad.archives. gov/aad/createpdf?rid=241658&dt=2532&dl=1629

American Embassy Tunis. (1977c, December). *The Tunisian governmental crisis– a description and assessment*. Retrieved from http://aad.archives.gov/aad/createpdf?rid=302307&dt=2532&dl=1629

American Embassy Tunis. (1978a, January). *UGTT version of general strike and aftermath*. Retrieved from http://aad.archives.gov/aad/createpdf?rid=10419&dt=2694&dl=2009

American Embassy Tunis. (1978b, October). *Taking stock in Tunisia: An analysis of the government*. Retrieved from http://aad.archives.gov/aad/createpdf?rid=267550&dt=2694&dl=2009

Beinin, J. (2015). *Workers and thieves: Labor movements and popular uprisings in Tunisia and Egypt*. Stanford: Stanford University Press.

Bellin, E. (2002). *Stalled democracy: Capital, labor, and the paradox of state-sponsored development*. Ithaca: Cornell University Press.

Bin Hasan, S. (2014, July 09). *Annaqaba fi Tunis* [Trade Unions in Tunisia]. Retrieved from http://ifriqiyah. com/detail/27302

Bishara, D. (2012). The power of workers in Egypt's 2011 uprising. In B. Korany & R. El-Mahdi (Eds.), *Arab spring in Egypt: Revolution and beyond* (pp. 83–103). Cairo: American University Cairo.

Bou Nassif, H. (2015). A military besieged: The armed forces, the police, and the party in Bin 'ali's Tunisia, 1987–2011. *International Journal of Middle East Studies, 47*, 65–87.

Buehler, M. (2015). Labour demands, regime concessions: Moroccan Unions and the Arab uprising. *British Journal of Middle Eastern Studies, 42*(1), 88–103.

Chibber, V. (2005). From class compromise to class accommodation: Labor's incorporation into the Indian political economy. In M. Katzenstein & R. Ray (Eds.), *Social movements in India: Poverty, power, and politics* (pp. 32–61). Lanham: Rowman and Littlefield.

Disney, N. (1978). The working class revolt in Tunisia. *MERIP, 67*, 12–14.

Gall, C. (2014, May 13). Tunisian discontent reflected in protests that have idled mines. Retrieved from http://www.nytimes.com/2014/05/14/world/africa/tunisian-discontent-reflected-in-protests-that-have-idled-mines.html?_r=0

Gobe, E. (2010). *The Gafsa mining basin between riots and a social movement: Meaning and significance of a protest movement in Ben Ali's Tunisia* (Working Paper). https://hal.archives-ouvertes.fr/file/index/ docid/557826/filename/Tunisia_The_Gafsa_mining_basin_between_Riots_and_Social_Movement.pdf

International Labor Organization. (n.d.). Retrieved from http://laboursta.ilo.org/STP/guest

Jebnoun, N. (2014). In the shadow of power: Civil–military relations and the Tunisian popular uprising. *The Journal of North African Studies, 19*(3), 296–316.

Memorandum for the President. (1971, January 22). *Transfer of power in Tunisia*. (POL 15-1 TUN, RG 59). Washington, DC: National Archives.

Moore, C. H. (1965). *Tunisia since independence: The dynamics of one-party government*. Berkeley: University of California Press.

Reuters. (2016, January 19). *Main Tunisian union, industry agree wage hike in private sector*. Retrieved from http://af.reuters.com/article/topNews/idAFKCN0UX1T3

Trouble in Tunisia: Dying to work for the government. (2016, January 30). *The Economist*. Retrieved from http://www.economist.com/news/middle-east-and-africa/21689616-unemployment-undermining-tunisias-transition-dying-work-government

US Geological Survey. (n.d.). Retrieved from http://minerals.usgs.gov/minerals/pubs/commodity/phosphate_ rock/

Wazara Ash'ūn Al-i'jtimā'ia [Ministry of Social Affairs]. (2014, November). *Dlīl Al-āḥṣā'īāt Al-i'jtimā'ia 2014* [Manual of Social Statistics 2014]. Retrieved from http://www.social.tn/fileadmin/user1/doc/ annuaire_2014_version_final.pdf

Webmanagercenter.com. (2010, January 6). *tūnis: tqdīrāt intāj al-nuft wālghāz al-tabī'ī l'ām 2010* [Tunisia: Estimated production of oil and natural gas 2010]. Retrieved from http://ar.webmanagercenter.com/ 2010/01/06/1929/

The World Bank. (2014, May 24). *The unfinished revolution: Bringing opportunity, good jobs and greater wealth to all Tunisians*. Retrieved from http://documents.worldbank.org/curated/en/2014/05/20211980/unfinished-revolution-bringing-opportunity-good-jobs-greater-wealth-all-tunisians

Zemni, S. (2013). From socio-economic protest to national revolt: The labor origins of the Tunisian revolution. In N. Gana (Ed.), *The making of the Tunisian revolution: Contexts, architects, prospects* (pp. 127–146). Edinburgh: Edinburgh University Press.

Appendix: Annual strikes and lockouts 1961–2014

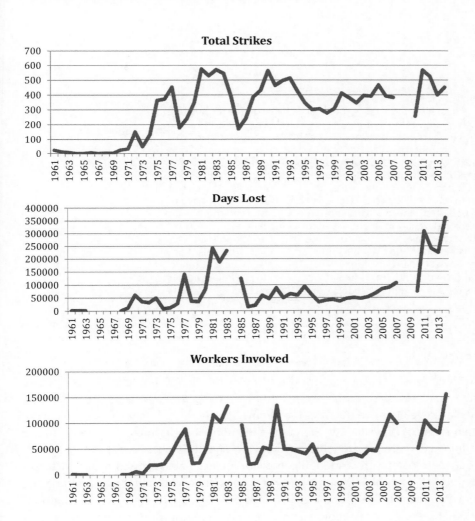

The legacy of compliant activism in autocracies: post-Communist experience

Alexander Libman and Vladimir Kozlov

ABSTRACT

Compliant activism – that is, political activity of the population, either fully supporting the regime, or merely criticizing individual shortcomings of its policies – strengthens authoritarian rule. However, compliant activism can over time turn into non-compliant one. Hence, the regimes need to ensure that the norms of compliant activism are internalized by the society and become self-enforcing. We use the case of the Communist legacies in Russia to show that compliant activism can, indeed, become highly persistent and outlive the regime, where it emerged. Using cross-regional variation in the levels of compliant activism in the contemporary Russia, we demonstrate that it is strongly affected by the variation in the membership share of the Communist Party of the Soviet Union in the 1970s. The results have broader implications beyond the Russian case and provide relevant insights for studying political activism in autocracies.

1. Introduction

Dealing with citizens' political activism is a complex task for authoritarian leaders. There are strong incentives to suppress even the most limited forms of activism, since over time they may develop into a threat to the regime. But there are also incentives to encourage certain forms of activism – to overcome the information asymmetry or to boost the regime legitimacy. Therefore, from the point of view of authoritarian leaders, there is a distinction between 'compliant' and 'non-compliant' political activism. Compliant activism can be defined as political activism, involving actions either indisputably supporting the regime, or criticizing some policies or their implementation, but at the same time supporting most other features of the regime and, in particular, embracing the assumption that the shortcomings criticized can be corrected only through channels created and maintained by the regime. Non-compliant activism involves criticisms of the key elements of the regime (e.g. the way political leadership is formed), calling for a regime change (on similar concepts in the literature see Bahry & Silver, 1987, 1990; Seligson, 1980).

Supplemental data for this article can be accessed here http://dx.doi.org/10.1080/13569775.2016.1206275.

The main problem for the authoritarian leaders is that over time compliant activists can turn into non-compliant ones, for example, if they become dissatisfied with the outcomes of their effort in terms of improving their personal and general social situation. In this case, encouraging or even tolerating compliant activism could in the long run turn into a risk for the regime: compliant activists obtain political and organizational experience, which make them better able to implement non-compliant activities. A possible solution to this problem from the perspective of an authoritarian regime is ensuring that the compliant activism is internalized as a social norm by crucial social groups. Göbel (2011) highlights the importance of manipulating norms, behavioural practices and attitudes for authoritarian regimes; if these norms become self-enforcing through societal mechanisms (Leipold, 2006), stability of the regime increases. These mechanisms include, for example, adjustment of beliefs (i.e. certain types of behaviour are expected to yield higher payoffs than others), social sanctions (i.e. those behaving in an 'inappropriate way' are ostracized by other members of the group they belong to), or learning (i.e. certain behaviour is replicated because switching to a different type of behaviour requires high learning costs).

The goal of this paper is to provide empirical evidence regarding the ability of regimes to turn compliant activism into a lasting self-enforcing social norm. For this purpose, we investigate the legacies of the Communist regime in Russia (on its importance see Beissinger & Kotkin, 2014). We look at the activity of Russians in submitting human rights violations complaints to the Office of the Federal Ombudsperson (*federal'nyi upolnomochennyi po pravam cheloveka*) in 2004–2012. This type of activity, as it will be discussed, is very much in line with the logic of compliant activism (Henry, 2012). We attempt to explain the large variation in the number of complaints submitted in different regions of the Russian Federation. For this purpose, we look at a particular form of Communist legacies: those created by the spread of membership in the Communist Party of the Soviet Union (CPSU) across regions of Russia in the 1970s. Our hypothesis is that the CPSU membership 'activated' various societal mechanisms making compliant activism self-enforcing. Extant studies show that regions of Russia were characterized by substantial differences in the share of the CPSU members in their population and that these differences had an effect on the outcomes of sub-national post-Communist political transition. We show that stronger legacies of the CPSU are associated with higher compliant political activism – larger number of complaints submitted to the Ombudsperson. At the same time, regions with a larger share of CPSU members in the past are characterized by lower levels of non-compliant activism – public protests.

The paper is organized as follows. The next section presents the theoretical logic of the study, showing why authoritarian regimes favour compliant activism. Section 3 describes how CPSU membership could have turned it into a self-enforcing norm. Section 4 demonstrates that the human rights violations complaints to the Ombudsperson are indeed a form of compliant activism. Section 5 reports the statistical analysis, proving that there is a correlation between the CPSU saturation and the compliant activism. Section 6 analyses the persistence of legacies, proving that legacies are stronger in regions where CPSU saturation became larger at an earlier point of time in history. Section 7 argues that the compliant activism is important for the contemporary Russian regime, but also that the results reported in this paper are relevant outside the specific Russian context.

2. Theory

In the eyes of authoritarian regimes, different forms of compliant activism have different advantages. For example, compliant activism based on unambiguous support of the regime – participation in pro-regime organization and parties, public manifestations and propaganda campaigns – is important to create the image of invincibility of the regime among the ruling elites (Magaloni & Wallace, 2008). Critical non-compliant activism (which we will focus at in this paper)[1] also produce a number of important effects autocracies could benefit from.

First, compliant activism can reduce the information asymmetries which autocracies face. The ability of the bureaucratic hierarchies of autocracies to collect accurate information is limited (Prendergast, 1993), and regimes are interested in encouraging people to provide additional information to the government (in particular on the issues of potential public concern). If the compliant activism is suppressed, regime faces the 'dictator's dilemma' (Wintrobe, 1998): even the most loyal subjects will be afraid of informing the leaders of possible problems and risks essential for regime's survival. Furthermore, compliant activism distracts people from possible 'non-compliant' activism. By accepting complaints (and even, in some cases, reacting to them), the regime demonstrates its 'openness' to the public, showing that many concerns can be solved without resolving to protests: otherwise even high costs of protests may not be enough to discourage people from acting upon their grievance. To some extent, compliant activism allows for cooptation of potentially more active or more discontent groups of the society by the regime (Gerschewski, 2013). At the same time, compliant activism limits the toolbox of potential opposition: if the public cannot clearly distinguish between the (apparently similar) forms of compliant activism pursued by groups loyal to the regime and actions of the opposition, it becomes more difficult for the latter to mobilize mass support.

Second, by keeping channels of compliant activism open, the regime can increase its legitimacy, particularly in case of electoral autocracies that imitate democratic institutions. Many of these regimes base their legitimacy on a claim that they are as democratic as other, acknowledged democratic countries (Schedler, 2002), although there is typically a caveat that there is something 'distinctive' about the national version of 'democracy'. To sustain this claim, regimes need their population to 'play along' – to use official channels of complaining or to vote for 'opposition' parties, which criticize some governmental policies, but at the same time are ready to unambiguously support the regime in case crucial decisions are made. Legitimacy is important not only vis-à-vis the domestic actors, but also vis-à-vis the international partners (successful electoral autocracies manage to project the image of democracies for decades). Finally, complaints to authorities as a specific form of compliant activism are important for authoritarian regimes, because complaints are an individual act; hence, encouraging complaints discourages people from collective action, which can pose a bigger problem for the regime.

Thus, it is not surprising that authoritarian regimes utilized and even encouraged compliant activism and, in particular, submission of complaints to state officials, which became an important part of political and social life, for example, in the Soviet Union (Alexopoulos, 1999; Dimitrov, 2014b; Fitzpatrick, 1996, 1999; Friedgut, 1979; Merl, 2012), German Democratic Republic and Third Reich (Bouma, 2014; Merl, 2012) and Socialist Bulgaria (Dimitrov, 2014a). A large contemporary research focuses on the role complains play in the functioning of the Chinese authoritarianism (Dimitrov, 2015; Lee & Zang, 2013; Luehrmann, 2003; Nathan, 2003; Thireau & Linshan, 2003). Meng, Pan, and Yang (2014) and Chen, Pan, and Xu (2015) use field and survey experiments in China and show that governments are indeed responsive to certain types of complaints, and complaints can be effectively used by the higher level government as a control mechanism over lower level administrators and thus contribute to regime survival.

However, as mentioned, the boundary between compliant and non-compliant activism is uncertain. Dissatisfaction with the way government deals with complaints (which is very likely to increase over time, if the roots of the problem are in the nature of the regime) reduces the trust into government and encourages non-compliant activism, with potential dissidents being better prepared to it due to the knowledge and experience acquired. Compliant activism can be used by anti-regime forces as part of their strategy (legitimizing it among some of the regime supporters or giving some sort of protection from the counter-actions of the regime): even in the Soviet Union the dissident movement started from the demands to 'respect the Soviet constitution' (Pastrukhov, 2013). The argument that compliant activism could turn into non-compliant one has been made for contemporary Russia (Clement, 2008) and China (Li, 2008).

Therefore, merely creating institutions and channels allowing for compliant activism (e.g. submission of complaints) is insufficient for the authoritarian government.[2] It also needs to make sure that there are no attempts to use these channels for non-compliant political action. The regime succeeds in achieving this task in particular if the compliant activism is internalized as a behavioural norm by the society or, at least, its important groups. For this purpose, the regime needs to create an environment where the societal mechanisms making compliant activism self-enforcing are particularly effective. Examples of this environment are loyal youth organizations or dominant political parties. Other tools like media (reporting on compliant activism and even becoming a tool of compliant activism by publishing letters from the public) can also play an important role. In this paper, we show that internalized norm of compliant activism can outlive the regime they originate from and contribute to the stability of the subsequent authoritarian regime.

3. CPSU and compliant activism

The Soviet regime used various forms of compliant activism based on complaints and petitions throughout its history. In the Stalin era, compliant activism became element of the repressions, with people strongly encouraged to report on possible 'enemies of the people' (Nekhamkin, 2014). In the post-Stalin era, Soviet citizens were invited to submit various forms of complaints, identifying individual deficits (*otdel'nye nedostatki*) of the existing practices. These complaints could have been submitted to the party committees or take form of the letters to the press. Some of these complaints were followed by investigations and interventions of the party authorities.

The compliant activism flourished within the ranks of the CPSU – the key institutions of the Soviet era. The behaviour of the members of the party was guided by two sets of norms: the formal and the informal ones. The formal norms prescribed party members to be the most loyal adherents of the Soviet ideology, in particular, by identifying individual shortcomings of how governmental policies were implemented (e.g. if they were caused by the behaviour of individual bureaucrats or officials) and reporting them to the superiors, at the same time fiercely protecting the regime. The Rules of the CPSU as of 1971 explicitly requested all members to 'bravely uncover the drawbacks and request their correction, … report any actions damaging the state and the party to the party institutions, including the Central Committee'.[3] There is empirical evidence that lower level party organizations were encouraged to file complaints regarding provision of social benefits or public goods issues (Bittner, 2003; Lussier, 2011). On the informal level, numerous studies confirm that the party was seen primarily as a career vehicle: members of the CPSU, while using the loyalist rhetoric, had little faith in the Soviet ideology and were more interested in using their position as an instrument of career advancement (Furman, 2010; Glazov, 1988; Shlapentokh, 1989; Titma, Tooding, & Tuma, 2004). From this perspective, compliant activism allowed a CPSU member to pay lip service to their ideological duties and to distinguish oneself from other possible competitors for attractive positions (DiFranceisco & Gitelman, 1984).

It is plausible to suggest that over time in this environment compliant activism was internalized as a social norm by the CPSU members. There are two mechanisms which could have led to this result. On the one hand, members of the CPSU were subject to severe indoctrination – both through official channels (though one could doubt how effective this propaganda actually was, especially in the late Soviet era), but also through contacts to and socialization among experienced party members, conveying informal rules and practices to new members (Mitrokhin, 2009). Both formal and informal levels of indoctrination, as mentioned, encouraged compliant activism. On the other hand, by regulating access to the CPSU membership which was associated with substantial benefits (Gerber, 2000), the Soviet regime also increased the attractiveness of compliant activism: party candidates (i.e. those aspiring career and wealth) had to demonstrate compliant activism in various forms to join the CPSU (Belonogov, 2015). Repetition of actions is likely to turn conscious adherence to certain norms into 'habitual second nature' (Eisenberg, 1999, p. 1260).

Compliant activism associated with unconditional support of the party line was clearly a benefit for a career-oriented CPSU member. Compliant activism associated with complaints or other forms of criticizing the 'individual deficits' was riskier, since complaints could damage another (influential) party member; but in case of success (i.e. if complaints were notices by higher level officials and considered valuable and important) the payoff for petitioners was substantial. The lack of complaints, on the other hand, could under certain circumstances damage one's career as a sign of 'lack of initiative' and 'effort'. The empirical evidence also confirms that at least some forms of compliant activism were indeed typical for the members of the CPSU (Bahry & Silver, 1990; Hough, 1976b).

The self-enforcing norms of compliant activism were likely to survive even after the disappearance of the original incentives created by the Communist regime (and, therefore, outlive the party itself). First, this persistence can be explained by learning effects: experience with filing complaints and contacting the authorities could be used in various political environments, especially given the strong continuity in the Soviet and post-Soviet bureaucratic cultures. Second, full political apathy of individual (former) Communists could be criticized by other Communists (an important social group they belong to) as a sign of one's weakness and unwillingness to undertake necessary effort to improve one's situation. At the same time, third, if the majority of members of a certain group (e.g. Communists) use compliant activism, it is more difficult to mobilize them to participate in non-compliant actions. Smaller number of participants in non-compliant activities makes them less likely to succeed, reinforcing the commitment of the members of the group to compliant activism.

The experience of the Perestroika and of the post-Soviet democratization could have challenged the confidence of the (former) CPSU members in compliant activism, if participation in non-compliant activism during that era resulted in higher payoffs. However, after the fall of the USSR party members remained more economically successful than the rest of the population (Geishecker & Haisken-DeNew, 2004) and played an important role in the new ruling elites of Russia. In this sense, they performed better than most of the former dissidents and opposition activists.

The membership in the CPSU was unequally distributed across the territory of the USSR and the Russian Soviet Federative Socialist Republic (RSFSR) – the present-day Russia. While in some regions the share of the CPSU members ('party saturation', see Hough, 1976a) was very high, in others there were relatively few party members. These differences were driven by both supply of and demand for party membership. On the one hand, the Soviet leadership regulated the quotas allowed to individual regions, as well as social (workers, peasants, *intelligentsia*) and ethnic groups, to join the party (Alekseev, 2011; Jones & Grupp, 1984). On the other hand, CPSU membership was also particularly attractive for some groups, especially those with higher income and social status and better education (party membership was a necessary prerequisite for attractive careers in administration, media or diplomatic service). Therefore, the extent to which the CPSU fostered compliant activism (as indoctrination and as requirement to access) in the broader population also varied from region to region. In regions, where larger share of the population was allowed to join the party, the practices of compliant activism were likely to become more widespread, eventually also among those not belonging to the CPSU through the horizontal diffusion of norms (Bisin & Verdier, 2010). In regions, where the share of the CPSU members was smaller, this diffusion was much more limited.

A number of studies have investigated the effects of the Communist legacy on the contemporary political institutions in Russian regions. Libman and Obydenkova (2015) and Lankina, Libman, and Obydenkova (2016) have shown that the regions of Russia with higher CPSU saturation in the Soviet era developed into less democratic polities in the 2000s. This variation in the levels of sub-national democracy survived in spite of Putin's centralizing policies. The extant studies explain the survival of the CPSU legacies by two factors. On the one hand, it is linked to the specifics of the sub-national bureaucracies: in regions with higher CPSU saturation, the continuity of the bureaucratic personnel between the post-Soviet and the Soviet eras was higher; therefore, old Soviet practices were more likely to persist in the bureaucratic behaviour. On the other hand, there seems to be substantially lower level of protest activity in the regions with stronger CPSU legacy. To show this, Libman and Obydenkova (2015) use data from a public opinion survey on protest sentiment in the Russian regions in the second half of the first decade of the 2000s. Lankina et al. (2016) utilize a data set on the actual number of protests in the regions of Russia in 2007–2012 (more on the data set see Lankina, 2015). They demonstrate that a higher share of the CPSU members in the 1970s was associated with a lower number of political and economic protests and lower willingness to engage in protest. It means that higher share of the CPSU members in the Soviet era was associated with lower level of *non-compliant activism* (political public protests are the most obvious form of it) as late as early 2010s; this fact plays an important role in the research design of our paper.

4. Complaints to the Ombudsperson as a tool of compliant activism

Even if the informal norms favour compliant activism, in order to function it requires a further condition to be fulfilled: the regime should create and maintain institutional channels, through which compliant activism is possible. In Russia one can indeed observe various channels of this sort: we investigate one of these, associated with submitting complaints to the Office of the Ombudsperson of the Russian Federation. The position of a federal Ombudsperson was introduced in Russia in 1993; the first Ombudsperson was appointed in 1994, and, since then, the position was occupied by five individuals (during the period of our investigation, it was Vladimir Lukin). We are interested in the functioning of the Office of the Ombudsperson in the 2000s, when Putin managed to consolidate the Russian authoritarian regime; even although the position of the Ombudsperson was during this period mostly occupied by individuals known for their 'pro-democratic' convictions, by accepting the office they became integrated in the political hierarchy of the regime and, therefore, the use of the Office of the Ombudsperson for compliant activism became possible.[4]

The Ombudspersons are appointed by the federal parliament and, as their main task, have to consider complaints submitted by individuals (Russians and foreigners) regarding the human rights violations. The Ombudspersons consider only cases, which have already been subject of court or administrative procedures and rejected by these institutions (with the exception of individuals serving a prison sentence, which may submit their complaints directly to the Ombudsperson). Complaints can be submitted in written form or via Internet by a victim of the human rights violation or a legal representative, and should be accompanied by copies of the court or administrative decisions; one can also submit a complaint in person to the staff of the Ombudsperson in Moscow. The complaint should be made within a year after the violation happened; anonymous complaints and complaints regarding decisions of the federal and regional parliaments are not accepted. The concept of the 'human rights violations' is very broad and includes all forms of abuse or illegal action (or inaction) of the governmental agencies: complaints against private persons are not accepted (but one can submit a complaint against an individual acting as a governmental official – for example, a policeman or a judge).

Empirically, most complaints seem to concern the criminal prosecution, due process and penitentiary system, as well as social and economic rights (e.g. housing and labour disputes); there are very few complaints concerning political rights. In 2012, for example, 57% of all complaints concerned civil rights – typically prosecution, actions of courts and penitentiary; 27% concerned social rights (mostly associated with the right to housing); and 13% concerned economic rights – labour disputes and private property protection.[5]

The rights of the Ombudsperson to intervene on behalf of these complaints are extremely limited. Ombudspersons do not have the authority to revisit decisions of courts or administrative decisions. They can only request explanations from governmental agencies (which, according to the law, these agencies are obliged to provide). In case the Ombudspersons find complaints to be relevant, they submits recommendations to authorities. They may also assist the victims of human rights violations in further litigation. In 2012, in 51.8% of the cases a complaint was made the Ombudsperson simply advised the individuals on further options to protect their rights through litigation or administrative process; in 26.9% the Ombudsman acted on complaint, and only in one quarter of these cases did the governmental agencies implement any changes based on recommendations of the Ombudsperson (12.2% of complaints were rejected as not meeting the criteria of the Ombudsperson).

Thus, on the one hand, submitting a complaint to the Ombudsperson does not challenge the regime in any way (individual bureaucracies have no reasons to fear the Ombudsperson as well; there is no evidence of personal resignations or any other punishments because of the complaints). On the other hand, complaints provide alternative source of information on possible problems in the regions at an early stage, which can be useful for the political leadership. Furthermore, complaints imitate an additional channel of protecting human rights, possibly distracting some of discontent from non-compliant activism. Finally, the activity of the Ombudsperson (regardless of the intentions of the individual occupying this position) is used by the propaganda to prove the respect of the Russian leadership to human rights and to the protection of interests of citizens. Thus, submitting complaints to the Ombudsperson can be interpreted as compliant activism and therefore could be influenced by the legacies of the CPSU in the way described above.[6] This is what we test empirically in the remaining part of the paper.

5. Statistical analysis

Our main hypothesis is that the compliant activism should be more frequent in the regions, where the CPSU saturation in the past was higher. In order to test it, we regress the proxy of compliant activism on the party saturation indicator, as well as other controls. As the dependent variable, we use the *average annual number of human rights violations complaints per 100,000 residents* in 2004–2012. We use this variable rather than the total number of complaints to account for the fact that the flow of complaints from the more populous regions should generally be larger. Our key explanatory variable is the *share of the members of the CPSU in the regional adult population in the 1970s*. The CPSU membership rate is measured for each region of the former RSFSR, which with some small exceptions coincide with the regions of the Russian Federation.

Unfortunately, the Soviet statistics did not provide any information on the party saturation in individual RSFSR regions. However, the size of individual regional party organizations can be inferred from the regularly published reports of the party congresses (s'yezd).[7] The congresses took place within regular (typically five-year) intervals. For our baseline specification, we used the data of the XXV congress, which took place in 1976. This year was chosen as almost the middle of the Stagnation era (the rule of Brezhnev, Andropov and Chernenko, 1964–1984). Stagnation era was the period of relative stability of the Soviet society (at least it was perceived as such by the population, see Yurchak, 2005) and therefore should have allowed for formation of more persistent behavioural patterns than more turbulent times. We expect the party saturation to have a positive and significant impact on the human rights violations complaints activity in the region. The regressions also use a set of controls: proxies of regional social and economic development (income per capita, urbanization and level of education); of the regional culture (share of ethnic Russians); and of the geographical location of the region (distance from the City of Moscow).[8] Our sample includes all regions of Russia with a few exceptions.[9]

Table 1 reports the main results. Regression (1) is the baseline. In regression (2), we substitute the share of ethnic Russians by a dummy for ethnic republics: it is possible that this status is a necessary prerequisite for the region to be able to develop an independent political culture. Regressions (3)–(5) include indicators characterizing the sub-national politics and economic institutions (indices of sub-national democracy, corruption, and electoral manipulations). In regression (6), we replace the income per capita measure by a measure of subjective well-being, based on a survey of the FOM of 2010. The variable captures the share of respondents, who claimed that they are generally happy with the situation in the region. People's actions are based on subjective well-being and not on objective income: the same levels of income may receive different subjective evaluation.

Table 1 shows that party saturation in the 1970s has a positive effect on the number of complaints per capita. In fact, the correlation between the number of complaints per capita and the party saturation can be easily observed visually, if one presents these two variables using a scatterplot (see Figure 1). Numerous robustness checks confirm our findings.[10]

As mentioned, hypothetically, the institutions created for compliant activism can also be used by non-compliant activists as part of their strategy of challenging the regime. However, in our case we can exclude this possibility, since, as mentioned, the previous research by Lankina et al. (2016) and Libman and Obydenkova (2015) has shown that

Table 1. Determinants of complaints activism, dep. var.: average number of complaints per capita, 2004–2012.

	(1) OLS	(2) OLS	(3) OLS	(4) OLS	(5) OLS	(6) OLS
Income per capita, 2004–2012	0.000	0.000	0.000	0.001	0.000	
	(0.001)	(0.001)	(0.001)	(0.001)	(0.001)	
Urbanization, 2010	−0.011	0.049	0.016	0.079	−0.011	0.017
	(0.120)	(0.108)	(0.145)	(0.128)	(0.122)	(0.129)
Share of ethnic Russians, 2010	0.044		0.052	0.012	0.044	−0.040
	(0.043)		(0.041)	(0.051)	(0.059)	(0.061)
Education, 2010	−27.292	−36.331	−27.953	−59.945**	−27.274	−22.581
	(26.057)	(26.407)	(26.317)	(27.874)	(25.950)	(20.496)
Distance from Moscow	−0.533*	−0.553*	−0.542*	−0.449	−0.534*	−0.380
	(0.306)	(0.301)	(0.308)	(0.290)	(0.311)	(0.283)
CPSU saturation, 1970s	2.065***	2.253***	1.924***	2.006***	2.065***	2.317***
	(0.571)	(0.603)	(0.623)	(0.598)	(0.571)	(0.604)
Dummy republic		−0.098				
		(2.798)				
Democracy, 2001–2010			−0.110			
			(0.195)			
Corruption, 2010				10.639**		
				(5.011)		
Culture of falsifications					0.000	
					(0.001)	
Subjective well-being, 2010						−0.081
						(0.080)
Constant	6.424	6.559	8.400	4.828	6.457	12.788
	(7.438)	(7.957)	(7.449)	(8.209)	(8.996)	(7.985)
Observations	71	71	71	65	71	63
R^2	0.311	0.298	0.315	0.307	0.311	0.273

Note: Robust standard errors in parentheses.
***Significant at 1%.
**Significant at 5%.
*Significant at 10%.

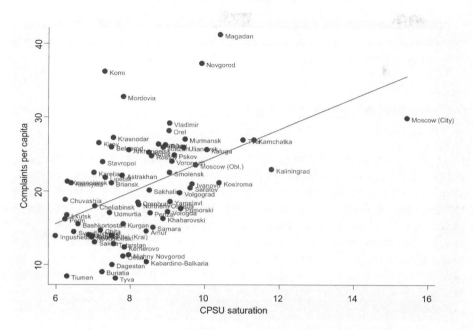

Figure 1. Correlation between the number of complaints per capita and CPSU saturation, linear correlation.

the level of non-compliant activism in the regions with higher CPSU saturation in the past was significantly lower than in other regions. Hence, our results can be interpreted in the following way: in Russia CPSU legacy makes people *less* likely to use political instruments risky for the regime (public protests), but *more* likely to use instruments, which do not pose any challenge to the regime (complaints to the Ombudsperson). This is what one would expect if there were a strong internalized norm of compliant activism – and it would fit the preferences of the regime regarding the public political activity.

The correlation between the CPSU legacy and the compliant activism could be driven by an omitted variable. Specifically, regions with stronger CPSU legacy could have higher level of the actual human rights violations (which we cannot observe directly), which would drive people to use the compliant activism more often. However, if our effects were indeed driven by worse human rights situation in the regions with stronger CPSU legacies, we would also observe more frequent political protests (non-compliant activism) in these regions – which is not the case.

The combination of high compliant activism and low non-compliant activism could also be observed, if the regions with higher CPSU saturation in the 1970s also had higher level of repressiveness in the 2000s: then the compliant activism would remain the only tool at the disposal of the public. In order to deal with this problem, we estimate two further specifications controlling for different dimensions of the repressiveness in the Russian regions. First, we control for the repressiveness of the regional courts: how likely are the courts to impose harsher punishments for similar crimes.[11] Second, we use the data of the website politzeki.ru, containing a detailed list of more than two hundred cases of politically motivated prosecution (e.g. for the participation in public protests, blogging activity, and activity of opposition media). We construct a variable equal to one for all regions, where at least one case classified as political prosecution was reported.[12] Our main findings are confirmed controlling for the level of repressiveness in the region.

6. Origin and persistence of legacies

6.1. Origin of legacies

By choosing the party saturation in 1976 as our main explanatory variable, we face two problems. First, it is not clear whether the results would be robust to selecting another year – possibly, 1976 was (for some reasons) an outlier. Second, and more fundamentally, the legacy argument suggests that internalization of behaviour unfolds over time. By measuring the explanatory variable at a single time point, we cannot prove that there is an 'accumulation' of legacies going on. For this purpose we have to compare, for example, regions where the party saturation became substantial at an early point in time and regions where it happened only at a later point in time – the latter should exhibit lower persistence of legacies (see Pop-Eleches and Tucker (2014) for a similar discussion).

To deal with this problem, we collected additional data on the party saturation in the regions of Russia, using other party congress reports than that of 1976.[13] In our analysis, we focus on the post-Second World War era, because before that the party membership was much smaller and admission to the party was governed by much more restrictive rules. In addition, between 1939 and 1952, there were no congresses, so no data on the party saturation is available (and the Great Purge eliminated numerous Communists, who joined the party before 1936–1938). Finally, until mid-1950s the territorial division of the RSFSR was substantially different from the modern division of the Russian Federation, and therefore one cannot match the Soviet regions of that era and the post-Soviet regions. This is the reason why we also do not consider the first post-war congress of 1952. Therefore, we have collected data for the subsequent congresses preceding 1976 – those of 1956, 1959, 1961, and 1966 (in 1971, the congress report did not contain any information on the regional origin of delegates).[14] Furthermore, we have collected data for the congress of 1986 and the conference (lower level party event similar to congress) of 1988 – the last assemblies, which were convened when the Soviet regime was still relatively stable.[15]

Using these data, we, first estimate the baseline regression of the paper, replacing the party saturation of 1976 by party saturation of other periods. Table 2 reports our results. One can see that the significant and positive effect on the number of complaints we reported above persists regardless of the point of time when the party saturation was measured – thus, it is not the case that 1976 was an outlier.

Furthermore, we attempt to provide evidence on how the accumulation of legacies happened over time. For this purpose, we compute the growth rate of the CPSU membership share in the regions of the RSFSR between 1959 (for 1956, the set of regions was still not entirely compatible to that of the subsequent periods; and several other measurement issues were present) and 1988.[16] On average, the party saturation almost doubled over this period, but the variation across provinces was substantial: in some regions it more than tripled, while in a small group of regions the share of party members declined. Then we

Table 2. Marginal effect of the CPSU saturation in different time periods on the number of complaints per capita.

CPSU membership rate	Dep. var.: average complaints per capita, 2004–2012	Dep. var.: complaints per capita, 2004	Dep. var.: complaints per capita, 2012
1956	2.149***	2.338**	2.183***
1959	1.764**	1.284	1.956***
1961	1.960**	2.926**	1.502**
1966	1.680**	2.991***	0.807
1986	1.430*	2.630**	0.459
1988	1.797**	3.012**	0.534

Notes: All control variables of the baseline specification included. Robust standard errors applied.
***Significant at 1%.
**Significant at 5%.
*Significant at 10%.

estimate our baseline regression, using both the *share of party members in 1959* and the *growth of party membership share in 1959–1988* as explanatory variables. Both turn out to be significant and positive.[17] To compare the relative influence of these two variables, we compute the standardized beta coefficients.[18] For the CPSU membership share, it is 0.524; for the CPSU growth rate it is 0.390. Through this procedure, we separated the effect of early 'accumulation' of legacies (i.e. high share of CPSU members already in 1950s) from the effect of late 'accumulation' (i.e. low initial CPSU saturation, but high growth rates of the CPSU membership, resulting in high CPSU saturation at a later point of time). Both regions with early and with late accumulation exhibit high number of complaints in the 2000s, but the effect of early accumulation is, as the standardized beta coefficients show, quantitatively stronger. It means that the earlier the share of the CPSU members in the region became high, the stronger the legacy effect is.

The CPSU membership rates extracted from individual congress reports are highly correlated with each other.[19] It leads to a further issue: it is possible that the persistent CPSU membership actually reflects an unobserved underlying characteristic of the regions, which is driving our results – that is, regions, which are characterized by high party saturation, also have other features, which make them more likely to exhibit high level of compliant activism. However, we can refute this interpretation based on the available evidence. Lankina et al. (2016) investigate the factors determining the CPSU membership rates in individual Russian regions in mid-1970s, and conclude that they are driven primarily by the following factors: the share of ethnic Russians (non-ethnic regions typically had higher CPSU membership shares) and the level of education of the regional population (although the CPSU presented itself as a party of the workers, the extant research clearly shows that in the post-war era it was more attractive for the educated strata of the population, which intended the membership as a career ladder) – both before the establishment of the Communist rule (literacy in the 1890s) and during Communist times (university education in the 1970s).

The role of the ethnic factor is less important for us, since, as we will show in what follows, our effects are entirely driven by non-ethnic regions. The results for the education are more important: one could hypothetically argue that the effects we observe are driven by the legacies of education and not by the CPSU legacies. However, if we again look at the available research, it appears unlikely. As for the pre-Communist education levels, the extant literature (Darden & Grzymala-Busse, 2006) typically points out that it was more likely to 'immunize' the population from the impact of Communist indoctrination, increasing the likelihood of the democratic transition. But, as mentioned, regions with high CPSU membership share are characterized by significantly *lower* non-compliant activism, which would contradict the 'immunization' thesis. In fact, Lankina et al. (2016) demonstrate how Soviet Union managed to 'appropriate and to subvert' the educated strata *through* the CPSU membership. As for the Soviet-era education, while hypothetically it could have made people more compliant to the demands of the regime, there is a large body of research showing that it is not the case: in the post-Communist Russia education was strongly correlated with support of democratization (see survey in Brym, 1996). In spite of survival of numerous Soviet legacies in the post-Soviet educational system (Kovzik & Watts, 2001), in early 2010s education was again positively correlated with mass protest participation (Hagemann & Kufenko, 2016). Thus, the results we report are exactly the opposite to those one should expect if the effect were driven by the regional education levels.

6.2. Persistence of legacies

How can one explain the survival of the old Soviet norm after the collapse of the USSR? First, many former CPSU members remained active in the first decades after the transition (and, as mentioned, were typically very successful in terms of their economic and political adaptation) – they could have to some extent continued to follow the norms they internalized in the Soviet period. Second, norms could be inherited through vertical diffusion, that is, intergenerational transmission within families (Bisin & Verdier, 2010), as well as through the educational establishments (where the share of former Communists remained relatively large and they often determined the curricula). Third, compliant activism could have remained an attractive practice in the post-Soviet era as well. Compliant activism is, to some extent, encouraged by the Putin regime since 2000: in the Putin's Russia, various institutions (including the highest level – the presidential administration – but also local and regional administrations and the ruling party United Russia) accept complaints from the public.[20] While the effectiveness of these complaints in terms of actually affecting policies remains low, practices of compliant activism is strengthened through the sheer existence of these channels, because the old behaviour could have been replicated and reproduced.

How strong is the effect of the CPSU legacies on complaints over time? In order to study this question, we run a series of regressions, using the number of complaints per capita *in each particular year* from 2004 to 2012, rather as the average number of complaints, as the dependent variables.[21] The results are presented in Figure 2, where we plot the marginal effect of the CPSU legacy with the 95% confidence intervals from each of the regressions. Figure 2(a) reports the results for the full sample of regions. The marginal effect of the CPSU legacy decreases over time; for 2012, we actually find no significant effect. Overall, the marginal effect goes down by more than two times between 2004 and 2012.[22] This dissipation of the CPSU legacy over time is consistent with the explanation linking CPSU legacy to the activity of the former Communists themselves, who over time move into retirement or become otherwise inactive.

However, there exists a difference between ethnic republics and the rest of Russia. If we exclude the ethnic republics (Figure 2(b)), the decline of the effect of party saturation

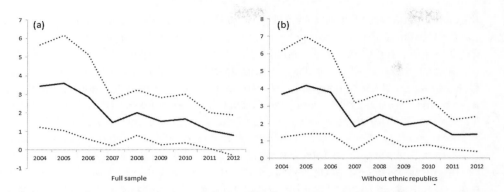

Figure 2. Marginal effect of CPSU saturation on the number of complaints per capita in individual years, 95% confidence intervals.

happens much more slowly; the beta coefficient for this sub-sample has been roughly the same as for the full sample in 2004, but was almost two times larger than for the full sample in 2012. For the sub-sample of non-ethnic republics, CPSU legacy remains significant in 2012 as well. The lack of legacy persistence in ethnic regions could be associated with several factors. First, ethnic republics have been substantially more active in developing their own political culture and institutions, diminishing the impact of Soviet legacies. Second, ethnic republics developed closed political systems, generally trying to prevent any unauthorized contact of their public with federal officials (including complaints to the Office of the Ombudsperson). The average number of per capita complaints in ethnic republics is significantly lower than in other regions of Russia. Third, political relations in ethnic republics are to an even larger extent than in other regions of Russia governed by informal ties and personal networks (the importance of these informal networks could have increased under Putin's centralization process, which standardized formal political institutions across Russian regions). Informal networks are typically successful if all conflicts are resolved within the network itself; formal complaints to a federal institution are problematic from this point of view.

Ethnic republics of Russia are heterogeneous as well: therefore, we implement a further test, replicating annual cross-sectional regressions excluding only the ethnic republics of the Northern Caucasus (Adygeia, Kabardino-Balkaria, Karachaevo-Cherkessia, Northern Ossetia, Ingushetia, and Dagestan). In this case already, we find a significant effect of the CPSU legacies as late as 2012. Northern Caucasus is part of Russia with particularly strong informal networks and high specificity of political culture. Furthermore, high level of unrest and terrorist activity and respective high activity of the federal law enforcement and security services (which regularly introduce the so-called 'counter-terror operation' regime, providing them with larger authorities and restricting the rights of the citizens) makes Northern Caucasus unusual in terms of both citizen's willingness and ability to submit human rights violations complaints.

Table 2 reports the marginal effects of the CPSU saturation measured at different points in time of the Soviet era on the number of complaints per capita in 2004 and 2012. One can see that if we take an earlier proxy (i.e. capture the impact of legacies in regions, where party saturation was high at an early stage), the effect of the CPSU legacy remains significant throughout 2004–2012. If we take a later proxy (i.e. look at both regions, where the share of the CPSU members was relatively high at an early stage, and regions, which increased their CPSU membership share over time), the effect is present only for 2004, but not for 2012. It means that after the fall of the USSR the impact of legacies, which were based on a relatively early formation of large share of CPSU members in the regional population (and thus could have been internalized over a longer period of time), was more persistent than the impact of legacies, which formed at a later stage (and thus were less internalized).

The effect we observe is therefore related to the insufficient degree of internalization of behavioural patterns in regions, where high CPSU saturation levels existed for a shorter period of time. It also partly explains the difference between ethnic and non-ethnic regions. Already in the 1950s, ethnic republics had on average a significantly lower CPSU membership share (in 1956, it was 3.0% of the population versus 3.7% in the non-ethnic regions). At the same time, they were also characterized by significantly lower CPSU membership share growth rates in 1950s–1980s (in non-ethnic republics the CPSU membership share increased in 1959–1988 by 3.4% points versus 2.1% points in republics). Thus, the accumulation of the legacies in republics was slower than in non-ethnic regions.

7. Conclusion

It remains to summarize the results of our investigation. We demonstrated that in the post-Soviet Russia the legacy of compliant activism of the Soviet past survived after the fall of the USSR. In particular, we looked at the legacy of party saturation of the 1970s, which was higher in some regions of Russia than in others. We showed that larger party saturation in the 1970s led to stronger compliant activism in the 2000s (in form of submission of complaints to the Office of the federal Ombudsperson), although, according to other studies, the level of non-compliant activism (public protests) in these regions was lower. Over time, the effect of the CPSU legacy seems to go down, but for non-ethnic regions (in particular, regions excluding the ethnic republics of the Northern Caucasus) it remains significant as late as 2012. The effect is stronger for regions, where large party saturation emerged at an earlier point of their history: thus, it indeed appears that legacies have a more substantive and persistent effect if the period of the internalization of particular norms was longer.

The ability of authoritarian regimes to create a self-enforcing norm of compliant activism increases the survival chances of these regimes. Even if the effect is insufficient to save the regime itself (as it clearly happened in the Soviet case), compliant activism is likely to encourage the formation and the stabilization of a new autocratic regime after the fall of the old one, at least as long as the legacy does not dissipate. For the Putin regime, compliant activism can be important for three reasons. It strengthens its legitimacy claim (which is linked to the self-identification of the regime as based on the strict adherence to the law). It allows the regime to mobilize the public in its support and thus to counteract the opposition movement, at the same time avoiding the situation that the pro-regime activism creates new leaders of public opinion independent of the Kremlin or constraints the policy choices of the regime (forced to take the position of the activists into account). It provides information on the possible 'weak spots' in the economy and society generating discontent and therefore improves the selective allocation of funds inevitable in the environment of economic stagnation Russia entered in 2013.

While the paper concentrated on a particular country case, it has implications beyond Russia. Evaluating political activism in non-democratic countries is a difficult task for researchers and policy-makers. It is challenging to distinguish the activities threatening the regime and setting the preconditions for further democratization from mere power struggles within the elite or activities actually strengthening the regime. Our study highlights that autocracies can at least in some cases successfully cultivate compliant activism and turn it into persistent behavioural norms. As a result, caution is required while observing supposedly critical activism in some of the authoritarian regimes. Many observers are prone to seeing them as signs of growing unrest destabilizing the regime. However, regimes can be successful in keeping criticism within boundaries, where it merely serves as a pillar of the autocracy. Even more, in countries where the practices of compliant activism are well-established, it will take a lot of time for them to disappear even after the regime change: they can in fact turn out to be more viable than the new political practices, which emerged after the end of the regime.

Notes

1. Criticism is a form of compliant activism, as long as only individual shortcomings are criticized and cooperation with the regime is seen as the only tool to solve the problems; if the criticism suggests that problems can be solved only through regime change, it is a form of non-compliant activism.
2. By 'creating institutions and channels for complaints', we mean establishing formal procedures through which individuals can submit their complaints to the government, and the government pledges to consider them. If the government does not accept complaints or discourages people from submitting them, petitioning, regardless of the original intentions, becomes part of non-compliant activism (an example in the Russian history is the Red Sunday in 1905 – an attempt of workers to petition the Tsar, followed by the use of force by the government). To make compliant activism possible, the government should explicitly indicate that submitting complaints through certain procedures is permissible. In Russia, the Office of the Ombudsperson functions in this capacity; another example is the 2006 Law on Citizens Appeals, which regulates how people can submit complaints to individual agencies and ensures some level of responsiveness.
3. Translated by the authors. The text of the Rules is available at www.leftinmsu.narod.ru/polit_files/books/Ustav_kpss.html, accessed 1 May 2015. The picture of a CPSU member uncovering flaws in the actions of local administration – for example, the enterprise management – has been frequently used in the Soviet literature and movies.
4. Online Supplementary Material A9 shows how the evolution of Russia during the period of a more pluralistic politics of the 1990s affected the design of the Office of the Ombudsperson and its role in the compliant activism practices. See also Finkel (2012).
5. See the websites of the Ombudsperson: www.ombudsmanrf.org and www.ombudsman.gov.ru, accessed 1 June 2015.
6. The fact that political rights (e.g. electoral manipulations) enjoy so little attention by the petitioners fits our interpretation: political rights are particularly difficult to be explained as examples of 'individual shortcomings' and clearly linked to the nature of the regime itself.
7. See Online Supplementary Material A5.
8. See Online Supplementary Material A1.
9. See Online Supplementary Material A2.
10. See Online Supplementary Material A3.
11. See Online Supplementary Material A4.
12. Looking at the number of cases is not reasonable, first, because of the small number of overall cases, and second, because individuals are often prosecuted as part of large trials (e.g. for

participating in a non-sanctioned manifestation). The data were extracted as of December 2015.

13. Online Supplementary Material A6 reports the development of the party membership over time.
14. On issues of measurement see Online Supplementary Material A8.
15. The last congress of 1990 happened amidst the Perestroika struggles and is therefore not comparable to the rest.
16. It is computed as the ratio of CPSU membership share in 1988 to the CPSU membership share in 1959.
17. The beta coefficients are 3.381 (significant at 1% level) and 5.806 (significant at 5% level), respectively.
18. Standardized beta coefficients show by how many standard deviations the dependent variable increases if the independent variable goes up by one standard deviation. They are used to compare the impact of various covariates with different units of measurement in a regression.
19. See Online Supplementary Material A8.
20. The costs of submitting complaints to all these institutions go down over time (also because complaints are more frequently accepted online).
21. We use the same set of control variables as in Table 1 (specification (1)). For income per capita, we use annual data instead of the average over 2004–2012.
22. The average number of complaints per 100,000 people went down from 20.9 in 2004 to 17.3 in 2012 as well; hence, we also compute the standardized beta coefficients, which measure the effect of the change of the predictor by one standard deviation. This measure also goes down over time. See also the Online Supplementary Material A10.

Acknowledgements

The authors appreciate the helpful comments of the Editors, two Referees, and of the participants of the ASEEES congress (Philadelphia, 2015), in particular Amanda Gregg, and of the 8th Joint IOS/APB/EACES Summer Academy on Central and Eastern Europe. All mistakes remain our own. Alexander Libman is grateful to the International Center for the Study of Institutions and Development of the National Research University Higher School of Economics for the generous support. The article was prepared within the framework of the Basic Research Program at the National Research University Higher School of Economics (HSE) and supported within the framework of a subsidy by the Russian Academic Excellence Project '5–100'.

Disclosure statement

No potential conflict of interest was reported by the authors.

References

Alekseev, A. (2011). Tridtsat' let v stroyu (moye chlenstvo v KPSS). *Teleskop, 3*, 7–12.

Alexopoulos, G. (1999). Victim talk: Defense testimony and denunciation under Stalin. *Law and Social Inquiry, 24*, 637–654.

Bahry, D., & Silver, B. D. (1987). Intimidation and the symbolic use of terror in the USSR. *The American Political Science Review, 81*, 1065–1089.

Bahry, D., & Silver, B. D. (1990). Soviet citizen participation on the eve of democratization. *The American Political Science Review, 84*, 821–847.

Beissinger, M., & Kotkin, S. (Eds.). (2014). *Historical legacies of communism in Russia and Eastern Europe.* Cambridge: Cambridge University Press.

Belonogov, Y. (2015). Formy vneshtatnoy aktivnosti v apparatnoy deyatel'nosti organov mestnoy politicheskoy administratsii SSSR v 30-e gody. *APROPRIORI, 2*, Article 10, 1–16.

Bisin, A., & Verdier, T. (2010). *The economics of cultural transmission and socialization* (Working Paper No. 16512). Cambridge, MA: NBER.

Bittner, S. V. (2003). Local Soviets, political order, and welfare under Stalin: Appeals from Moscow's Kiev raion. *Russian Review, 62*, 281–293.

Bouma, A. (2014). Strategies of complaint: Interest organizations of GDR Staatssicherheit coworkers after German reunification. *Laboratorium, 6*, 27–54.

Brym, R. J. (1996). Re-evaluating mass support for political and economic change in Russia. *Europe-Asia Studies, 48*, 751–766.

Chen, J., Pan, J., & Xu, Y. (2015). Sources of authoritarian responsiveness: A field experiment in China. *American Journal of Political Science, 60*, 383–400.

Clement, K. (2008). New social movements in Russia: A challenge to the dominant model of power relationship? *Journal of Communist Studies and Transition Politics, 24*, 68–89.

Darden, K., & Grzymala-Busse, A. (2006). The great divide: Literacy, nationalism, and the Communist collapse. *World Politics, 59*, 83–115.

DiFranceisco, W., & Gitelman, Z. (1984). Soviet political culture and 'covert participation' in policy implementation. *The American Political Science Review, 78*, 603–621.

Dimitrov, M. K. (2014a). What the party wanted to know: Citizen complaints as a "barometer of public opinion" in Communist Bulgaria. *East European Politics and Societies and Cultures, 28*, 271–295.

Dimitrov, M. K. (2014b). Tracking public opinion under authoritarianism. *Russian History, 41*, 329–353.

Dimitrov, M. K. (2015). Internal government assessments of the quality of governance in China. *Studies in Comparative International Development, 50*, 50–72.

Eisenberg, M. A. (1999). Corporate law and social norms. *Columbia Law Review, 99*, 1523–1592.

Finkel, E. (2012). The authoritarian advantage of horizontal accountability. *Comparative Politics, 44*, 291–310.

Fitzpatrick, S. (1996). Supplicants and citizens: Public letter-writing in Soviet Russia in the 1930s. *Slavic Review, 55*, 78–105.

Fitzpatrick, S. (1999). *Everyday Stalinism: Ordinary life in extraordinary times.* Oxford: Oxford University Press.

Friedgut, T. H. (1979). *Political participation in the USSR.* Princeton, NJ: Princeton University Press.

Furman, D. (2010). *Dvizhenie po spirali: Politicheskaya sistema Rossii v riadu drughikh sistem.* Moscow: Ves Mir.

Geishecker, I., & Haisken-DeNew, J. P. (2004). Landing on all fours? Communist elites in post-Soviet Russia. *Journal of Comparative Economics, 32*, 700–719.

Gerber, T. P. (2000). Membership benefits or selection effects? Why former Communist party members do better in post-Soviet Russia. *Social Science Research, 29*, 25–50.

Gerschewski, J. (2013). The three pillars of stability: Legitimation, repression and co-optation in autocratic regimes. *Democratization, 20*, 13–38.

Glazov, Y. (1988). *To be or not to be in the party: Communist party membership in the USSR.* Dodrecht: Kluwer.

Göbel, C. (2011). Authoritarian consolidation. *European Political Science, 10*, 176–190.

Hagemann, H., & Kufenko, V. (2016). Economic, structural, and socio-psychological determinants of protests in Russia during 2011–2012. *Economics of Transition, 24*, 3–30.

Henry, L. A. (2012). Complaint-making as political participation in contemporary Russia. *Communist and Post-Communist Studies, 45*, 243–254.

Hough, J. F. (1976a). Party 'saturation' in the Soviet Union. In P. Cocks, R. V. Daniels, & N. W. Heer (Eds.), *The dynamics of Soviet politics* (pp. 117–134). Cambridge, MA: Harvard University Press.

Hough, J. F. (1976b). Political participation in the Soviet Union. *Soviet Studies, 28*, 3–20.

Jones, E., & Grupp, F. W. (1984). Modernisation and ethnic equalisation in the USSR. *Soviet Studies, 36*, 159–184.

Kovzik, A., & Watts, M. (2001). Reforming undergraduate instruction in Russia, Belarus and Ukraine. *The Journal of Economic Education, 32*, 78–92.

Lankina, T. (2015). The dynamics of regional and national contentious politics in Russia: Evidence from a new dataset. *Problems of Post-Communism, 62*, 26–44.

Lankina, T., Libman, A., & Obydenkova, A. (2016). Appropriation and subversion: Pre-Communist literacy, Communist party saturation, and post-Communist democratic Outcomes. *World Politics, 68*, 229–274.

Lee, C. K., & Zang, J. (2013). The power of instability: Unraveling the microfoundations of bargained authoritarianism in China. *American Journal of Sociology, 118*, 1475–1508.

Leipold, H. (2006). *Kulturvergleichende Institutionenökonomik*. Stuttgart: Lucius & Lucius.

Li, L. (2008). Political trust and petitioning in the Chinese countryside. *Comparative Politics, 40*, 209–226.

Libman, A., & Obydenkova, A. (2015). CPSU legacies and regional democracy in contemporary Russia. *Political Studies, 63*, 173–190.

Luehrmann, L. M. (2003). Facing citizen complaints in China, 1951–1996. *Asian Survey, 43*, 845–866.

Lussier, D. N. (2011). Contacting and complaining: Political participation and the failure of democracy in Russia. *Post-Soviet Affairs, 27*, 289–325.

Magaloni, B., & Wallace, J. (2008, April). *Citizen loyalty, mass protest and authoritarian survival*. Paper presented at the conference on 'Dictatorships: Their governance and social consequences', Princeton, NJ.

Meng, T., Pan, J., & Yang, P. (2014). Conditional receptivity to citizen participation: Evidence from a survey experiment in China. *Comparative Political Studies*. Advance online publication. doi:10.1177/0010414014556212

Merl, S. (2012). *Politische Kommunikation in der Diktatur*. Göttingen: Wallstein.

Mitrokhin, N. (2009). Apparat TsK KPSS v 1953–1985 godakh kak primer 'zakrytogo' obshchstva. *Novoye Literaturnoye Obozrenie, 100*, 607–630.

Nathan, A. J. (2003). Authoritarian resilience. *Journal of Democracy, 14*, 6–17.

Nekhamkin, V. (2014). Donos kak sotsial'no-psikhologicheskiy fenomen. *Istoricheskaya Psikohologiya i Sotsiologiya Istorii, 2*, 63–79.

Pastrukhov, V. (2013). U konstitutsionnoy cherty. *POLIS, 1*, 7–31.

Pop-Eleches, G., & Tucker, J. (2014). Communist socialization and post-Communist economic and political attitudes. *Electoral Studies, 33*, 77–89.

Prendergast, C. (1993). A theory of "yes man". *American Economic Review, 83*, 757–770.

Schedler, A. (2002). The menu of manipulation. *Journal of Democracy, 13*, 36–50.

Seligson, M. (1980). Trust, efficacy and models of political participation: A study of Costa Rican peasants. *British Journal of Political Science, 10*, 75–89.

Shlapentokh, V. (1989). *Public and private live of the Soviet people*. New York, NY: Oxford University Press.

Thireau, I., & Linshan, H. (2003). The moral universe of aggrieved Chinese workers: Workers' appeals to arbitration committees and letters and visits offices. *The China Journal, 50*, 83–103.

Titma, M., Tooding, L. M., & Tuma, N. B. (2004). Communist party membership: Incentives and gains. *International Journal of Sociology, 34*, 72–99.

Wintrobe, R. (1998). *The political economy of dictatorship*. Cambridge: Cambridge University Press.

Yurchak, A. (2005). *Everything was forever, until it was no more: The last Soviet generation*. Princeton, NJ: Princeton University Press.

Context, image and the case of the Shahbag movement

Sanchari De

This research discusses the importance of a photograph of an accused war criminal, Abdul Kader Molla, during the period immediately before the emergence of the Shahbag movement in Bangladesh. The image captures Kader Molla flashing a V sign, and it was taken in the moments after he had been sentenced to life imprisonment by the International Crimes Tribunal in Bangladesh in 2013. After Kader Molla's punishment was revised to a death sentence, a number of images were circulated online of protesters flashing the same V sign. All these moments pose a key question which this research seeks to answer: How does this image of Kader Molla signify a crucial point of reference for the mobilisation of the Shahbag movement? To provide an answer, this paper discusses a historical context of the tensions between people and the state in Bangladesh and how personalised memory can make such tensions visible.

Introduction

This research discusses the importance of a photograph of an accused war criminal, Abdul Kader Molla, during the period immediately before the emergence of the Shahbag movement in Bangladesh. The image captures Kader Molla flashing a V sign with his palm facing outwards, and it was taken in the moments after he had been sentenced to life imprisonment by the International Crimes Tribunal (ICT) in Bangladesh in 2013. This research is a part of a PhD thesis which uses the method of in-depth interviews with the key activists and participants associated with the Shahbag movement ($n = 22$, with future interviewees to be added). One of the recurring aspects of the interviews is that all key participants refer to this image of Kader Molla as a driving force in motivating them to participate in the movement. Moreover, during the course of the movement, the photograph was referred to, reproduced and recirculated in different forms. Cartoons was created, jokes were made and, finally, when the verdict was revised and Kader Molla was sentenced to death, an image of his wife, in which she is making the victory sign while on her way to meet Kader Moller for the last time, was circulated for sarcastic effect, as were images of protesters flashing the same V sign. All these moments pose a key question which this research seeks to answer: How does this image of Kader Molla signify a crucial point of reference for the mobilisation of the Shahbag movement? To provide an answer, this paper discusses a historical context of the tensions between people and the state in Bangladesh and how personalised memory can make such tensions visible. Focusing on the Shahbag movement in Bangladesh in 2013 as a case study, this paper will argue that the introduction of particular images within a context and network of deprivation of historical memory makes visible the tension and frustration within democratic states. Introduced in this preexisting context, the image of Kader Molla and its reception made visible the need for asserting people's sense of frustration and deprivation with the state. This research will refer to contemporary blog posts to underline the discursive context of deprivation in which history and memory could be evoked. In particular, it will examine how Kader Molla's image has some basic and obvious connotations for the people of Bangladesh by referring to blog discussions on the cultural struggles of Bangladesh in the twentieth century, namely the Language Movement of 1952 and the Liberation War and genocide of 1971.

A note on the method

This paper uses certain aspects of digital ethnography methodology and carries out a visual analysis of the image. Visuals often receive secondary status in the method of qualitative content analysis (Schrøder, 2012). However, visual analysis is important in identifying a given society's relationship with the past. It can underline not just how the past was captured, but how a captured moment mediates memory, nostalgia and the public's reception of these. Therefore, visual analysis is crucial in tracing visuals' sociocultural significance and the power relations in which certain visuals are produced (Rose, 2013). Sara Pink, Horst, and Postill (2016) propose digital ethnography as an approach for researching media environments before and during digital practices. They view media events as a means of understanding societal transformations, and suggest that mediation and private contexts are important in researching contemporary events:

> When it comes to researching events ethnographically, we need to go beyond the notion of the event as a public entity to consider ways in which it is mediated and how it is engaged within domestic and other nonpublic environments and contexts. (Pink et al., 2016, p. 148)

The research in this article draws on blog posts written immediately after the circulation of the photograph. The main blog posts discussed in the paper are from mukto-mona.com and were published between 4 February 2013 and 6 February 2013. This Bengali-language blog is crucial for its community posts on rationalism and scientific explanations of the universe as opposed to religious understandings. Moreover, from the very beginning of its creation, the community of bloggers associated with mukto-mona.com created a scope for critical political debates. In 2015, the blog became the focus of international news when religious fundamentalists in Dhaka assassinated the site's founder, Avijit Roy. Roy's wife (Rafida Ahmed Bonya, who is also a blogger and an activist) subsequently received Deutsche Welle's Best of Online Activism award for the site.

As the Shahbag Movement was not covered internationally and its localised context has not been researched in any particular depth, in conducting this research I also deployed a semistructured interview method to gain a deeper knowledge of the movement from twenty-two activists, artists and bloggers who physically participated in it. Some of them were arrested during the movement for 'demeaning the religion'. For ethical and security reasons, interviewees' identities are not revealed in this paper. As most of the interviewees are now seeking political asylum in other countries because of threats, the interviews were conducted mainly through online video-calling platform such as Skype. Some interviews were conducted in Kolkata in a face-to-face setting. Interviews were recorded with the consent of the interviewees, who were aware of their use for research purposes. They were transcribed mostly in their entirety, though in some cases only the relevant parts needed for the research were transcribed. Almost all the interviews were conducted in Bengali; as most interviewees preferred to talk in their mother tongue, and as my native language is also Bengali, its use facilitated smooth and long conversations, which are apt for the in-depth semistructured interview technique. All the interviews were translated into English during the transcription stage. Finally, the interviews were coded and structured according to relevant themes.

The Shahbag movement and the photo of Kader Molla: a brief introduction

In 2009, the Awami League government in Bangladesh established the ICT to investigate and prosecute the suspects of the 1971 genocide. In February 2013, Abdul Kader Molla was sentenced to life imprisonment rather than to capital punishment by the ICT. On 5 February 2013, people at the Shahbag Square in Dhaka gathered and demanded capital punishment[1] for Kader Molla. This movement gradually spread to several parts of Bangladesh. This image of Kader Molla flashing a victory sign was immediately broadcast on television. The instant reaction on social media platforms was the creation of pages with titles such as 'Hang Kader Molla and other War Criminals' and 'Shahbah Cyber Yuddha' [Shahbag Cyber War]. These pages continuously posted visuals with texts that reminded their audiences of the war crimes and of the contemporary political situation, with an emphasis on the connection between war criminals and religious fundamentalism. The reactions to this image of Kader Molla suggest a host of interconnected factors related to struggles with cultural memory and identity, with these relating memory of deprivation to the present sociopolitical situation. According to one participant,

> The Shahbag Movement started after Kader Molla made a V sign. People felt there might be some understanding between the government and the Jamaat. So people made a human chain in Shahbag Square and an event was created on Facebook to invite others to join the movement at around 3 p.m. (Interviewee 2, April 17, 2016, translation mine)

From this remark, it is possible to perceive that the people indicated by this participant expected justice from the ruling government. This expectation was directly linked to the practice of democracy, since the Awami League government promised before the election of 2008 to bring those who perpetrated war crimes to justice, a position which made young and educated middle-class voters hopeful about democracy and politics in Bangladesh:

> The freedom fighters were heroes in my heart. Later I saw how people accused of the genocide, who killed 3 million people, were in powerful positions in society and politics. They were making policies for Bangladesh. But as ordinary citizens, we were not capable of doing justice. So it was a demand from the youth to the Awami League government in the 2008 election. The young voters were over one crore [ten million]. (Interviewee 3, April 26, 2016)

Within this context of democratic expectation, the introduction and circulation of the photo of Kader Molla mobilised the narratives of struggles which are not often acknowledged in the official versions of history or in the official memorialisation processes.

The issue of war crimes cannot be separated from the cultural struggle for identity and recognition. The historical roots of the Liberation Movement of 1971 can be traced to the demand for federal status for the Bengali Language along with Urdu and English in 1948. Muhammad Ali Jinnah declared in 1948 that the language for Pakistan (including East Pakistan) will be Urdu alone. The formation of Bangladesh (formerly East Pakistan) as an independent state, therefore, was based on the aspiration for a state where ethnic and linguistic freedom could be practised. On 21 February 1952, students from different universities in the then East Pakistan gathered and demonstrated to demand Bengali as a state language along with Urdu. Many of the protesters were shot dead by the police. The 'Bengali' identity, in this sense, was more inclined to cultural aspects than religious ones. While in 1947 India and Pakistan were divided on the basis of religion, freedom of cultural expression and practice became important driving forces in the liberation of East Pakistan from West Pakistan. However, the confusion over identity was very prominent from the very birth of the nation. The debate over secular and Muslim identity was immediately felt in 1972 when, on the day on which the country's constitution was ratified, a procession of people in Dhaka chanted the slogan 'Joy-Bangla Joy-heen, Lungi Chhere Dhuti-pin' (Victorious Bengal has lost its victory as people prefer Dhuti over Lungi (translation mine)). Here the evocation of a men's garment called 'Lungi' refers to Muslim identity and 'Dhuti', also an item of men's clothing, to Hindu identity (see Yasmin, 2013). The Shahbag movement developed this debate, and it gradually became one of religion versus atheism.

The interviewees' perspectives shed light on the relevance of this context and its bearing on the Kader Molla image in three respects. First, the live television broadcast of this image and its publication in print media mobilised a sense of shared experience focused on remembering the Liberation War in contemporary everyday life. For example, interviewee 1 commented,

> When we grew up and started writing, we saw how Jamaat-e-Islami and Shibir [Chhaatro Shibir, a student union] tortured people, how they tortured the Hindu [minority] people. When I was a child, there was a Hindu family in my neighbourhood. I witnessed how Jamaat-e-Islami tortured them in 2001. We knew Jamaat-e-Islami had an alliance with war criminals … . They must be banned. In Germany, the Nazi Party is banned and hated … . When we started writing on blogs, naturally we started writing against Jamaat-e-Islami and politics based on religion. (Interviewee 1, interview, February 2016, translation mine)

Second, this image connotes the arrogance of a war criminal who had a privileged position in society:

> Before the Kader Molla verdict, there was another verdict on Bachchu Rajakar, and he was sentenced to death. He was the imam of Banani Masjid during the period of BNP [Bangladesh Nationalist Party] government. He used to preach about religion on ATN Bangla. So, this man escaped before he was captured. It was thought that he went to Pakistan first and then spent a few days in Sweden. Jamaat helped him financially. Actually, government was criticized, as he was able to escape after the verdict. The V sign made the protest stronger. A convicted criminal was showing the V sign to the martyrs and freedom fighters. (Interviewee 2, interview, April, 2016, translation mine)

Third, this image brings together two generations: the generation of people who witnessed the 1971 Liberation War and the generation who came immediately after them. Apart from knowing the state version of history, this second generation heard the stories of the 1971 war and genocide recollected from the personal memory of their family members. These two sources of information led the activists and bloggers to research more about this period of history on their own. Their individual experiences in democratic Bangladesh led to their seeking a way in which they could give vent to their concerns:

> We as young people realized that the people who were responsible for the genocide did not face trials. The Awami League government did not start any trial. Other governments which came later gave those war criminals opportunities in politics. They became ministers, members of the parliament and even prime ministers. During the era of Jia' ur Rahman one became prime minister. (Interviewee 1, interview, February 2016, translation mine)

Within this context, the image worked as a catalyst to bring together different forms of articulation of memory. Its circulation (first through television; later through social media platforms, the blogosphere and print media) communicated this frustration within the state. The generational struggle for an 'ideal' Bangladesh was merged into the image: past crimes were claiming victory in the present. News and counternews in mainstream media and blogosphere mediated the struggle to interpret a personalised sociocultural memory of the Liberation War of 1971. A mediation of the symbolic value inherent in the photograph created opportunity for moral shocks which derives from the memory of the 1971 Liberation War. In the next section, this paper discusses how photographic memories of the past can be relevant in the study of social movements in order to understand people's relationship with the state.

Photographs and social movements

Social movements and mass gatherings on streets during the period when the photograph was published were accompanied by an abundance of images. A moment captured in a photograph is not only capable of capturing attention at that specific moment but can also easily be reproduced in other mediums (Memou, 2015). Images captured either by professional journalists or by normal bystander or protesters and activists seem to declare an ontology of physical movements. Doerr, Mattoni, and Teune (2015) observe that

> It is hardly controversial to assume that movements are pivotally perceived through vision. Thus, clothing and bodily gestures, images and symbols, posters and videos are not only crucial forms of movements' representation but also potentially reach materials to answer central research questions in social movement studies. (p. 557)

However, visuals have been at the margins of the study of social movements. The use of visual methods for studying social movements is a rather new phenomenon. The visuals of social movements are often treated to generate a political message. Visual analysis of protest photographs could be helpful in determining how the content of an image could become a factor in mass mobilisation. However, in the absence of formal leadership and when there are numerous meaning-making processes at work through different media, turning the content of images into symbols could be more affective as invokers of memories and moral shock than the presence of a prominent leader. Olesen (2013) has shown how Khaled Said was transformed into a visual symbol of injustice by the strategic appropriation of the visual by activists. He goes on to analyse the interconnectedness of photograph, activism and society:

> In the process of infusing a photograph with injustice meaning, activists draw on injustice frames located in the political–cultural structure of society; second, once created, visual injustice symbols themselves enter the political culture and memory structure of society to become potential resources in subsequent activism. Visual injustice symbols thus both reflect and shape the society in which they emerge. (Olesen 2013, p. 5)

The importance of images and the power of photographs have triggered the imaginations of thinkers from different areas of study and research. For example, both French film critic Bazin (1967) and German film critic Siegfried Kracauer considered photographic memory in relation to subjectivity. For Kracauer (1965):

> Photography grasps what is given as a spatial (or temporal) continuum, memory images retain what is given only insofar as it has significance. Since what is significant is not reducible to either merely spatial or merely temporal terms, memory images are at odds with photographic representation. (pp. 50–51)

According to Ruchatz (2008), photographs offer a trace of memory more than they do an externalisation of it. The definitions of the concepts of externalisation and trace have been elaborated by Ruchatz, who states that 'whereas the concept of externalization foregrounds the instrumental and social character of media, the conception as trace stresses the autonomy of media technology' (p. 367). However, he further stresses that

> any photographic picture consists to different ratios of a mixture of selection and accident, of significant and insignificant elements. Photography produces an exceptional class of traces, insofar as they are regularly and intentionally produced as well as conventionally recognized as significant and signifying: Photographs show – but do not explain – what has caused them … . Before photographs can take on a symbolic meaning, for example, the objects in them have to be recognized by way of their iconicity. (p. 371)

For Ruchatz (2008), the concepts of trace and externalisation work together to signify both cultural and technological dimensions of a photograph, where 'memory and media interact'. During a protest, strategic uses of a photograph could prove to be important in affecting a crowd with the trope of memory to create moral shock:

> Jasper uses the term 'moral shock' to get at the first step. In the recruitment of strangers: when an event or situation raises such a sense of outrage in people that they become inclined toward political action, even in the absence of a network of contact. (Jasper & Poulsen, 1995, p. 498)

For 'moral shock' to take place, iconic photographs and symbols within images have to play important roles in leading a crowd to a political mobilisation. According to Hariman and Lucaites (2007), iconic 'photographs are not the only images that occur in these venues, of course, but they are images that occur repeatedly and in all of them' (p. 6). Hariman and Lucaites (2007) further comment that

> iconic photographs provide an accessible centrally positioned set of images for exploring how political action (and inaction) can be constituted and controlled through visual media. They are the images that you see again and again in the historical tableaus of visual media … . These images don't stop there, however, for they are also picked up by political cartoonists and by political demonstrators; used in commercial advertising and reproduced on T-shirts and all manner of promotional materials […] . (p. 5)

With regard to the Shahbag movement, the question is whether the image of Kader Molla can be considered iconic. In this case, an accused war criminal was turned into the 'face' of the movement instead of any leaders or protests. This is quite opposite to what happened in 2009 in Iran during the Green Movement, when Neda Agha Soltan was posthumously turned into the face of the movement. Even the murdered blogger Rajib Haider could not be turned into the 'face' of the Shahbag movement. As already mentioned, this imaged was reproduced in several cartoons and in other forms of protest materials. These multiple references and reproductions indicate the potential of this photograph to become an icon, with memory references playing an important role in turning the image into icon by stirring emotional associations with history and memory. In the case of Kader Molla's photograph, memory aspects condensed into the V sign, which symbolically represents the 'defeat' of the ideals behind the victory of Bengali Nationalism in the 1971 war. Hariman and Lucaites (2007) point out that iconic 'images were obviously highly specific memory and admiration, yet also somehow abstract representations whose value was far more symbolic than referential, and more a public art form than objects for connoisseurship' (p. 6). The Kader Molla photograph symbolically represents the context of frustration, suffering and 'defeat' of democratic ideals. As a result, this emotional impact needed for people to engage with a social movement seems to mobilise this context for a social movement.

In the following section, I will address how this photograph fits in the context of frustration evident in the blogosphere during this period. The introduction of the photograph transformed this context into a social movement event in which people could assert demands for justice. The discussions in the blogosphere indicate how people's expectations of the state were mobilised in the form of a social movement which circulated and recirculated a photograph which symbolised the 'victory' of people's causes of frustration, deprivation and injustice.

Bengali-language blogs and the meaning-making process

In Bangladesh, the history of the media is marked by censorship and mayhem. The press and the electronic media were not just under close supervision of the state, but journalists were also often attacked and confronted physical harassment. A number of laws, such as a new version of the Special Power Act 1974, were issued in 2011. According to this revised Act, prior permission and approval from the Ministry of Information would be needed before the broadcast of publicity materials related to the religious faith of minorities in Bangladesh. Apart from this, the Community Radio Policy (2008), the Right to Information Act (2009) and other pieces of legislation were meant to restrain the freedom of media. The introduction of the Internet in Bangladesh in 1996 opened up possibilities for creating an alternative forum for political, cultural and rational debates. As a result, Bengali-language blogging communities emerged. Within a decade, Bangladeshi blogs had become very popular platforms for Internet users to participate in political as well as sociocultural discussions (Haque, 2011). Blogging soon emerged as an alternative platform to express opinion about politics and other issues such as religion, atheism, homosexuality and other subjects that can be controversial in the physical sphere in a given context. Chowdhury's (2012) research on 'The Internet as a Public Sphere' examines discussions about liberation and radical Islamist issues on popular blogs. He found that such issues generated active and interactive participation among users. Civic issues were a prime concern of these blogs. In some cases, blogs even outperformed traditional media coverage in terms of their swiftness in communicating a piece of information (Chowdhury, 2012). However, this communication was not limited only to sharing and interpreting a piece of information. Instead, participation gradually transformed into activism.

The supreme manifestation of this process can be seen in the Shahbag movement. However, the popularity and practice of blogging were limited to the educated and urban middle class as a result of the digital divide and socioeconomic configuration of the country. Many bloggers within their small community tried to address the issue of secularism and often became part of various street demonstrations prior to the Shahbag movement. While talking about secularism, they often researched and investigated the history of the formation of Bangladesh, and they came to claim that secularism and freedom of cultural expression were the main ideas behind the liberation struggle of 1971. Started in 2001 by the late blogger, writer and activist Avijit Roy, mukto-mona.com was turned into a blog in 2004. It became a platform for free thinking and writing about science and scientific explanations opposed to religious explanations of the universe, and it provided a space where the intimate history of the 1971 liberation war and the idea of secular Bangladesh were revisited by many bloggers.

The reactions on online platforms immediately after the circulation of the Kader Molla image indicate that a number of people were expecting capital punishment for the war criminals. A mukto-mona.com blogger with the screen name Saiful (2013, February 5) called for a mass gathering. The Bengali-language blogs in Bangladesh that supported capital punishment for the war criminals gave a detailed, analytical and critical insight into the verdict of life imprisonment. The demand for capital punishment was unanimous in blog posts, as it was in comments on blog posts and on online newspaper reports. The comments on the blogs often tried to set out a strategy for the movement. For example, Shaiful Islam suggested the following for people who could not attend the main area of the protest:

> Friends, let's unite. Write slogans on a placard and make human chains. People's response will be aggravated. Wherever you are there must be a space for attracting people's attention. If you are studying in an educational institute, ask your friends. If you are working, inform your colleagues. Inform the people in your building. Where you are living, discuss it in the tea stalls. (Saiful, 2013, February 5, translation mine)

For blogs such as mukto-mona.com, Shahbag became a context for registering an alternative version of history to the mainstream one. While the mainstream media mainly talked about people's spontaneous participation in demanding capital punishment for Kader Molla and other accused war criminals, blog posts turned the issue into a context for contesting religious myths and politics and the process of the ICT in Bangladesh. This context was based on the demand for the justice for past crimes. For example, some of the comments on Saiful's posts read:

> @Avijit: Since I started opposing capital punishment, I have decided to stay firm against the verdict of capital punishment of any deeply abhorred, inhuman-like being. For this reason I do not want even Kader Molla to be hanged. However, since in Bangladesh capital punishment exists, and since Bachchu Rajakar was sentenced to death for lesser crimes than Kader Molla, this verdict is really surprising. (Safiq, 2013, February 6, translation mine)
> @Safiq: I am not sure about the concept of capital punishment. However, I was sure about capital punishment for Rajakar. (Rupan, 2013, February 6, translation mine)

In these comments, the sense of frustration and deprivation in contemporary sociopolitical life is evident. This sense of frustration brought forward the imagining of an 'ideal' nation based on the memories of the war of 1971. This 'ideal' nation was imagined to be free of religious biases and the politics of deprivation. The sense of frustration was created because this hope for the 'ideal' nation was disrupted by politics based on religion. The reference to religion and politics becomes clear in the discussion by a commenter with the profile name Orpheus, about the possibility of future collaboration between the present Awami League government and the Islamist party Jamaat-e-Islami:

> If Hazrat Ghulam Azam and Hazrat Nizami[2] are hanged until they are dead, or even if they are not, still in the name of these punishments they will be declared pious and the Awami League will form a coalition with Jamaat, because the trial will be done only once. (Orpheus, 2013, February 6, translation mine)

These comments indicate how religion and political strategies are wedded to the sociocultural life of Bangladesh. The formation of the nation called Bangladesh was based on ideas that would eventually turn the nation into 'Sonar Bangladesh' [Golden Bengal]. However, it seems, over the past forty-two years, the political uncertainties and upheavals meant that ruling governments never lived up to citizens' expectation of forming Sonar Bangladesh. As a result, participation in the Shahbag movement could be seen as struggle to assert the power of people who believed in the concept of Sonar Bangla, in which freedom of expression could be legitimised and practised against the power of political parties who failed to uphold the promises to create Sonar Bangladesh.

These discussions complemented the physical demonstration that took place in Shahbag Square itself. The cultural activities that took place alongside the demand for capital punishment for the war criminals – for example, religious minorities' singing of Baul songs and art students' drawing of cultural patterns and designs – indicate that Shahbag Square was treated as a space for expressing cultural freedom. Films such as *Guerrilla* (dir. Nasiruddin Yusuf, 2011) and *Amar*

Bandhu Rashed (*My friend Rashed*, dir. Morshedul Islam, 2011) were shown in the physical space of the protest. These films recall the struggle of the Liberation War. As a significant part of the crowd was made up of young people, this recollection of history should be studied in terms of an assertion of their presence within the broader history of the nation's formation, thereby suggesting a shared cultural existence. This shared cultural existence is the essence of the connectivity that the pro-Shahbag blogosphere tried to activate by referring to the nation's cultural history. For example, one of the dominant slogans of the movement, 'Tui Rajakar, Tui Rajakar' ('you are a traitor, you are a traitor', translation mine), refers to Humayan Ahmed's text *Bahubrihi*. During the movement, this slogan appeared in songs which spread rapidly and were compiled on new media platforms. In particular, a video clip was made from a television drama based on *Bahubrihi*, and it was circulated during the protest through YouTube along with slogans from the physical sphere and a newly made song by the Bangla band *Chirkut*.

Conclusion: images and the network of memory

Occupations of urban spheres are significant because they demonstrate the relational aspect of crowd and networks within a particular cultural framework. Historical circumstances in this regard are important as these could be a determiner of a larger sociopolitical and cultural space where online activities take place. Movements such as Shahbag offer the scope and possibility for viewing demonstrations as more than a reflection of people's engagement with the larger technological as well as sociocultural infrastructure of a society. The Shahbag movement also demonstrates how a mass gathering could be seen as a visible manifestation of memories which declare people's tensions and struggles within a democratic state. In this paper, I discussed the importance of an image which acted as a material codification of this tension and struggle. This image activated the network of memory hidden from official versions of history, thereby initiating a meaning-making process that gave rise to a social movement.

Doerr, Mattoni, and Teune (2015) give a detailed literature review on how visuals echo social movements. Their main contribution is to consider visuals in social movements from the point of view of performance and mediatisation. In a similar vein, McLagan and McKee (2012) examine political acts manifested through media forms. Their analysis is based on two interconnected levels:

> First, it requires close attention to the formal, aesthetic, rhetorical, and affective dimension of the images, performances, and artefacts that George Marcus has called 'the activist imaginary'. Second, it requires an examination of the processual aspect of this imaginary, which is to say the whole network of financial, institutional, discursive and technological infrastructures and practices involved in the production, circulation, and reception of the visual-cultural materials. (McLagan & McKee, 2012 p. 1)

This study by McLagan and McKee (2012) examines how both visuals and their perception through media work together to underline the political struggle with memory through nongovernmental manifestations. In this regard, it can be said that the introduction of an image in an already created context consists in a number of sociopolitical issues, and the reception of the image denotes social relations that are not limited to its contents only. This discussion obviously opens up the possibility of a mediation of aesthetics of protest manifestations. Although the image that I have considered has been codified in a very localised context, the analysis and study of the image and its circulation and reception through different media platforms suggest that alternative history and personalised memory can be made visible through digital media platforms. This visibility further creates opportunities for people to become engaged with politics and gives a form of protest to cultural and historical struggles for identity and democracy.

Disclosure statement

No potential conflict of interest was reported by the authors.

Notes

1. The issue of capital punishment arguably makes the movement's demand controversial on humanitarian grounds. Here in this paper the demand for capital punishment is considered as a demand for highest punishment in the constitution of Bangladesh. This demand for execution in a democratic state has meaning beyond the simple taking of the life of a human being. However, in this paper, Bangladesh's democracy and the legal existence of capital punishment have not been discussed. The aim of this paper is focused on the context of history rather than on the constitutional existence of capital punishment in Bangladesh.
2. Here the author satirically refers to the accused war criminals Ghulam Azam and Motiyur Rahman Nizami.

References

Bazin, A. (1967). The ontology of photographic image. In Hugh Gray (Ed.), *What is cinema?* (Hugh Gray translated, Vol. 1). Berkeley: University of California Press.

Chowdhury, M. Z. (2012). The internet as a public sphere: Blogging 'liberation war vs Jamaat' issue in somewherein … blog, a case study. Retrieved from http://www.academia.edu/2241606/The_Internet_as_a_public_sphere_Blogging_Liberation_war_vs_Jamaat_issue_in_somewherein … blog_a_case_study

Doerr, N., Mattoni, A., & Teune, S. (2015). Visuals in social movements. In D. Porta & M. Diani (Eds.), *Oxford handbook of social movements* (pp. 557–566). Oxford: Oxford University Press.

Hariman, R., & Lucaites, J. L. (2007). *No caption needed: Iconic photographs, public culture, and liberal democracy.* Chicago, IL: University of Chicago Press.

Haque, F. (2011). Bangla blog community: Opinion, virtual resistance or the hunger for creating community of the detached people. *Yogayog, 10,* 151–178.

Islam, M. (dir.) (2011). Amar Bandhu Rashed [My Friend Rashed]. Bangladesh: Monon Chalachitra & Impress Telefilm Ltd.

Jasper, J. M., & Poulsen, J. D. (1995). Recruiting strangers and friends: Moral shocks and social networks in animal rights and anti-nuclear protests. *Social Problems, 42*(4), 493–512.

Kracauer, S. (1965). Photography. In T. Y. Levin (Ed.), *The mass ornaments: Weimer essays* (pp. 47–63). Cambridge: Harvard UP.

McLagan, M., & McKee, Y. (2012). Introduction. In Meg McLagan & Yates McKee (Eds.), *Sensible politics: The visual culture of nongovernmental activism* (pp. 9–26). New York: Zone Books.

Memou, A. (2015). *Photography and social movements: From the globalization of movement (1968) to the movement against globalization (2001).* Manchester: Manchester University Press.

Olesen, T. (2013). *Research in social movements, conflicts and change.* Retrieved from http://www.emeraldinsight.com/doi/full/10.1108/S0163-786X(2013)0000035005

Orpheus. (2013, Fenruary 6). Re: We demand to free Grandpa Kader [web log comment]. Retrieved from https://blog.mukto-mona.com/2013/02/06/33186/

Pink, S., Horst, H., & Postill, J. (2016). *Digital ethnography: Principles and practice.* London: Sage Publications.

Rose, G. (2013). *Visual methodologies* (3rd ed.). London: Sage.

Ruchatz, J. (2008). The photograph as externalization and trace. In A. Erll (Ed.), *Cultural memory studies an international and interdisciplinary handbook* (pp. 367–378). Berlin: Walter de Gruyt.

Rupan. (2013, Fenruary 6). Re: We demand to free Grandpa Kader [web log comment]. Retrieved from https://blog.mukto-mona.com/2013/02/06/33186/

Safiq, Islam. (2013, February 6). Re: We demand to free Grandpa Kader [web log comment]. Retrieved from https://blog.mukto-mona.com/2013/02/06/33186/

Saiful, Islam. (2013, February 5). We demand to free Grandpa Kader [Kaderdadur Mukti Chai][web log post]. Retrieved from https://blog.mukto-mona.com/2013/02/06/33186/

Schrøder, K. (2012). Discursive realities. In K. B. Jensen (Ed.), *A handbook of media and communication research: A qualitative and quantitative methodologies* (2nd ed.) (pp. 106—130). London: Routeledge.

Yasmin, L. (2013). Religion and after: Bangladeshi identity since 1971. Retrieved from https://www.opendemocracy.net/opensecurity/lailufar-yasmin/religion-and-after-bangladeshi-identity-since-1971

Yusuf, N. (dir.). (2011). *Guerilla*. Bangladesh: Ashirbad Cholochitra.

Social movements and constitutional politics in Latin America: reconfiguring alliances, framings and legal opportunities in the judicialisation of abortion rights in Brazil

Alba Ruibal

One of the main innovations in the interaction between social movements and the state in Latin America since the democratisation processes is the use of courts as venues for social change and the intervention of social actors in constitutional politics. Drawing from the empirical study of the process of strategic litigation for abortion rights in Brazil, this paper aims to show what type of changes can take place when social actors set out to pursue a legal strategy on a highly controversial matter, and in a transitional context, where courts are in the midst of a redefinition of their institutional role in the political system, and movements have not yet been central actors in judicialisation processes. The study highlights how feminist organisations adapted their framing of the abortion issue and developed new alliances with legal actors in order to pursue a rights strategy and to interact with the constitutional court. It also points out how, when dealing with the abortion controversy, the Brazilian constitutional court (*Supremo Tribunal Federal*) expanded the legal opportunity for the participation of civil society actors and, in its 2012 decision that liberalised the abortion law, acknowledged the legal arguments advanced by social actors in this field.

Introduction

One of the main innovations in the interaction between social movements and the state in Latin America since the democratisation processes is the use of courts as venues for social change and the intervention of social actors in constitutional politics. The displacement of part of movements' actions to the legal arena has taken place particularly following constitutional and judicial reforms throughout the region, which expanded the legal opportunity for citizens' rights claims through the creation or reform of constitutional courts and the inclusion of new constitutional rights and legal remedies.[1] This process has involved changes in the strategies, framings and organisational structures of civil society actors in order to carry out new forms of collective action, including in particular legal mobilisation and strategic litigation. It has also implied changes in court decision-making processes, in order to take into consideration the presence and voices of new actors in constitutional politics.

The abortion rights controversy is a privileged field in which to observe the shifting relationship between social movements and courts in Latin America, as well as the institutional and discursive changes it has involved. The highly restrictive legal framework of abortion in Latin America (see Lamas, 2008, pp. 68–69) has started to change during the past decade, as legislative reforms and constitutional court decisions have liberalised, to different extents, the abortion law in Colombia, Mexico City, Argentina, Brazil and Uruguay.[2] Constitutional Courts have been central actors in most of these cases, and have sided for the first time in the region with feminists' demands to decriminalise abortion under certain circumstances. They have done so by upholding legislative decisions or by expanding themselves the scope of exceptions to abortion criminalisation. During the same period, Constitutional Courts have also been key actors in backlash processes in the field of reproductive rights and have upheld the claims of counter-movements.[3] Finally, the abortion issue prominently includes the crucial problem of implementation and compliance with legal decisions, and the interaction between courts and social movements has also been important in this regards in the region.[4]

Brazil is one of the two cases in Latin America, together with Colombia, in which Courts liberalised the abortion law, motivated by constitutional claims submitted by feminist organisations. In 2012, after a process of strategic litigation carried out since 2004 by the Institute of Bioethics, Human Rights and Gender (ANIS) and its partners in this legal action, the Brazilian Constitutional Court (*Supremo Tribunal Federal*) legalised abortion in cases of anencephaly. This is a narrow though significant change, considering that the Brazilian abortion law is among the most regressive in the world – as it does not include an indication for cases in which women's health is at risk – and it had not been modified since 1940. Furthermore, this was the first case of strategic litigation for women's rights, as well as the first case on abortion rights decided by Brazil's highest Court. Finally, the case shows that the decision of Brazil's highest Court incorporated the legal concepts and framing advanced by social actors, which confirms the claim by democratic constitutionalism scholars who argue that social movements can be central actors in the generation of a discourse that begins from the bottom and that may influence the content of norms officially sanctioned by the state (Siegel, 2004, p. 15).

Through the study of the Brazilian case, this paper analyses the changes that can take place both at the level of civil society and courts when a movement, or one of its organisations, sets out to pursue a legal strategy, and to interact with constitutional courts, in a transitional context in which these are still novel processes. In particular, it aims to contribute to understand the conditions under which social movements are able to use superior courts and become significant actors in constitutional politics, in a setting where movements have not yet been central actors in judicialisation processes, and the legal opportunity to litigate before the constitutional court has been expanded, but the court is still in the midst of redefining its institutional role in the political system, and has not yet played a key role in rights adjudication.

Based on this case study, the paper points out three types of changes, along the three main analytical frameworks of social movement theory, and their application by legal studies. First, with regard to resource mobilisation, the case shows that, in the absence of its own support structure and legal expertise for strategic litigation, feminist actors established alliances with actors in the legal profession, who were external to the feminist movement. Second, with respect to framing, the pursuit of a legal strategy in this case entailed a moderation of the discourse and a renaming of the abortion procedure, in order to gain cultural resonance and public acceptance, which at the same time created intra-movement tensions. Third, with regards to opportunities, the case shows that the movement was able to use new institutional rules and legal instruments to reach the Court, and, most significantly, it shows that the Court itself, when dealing with the highly controversial abortion issue, expanded the legal opportunity for social actors' participation, opening new procedural opportunities for subsequent movements.

The analysis of the case study draws on semi-structured interviews conducted in 2013 with NGO activists, academics and jurists in three Brazilian cities: Rio de Janeiro, São Paulo and

Brasília, as well as on secondary sources and the case law. The paper's first section outlines the analytical perspective. The second section analyses the process of legal mobilisation, considering the organisational dimension, the construction of a new framing of the abortion issue in cases of anencephaly and the processing of the case before the *Supremo Tribunal Federal*, with emphasis on the expansion of the legal opportunity for the participation of social actors as well as on the reception by the Court of the legal concepts advanced by the claimants.

Analytical perspective: social movements and courts in transition

The three main analytical frameworks of social movement theory have been used and further developed by socio-legal studies and constitutional theorists – particularly Reva Siegel – in their analysis of the interaction between social actors and the legal system. This section outlines the main insights of these frameworks, as applied in legal studies, for the analysis of the dynamics between courts and social actors particularly in a transitional context. By a transitional setting we mean one in which social movements' participation in constitutional politics as well as courts' role in the protection of rights are still recent processes, and legal practices and institutions are being reconfigured.

In the first place, drawing on the resource mobilisation paradigm developed by social movement theory, Epp (1998), working in the field of legal mobilisation studies, has pointed out the importance of the organisational dimension for the development of strategic rights advocacy, and has advanced the influential concept of *support structure for legal mobilisation*, which includes the presence of public interest lawyers, rights advocacy organisations and the availability of financing sources to sustain litigation (p. 18). In transitional contexts, where social movements have not yet developed their own support structure and legal expertise, we can expect that the decision by social actors to pursue a legal strategy leads them to search for new types of organisational means to carry out these actions. In these cases, movement actors may start building their own resources for legal mobilisation, for example by creating new organisations oriented to the legal defence of rights, or they may recourse to alliances with partners and allies in the legal profession, outside of the movement, including state actors working in the legal field.

Secondly, in line with frame theory in social movement studies, democratic constitutionalism scholar Reva Siegel has developed a comprehensive theory about the influence of legal strategies on framing transformation.[5] She argues that movements willing to influence legal change must subject their claims and framing to what she calls the *public value* condition; that is, they must frame their idiosyncratic demands into a discourse that appeals to public values and shared constitutional understandings (Siegel, 2004, pp. 11–12). In this process, movements usually moderate their claims and rhetoric, especially when confronting a counter-movement (Siegel, 2006, pp. 1354–1365). For example, movements may search for cultural resonance by aligning their framing with the dominant discourse of the state (Ferree, 2003).[6] Resonance may also be searched by other means that do not imply an alignment with dominant institutional discourses, but nonetheless entail a moderation of movement claims. Movements may, for example, reframe an issue by renaming and re-categorising it, in an attempt at eluding the discussion of its most controversial aspects. In any of these cases, subjecting a movement's claims to the public value condition can provoke disagreement between the more legalistic and the more radical groups within the movement.[7] This type of intra-movement conflict is more likely to appear in a transitional context, where movements have a history of political mobilisation but have not yet pursued legal strategies, and the legal discourse appears as a new component of movement framings.

Finally, following the political opportunity approach in social movement theory, legal mobilisation studies have developed the concept of legal opportunity to refer to the institutional settings and dynamics within the state structure that are directly related to movements' recourse to law and the courts (Andersen, 2005; Hilson, 2002; Wilson & Cordero, 2006). This perspective assumes that there is a connection between institutional features and the types of claims and actors that reach the courts. In particular, the rules that regulate access and legal standing set incentives for parties to litigate and may affect the possibility of social movements to channel their claims through courts. Other types of rules, such as those that regulate public hearings and amicus curiae presentations, are also relevant for the interaction between courts and social actors. The relationship between courts and civil society may become an issue of particular concern by justices especially in contexts of redefinition of the institutional role of constitutional courts, following processes of political transition and judicial reform. In these contexts, highly contentious cases may become critical junctures for Courts to promote their interaction with social actors. As Siegel argues, in this type of case, justices may have an interest in citizens' engagement with constitutional interpretation, in order to make a decision informed by evolving social understandings and to find social support, which may allow courts to preserve their institutional authority (2001, p. 351). When dealing with these cases in transitional contexts, where courts have not yet modified their internal procedures in order to allow for the participation of external actors in their decision-making process, justices may find incentives to implement new institutional channels for social actors' claims; that is, they may decide to expand the legal opportunity, opening in this way new institutional venues for the claims of subsequent movements.

Feminist legal mobilisation for abortion rights in the case of anencephaly in Brazil
Support structure for legal mobilisation and new alliances for a feminist legal claim

During the past decades, Brazilian feminists have developed a strong movement for reproductive rights, and abortion rights in particular.[8] As in other Latin American cases, since the transition to democracy in the 1980s, the bulk of feminist advocacy for abortion law reform in Brazil has concentrated on pursuing legislative change. But, in Brazil – as in most cases in the region except from Uruguay and Mexico City – the political process under contemporary democratic governments has been closed so far for the liberalisation of abortion laws. As a result, despite several attempts at legislative reform, the Brazilian Criminal Code provisions drafted in 1940, which allow for abortions only in cases of rape and life-threatening circumstances, have not been modified by Congress. The acknowledgment by feminist organisations of the obstacles for the advancement of abortion legalisation through national politics has led a sector of the feminist movement in Brazil to turn to the judiciary in search of long-pursued reforms (Paranhos, 2012; Soares, 2012).

However, even after the constitutional reform of 1988, which brought about a more favourable legal opportunity for social movements' claims, the Brazilian feminist movement has not developed a strong legal expertise or a support structure for legal mobilisation. Several sociological factors contribute to explain the difficult relationship of feminist movements in Brazil – and in the region more generally – with legal systems that have historically reinforced patterns of gender discrimination. In the case of Brazil, interviewees for this study pointed out that one of the limitations for the development of legal mobilisation for women's rights is that there are still few feminist lawyers working in this field, and argued that this can be partly attributed to the lack of gender training at law schools, as well as to the lack of a human rights approach in legal education (Davis Mattar, 2012; Gonçalves, 2012). A further factor in this regards is that human rights movements in the country – which focus on issues such as public security, police violence and the violation of rights in the public space – have generally not included gender as a mainstream perspective. The lack of a gender approach by the human rights movement in Brazil can be partly explained by the fact that, since the dictatorship, this movement has been linked to the progressive sectors of the Catholic Church[9]; and the decisive fight of this sector of the Church against social injustice especially during the democratic transition did not include questioning gender injustices (Gebara, 1995, p. 131).

In addition, the characteristics of the field of public interest litigation in Brazil have contributed to a scarce legal mobilisation by social movements in general until recent years. Two main factors help explain why social movements have not been central actors in public interest litigation: the role of state officials and agencies in this field, on the one hand, and the preeminence of individual claims over collective petitions, on the other. With regards to the role of state actors in this type of legal cases, Botelho (2003, p. 90) explains that the provision of alternative legal services in the country, which had its origin in the initiative of lawyers who defended political prisoners during the dictatorship, was linked to some degree to the Church but most prominently to leftist political parties, in particular the Workers' Party (PT). Due to the ascension to national power of political actors that had been on the resistance side during the dictatorship in the first years of the transition, and due to the increasing difficulty to obtain external financing, since the late 1990s and throughout the 2000s a partnership between alternative legal services and the State was developed (Botelho 2003, p. 91). Furthermore, reinforcing the role of the state in this field, the Public Ministry has been a key actor in the development of a more rights-oriented justice system and has taken the lead in the field of public interest litigation (Sarmento, 2012)[10]. According to Hoffman and Bentes (2008, p. 114), the proactive stance of the this institution in the defense of citizens' rights contributed to downplay the role of civil society's actors in this field, although this trend has started to change in recent years.[11] With regards to the preeminence of individual demands, even in cases in which social movement activism was the driving force behind social change, legal claims were carried out by individuals rather than by social movements. This has been the case, in particular, regarding the impressive judicialisation of the right to health in Brazil since the 2000s, which has been pursued by individual demands (Ferraz, 2011, p. 78), while the *Movemento Sanitarista* (public health reform movement) has been one of the most influential social movements in Brazil in terms of its influence on legislation and public policy.

In this context, in Brazil, as it happened in other countries in the region, feminist organisations that intended to pursue litigation strategies had to start building their own organisational resources for legal mobilisation,[12] or they had to forge alliances with partners and allies in the legal profession, outside the feminist movement, including state actors. The latter was the strategy pursued by ANIS in Brazil when, in 2004, it decided to start a process of judicialisation of abortion rights in cases of anencephaly before the *Supremo Tribunal Federal* (STF). ANIS, founded in Brasilia in 1999, is a feminist NGO devoted to academic research, information, education and advocacy on bioethical issues related to human reproduction. Without counting on its own legal expertise, or on the presence of legal organisations within the feminist movement, this organisation searched from legal advice and support by external actors. In 2004, it held a meeting with then-Public Prosecutor Daniel Sarmento, in order to analyse the most effective way to carry out a legal strategy for abortion rights in cases of anencephaly that could have general effects. Sarmento is one of the main constitutionalist jurists working in the field of minority rights and sexual and reproductive rights in Brazil. He proposed to use the Allegation of Violation of a Fundamental Precept (*Argüição de descumprimento de preceito fundamental*, ADPF), which is one of four types of abstract review cases in Brazil – filed directly with the STF – and is only admitted when there is no alternative remedy to protect a fundamental precept of the Constitution.[13] Given Sarmento's position as a state official, he could not carry out the legal action, and suggested Luís Roberto Barroso – one of the most renowned Brazilian constitutionalists, who in 2013 became justice at the STF – as a possible litigant-lawyer in this case. Barroso agreed to carry out the legal demand pro bono (Paranhos, 2012).

The ADPF was still not a familiar type of claim in the Brazilian legal field, and a key issue to be resolved in this case was the selection of an appropriate actor, with legal standing to present the claim.[14] Given that national union confederations are among the actors legally allowed to submit abstract constitutional claims before the STF, Barroso suggested that the National Confederation of Health Workers (CNTS) would be a proper claimant, for it had already been granted legal standing in previous cases before the Court (Paranhos, 2012). The CNTS agreed to pursue the case on humanitarian grounds as well as due to the specific interest of the medical profession in the resolution of this issue (Barroso, 2004). Throughout the legal process, ANIS worked in partnership with Barroso, and provided bioethical and human rights arguments, as well as a theoretical and philosophical perspective to the argumentation of the case (Paranhos, 2012). The process of strategic litigation included various campaigns of public awareness, in which ANIS worked together with several other feminist organisations, in particular Catholics for Choice Brazil (*Católicas pelo Direito de Decidir*), GEA (Group of Studies on Abortion) and *Redesaúde* (Paranhos, 2012).

Reframing abortion in cases of anencephaly: The social construction of a legal claim, and intra-movement dissent

The core argument of the demand, which was presented by the CNTS before the STF on 17 June 2004, was that the interruption of the pregnancy of an anencephalic foetus does not fit into the penal definition of abortion, because anencephaly was a malformation incompatible with life outside of the womb, and therefore in such cases the factual support required by the law to criminalise abortion (the potentiality of life) was absent.[15] This argument had been developed by ANIS, and more specifically by Debora Diniz in her bioethical work and her ethnographic research.

In fact, this process had its origin in 2003, when Debora Diniz, ANIS's founder and Director – who is also Professor of Anthropology at the University of Brasilia and a leading actor in the abortion debate in Brazil – was carrying out ethnographic research at two public hospitals in Brasilia (*Hospital Regional da Asa Sul* and *Hospital Universitário de Brasília*) which provide legal abortion services. There, she was confronted with overwhelming cases of pregnant women who were going through medical treatment for cases of foetal anencephaly (Diniz, 2004, p. 23). She found that after receiving such a diagnosis, women did not use the word abortion, but they talked about anticipating unavoidable suffering and anticipating delivery. The same was found by Diaulas Costa Ribeiro during his work as Promoter of Justice for the Defense of Users of the Health System at the Public Ministry of Brasilia. This led them to redefine the procedure in this circumstance in order to have it reflect women's actual experiences (Diniz, 2004, pp. 22–23). The reasoning was that given that the abortion legislation aims to protect potential life, only the foetus with a physiological capacity to live outside of the womb could be subject to the crime of abortion; without that condition, there existed no juridical good to protect, and no grounds to prohibit a woman from interrupting her pregnancy (Diniz & Costa Ribeiro, 2003, p. 106). Within this framework, Diniz and Costa Ribeiro advanced a definition of the medical procedure in these cases as a 'therapeutic anticipation of birth', which became a central reference during the legal process.

The constitutional claim presented at the STF dealt with a condition that allowed the petitioners to circumvent the question of the beginning of life. They even framed the demand as a case that did not refer to abortion. In fact, the legal action, and its eight-year legal process before the STF, inevitably carved out a broad public discursive space on abortion and elicited a discussion that went far beyond the specific case of anencephaly, including broader arguments about women's reproductive freedoms. ANIS had anticipated the potentiality of the case in this regard, but it decided to maintain a type of discourse that allowed it to gain legitimacy to access the STF (Paranhos, 2012). By renaming the abortion procedure in cases of anencephaly, the legal strategy pursued by ANIS implied a moderation of the discourse by some feminist actors, in contrast with more radicalised feminist framings and strategies, which do not concede to elude the term abortion and ground their demands on a claim about women's right to their own bodies. This was one of the reasons why, especially at the beginning of the process, ANIS' legal strategy was critically characterised as 'gradualist' by some sectors of the movement, although with time most of them modified their opinion in light of the wide public debate provoked by the legal action (Paranhos, 2012).

This happened in the context of a large and diverse feminist movement in which, beyond basic agreements among the different sectors with regards to the abortion issue,[16] there exist strong disagreements regarding strategies and framing. Both types of disagreements are related to the pursuit of legal mobilisation. For example, while the more legalised sector of the movement, represented by *RedeSaúde* among others, holds that it is not always necessary to mention the word abortion (for, it is argued, it may discourage some actors, in particular doctors who do not talk about abortion but about the legal interruption of pregnancy and the exceptions in which it is lawful), more radical sectors, such as the Brazilian Women's Articulation, argue that not using the word abortion openly would mean a concession to false morals (Negrão, 2012). Another point of conflict refers to the convenience of pursuing a gradualist strategy: while some sectors defend working for the implementation of legal abortion and advocating for the extension of the indications model, other groups argue that emphasis should be placed on campaigning for unconditional abortion rights for all women (Rodrigues, 2012; Vieira Villela, 2012). For example, a member of the World March of Women maintains that while the gradualist approach contributes to placing the abortion issue on the public agenda, it circumscribes the limits of the abortion debate, consumes the energies of the movement and obliges it to develop a distorted argumentation, instead of openly advocating for abortion rights on grounds of women's autonomy and right to decide (Godinho, 2009, p. 65). Further disagreement within the movement is related to the idea of balancing constitutional values in the abortion controversy, although it has started to gain wider support (Corrêa, 2005, p. 212).

New legal opportunity and the incorporation of social actors' claims in court proceedings and decision

The demand was eventually upheld by the STF on 12 April 2012. The Court declared the unconstitutionality of the application of the abortion criminal law to cases of anencephaly, and established the right of pregnant women in that situation to have access to adequate medical procedures for the interruption of pregnancy, without previous judicial authorisation.

The eight-year process of the case before the Court took place at a time in which the STF was undergoing a process of redefinition of its institutional role. In fact, the legal opportunity for claiming citizen rights in Brazil had been expanded by the 1988 Constitution, which is well known globally for the inclusion of generous social provisions. The Constitution also widened the review powers of the STF, created new instruments for the defense of fundamental rights and expanded access for social and political actors to present claims before this Court.[17]

However, for several years after the promulgation of the 1988 Constitution, the bulk of the STF work concentrated on cases related either to economic governance or to the distribution of political power (Kapiszewski, 2011, p. 154), and the Court was not a significant player in the field of rights adjudication. Moreover, for some time it was seen as an appellate instance more than as a constitutional court (Martins, 2009, p. 46).[18] However, in recent years, the STF has gained influence in the political scene, and it has decided prominent rights-related cases, including issues such as access to AIDS medication (2000), stem-cell research (2008), same-sex civil unions (2011), racial quotas at universities (2012) and the demarcation of indigenous territories (2012) (see Barroso, 2012; Martins, 2009). The Court's decision on abortion rights in cases of anencephaly was part of this process.

In fact, according to the Justice in charge of organising and directing this case (Justice-Rapporteur), Marco Aurélio Mello, this has been one of the most important cases heard by the STF in its institutional history.[19] The controversial nature of the case, and its acknowledged institutional relevance for the Court help explain why, when dealing with it, the STF decided to expand the legal opportunity structure for the participation of social actors by convoking for the first time a public hearing at the STF, which was held in 2008, and was followed by three more.[20] The Justice-Rapporteur also accepted the request made in the ADPF that ANIS be admitted as amicus curiae in the case.[21]

The Court's decision was aligned with the arguments developed by the claimants, and originally constructed by ANIS. With a clear resonance with those arguments, in its opening paragraphs the decision frames the problem by stating that 'there is a difference between abortion and the therapeutic anticipation of birth' (ADPF 54, p. 32). It also declares that the question involves women's dignity, freedom, health and sexual and reproductive rights, and it mentions the tension between those rights and society's interest in the protection of its members, but concludes that in this case there is no real conflict between fundamental rights. In analysing the question of anencephaly, the decision draws heavily on scientific information presented at the public hearings. In fact, it explicitly states that 'the information and data revealed at public hearings greatly contributed to clarifying what anencephaly is' (ADPF 54, p. 46). On the basis of those arguments, it argues that there is no right to life or dignity of the unborn opposing women's rights, because life is not viable in the case of anencephaly. The decision also acknowledged the informational value of the opinions heard during public hearings with regards to women's agency to make a decision in these cases (ADPF 54, p. 80).

Conclusion

This paper has analysed the social construction of a legal claim that had its origin in the ethnographic research of feminist actors was further developed in an unconstitutionality action, and was eventually incorporated by the STF in its decision that liberalised the abortion law. In this regards, the case confirms democratic constitutionalism's argument that social movements can be key agents in the development of legal arguments that courts may incorporate into institutionalised law.

The study intended to show that the interaction between social movements and tribunals in this type of processes implies changes both at the level of social moments and courts: it leads to changes in terms of the discursive and organisational strategies of actors in civil society, as well as in courts' decision-making processes. In the Brazilian case, the study shows how the displacement of the movement's claims to the legal arena implied organisational changes in terms of the forging of new alliances with actors outside the feminist camp. In effect, in its intent to pursue a strategic litigation case before the STF, ANIS contacted renowned actors in the field of public law in Brazil, who provided their resources and legal expertise for the development of the case.

Secondly, the case study confirms Siegel's claim that movements usually moderate their framings when they intend to achieve legal change through courts. Most interestingly, the reframing of the abortion issue on cases of anencephaly had its roots in ANIS' ethnographic perspective and empirical work, which reflects the construction of a legal claim grounded on the discourse of the persons who were directly related to the situation that was being denounced.

Finally, the study also highlights how the intervention of social movements in constitutional politics on highly controversial cases can generate incentives for constitutional courts to incorporate the voices of these actors in the judicial decision-making process. In contexts of judicial transition, this may entail the implementation of institutional channels for the participation of social actors in court proceedings, such as public hearings, that had never been used before by the Court.

Disclosure statement

No potential conflict of interest was reported by the author.

Notes

1. Since the mid-1980s, most Latin American countries have carried out reforms to their judicial institutions, which have prominently included the empowerment of constitutional courts (Navia & Ríos-Figueroa, 2005).
2. In 2006, the Colombian Constitutional Court established that abortion should be legal in cases of rape, risk to the woman's life or health and serious foetal malformation. In 2007, Mexico City's Legislative Assembly legalised abortion during the first trimester. In 2012, the Brazilian *Supremo Tribunal Federal* legalised abortion in cases of anencephaly; Argentina's Supreme Court established that the rape exception introduced in 1921 covered all cases of rape; and Uruguay's National Congress decriminalised abortion during the first trimester.
3. Examples, among others, are Costa Rica's Supreme Court ruling in 2000 to prohibit in-vitro fertilisation (which was reversed by the Inter-American Human Rights Court in 2012) and the 2007 Chilean Constitutional Court ruling to declare unconstitutional the distribution of the emergency contraception pills.
4. In particular, the Colombian Constitutional Court has played a vanguard role in the implementation of abortion legal reform, and in countering backlash, by upholding feminist claims regarding the full implementation of its 2006 Decision that liberalised the abortion law (Roa & Klugman, 2014).
5. Other aspects involved in legal framing can be found in legal mobilisation studies (for example, Andersen, 2005; Marshall, 2003).
6. According to this perspective, in the West German case feminists aligned their frameworks with the official view on abortion, through the stigmatisation of abortion as a criminal and immoral act, and the depiction of women who decided to have an abortion as victims of this situation (Ferree, 2003, p. 304).
7. See Ferree (2003), Bagenstos (2009) and Vanhala (2011), working in the field of legal mobilisation, for thorough studies on intra-movement contestation on framing and tactics.
8. *RedeSaúde* (the National Feminist Network for Sexual and Reproductive Health and Rights), founded in 1991, is the biggest and most structured feminist network in the country, conjoining more than 300 entities (Negrão, interview, 2012), and the Brazilian Initiative for the Right to a Safe and Legal Abortion (*Jornadas Brasileiras pelo Direito ao Aborto Legal e Seguro*), created in 2004 as an offspring of *RedeSaúde*, is a single-issue coalition that coordinates different networks, organisations and advocates throughout the country.
9. In the first decade after the democratic transition, more than half of the groups that make up the National Movement for Human Rights were related to religious institutions, and particularly to the Catholic Church (Cleary, 1997, p. 268).
10. Hoffman and Bentes (2008, p. 114) affirm that the Public Ministry has played the role of a citizens' ombudsperson in the fields of health and education. In particular the Federal Public Ministry does not understand its role as an accusatory organ, but as a defender of human rights, minority rights and collective rights, and it is an independent power (Sarmento, Author interview, 2012).
11. While at the beginning of the 2000s, 9 out of 10 public interest actions were promoted by the Public Ministry, nowadays that proportion is 5 out of 10, which is due to the growth of the protagonism of civil society in this field (Sarmento, author interview, 2012).
12. This was the case in Colombia, where Colombian feminist lawyer Mónica Roa, supported by the organisation Women's Link Worldwide, established an office of this organisation in Bogota in 2005, with the specific aim of developing a litigation strategy for the liberalisation of the abortion law.

13. Fundamental precepts are more comprehensive than constitutional principles established in Articles 1–4, and they are not exactly defined by the Constitution or the legislation, so it is a competence of the STF to establish their scope and meaning.
14. The ADPF, as other abstract review petitions in Brazil, can be brought before the Court by several state actors, by the Federal Section of the Brazilian Association of Advocates (*Ordem dos Advogados do Brasil*), by any political party with representation in Congress and by national unions or class-representing entities (constitutional article 103).
15. ADPF 54/DF, *Supremo Tribunal Federal*, April 12 2012. The text of this decision can be retrieved from: http://www.stf.jus.br/arquivo/cms/noticiaNoticiaStf/anexo/ADPF54.pdf.
16. There exists consensus within the movement about the need to advocate for the legalisation of abortion during the first trimester, despite conservatives' accusations that the movement promotes abortion during the whole period of pregnancy (Soares, interview, 2012). The movement also shares the view that abortion should be framed not as a matter of privacy *vis-à-vis* the State, but as a right that should include the provision of the service by the State (Corrêa, 2005, P. 210).
17. Until then, there was an abstract claim of unconstitutionality, but its scope was limited and the only legitimated actor to present it was the attorney-general of the Republic who directly reported to the President.
18. The STF is both a constitutional court, in that it exercises concentrate abstract review, and it is also the ultimate appellate instance in concrete constitutional review cases.
19. Vote of Justice Marco Aurélio Mello, ADPF 54, Supremo Tribunal Federal, 12 April 2012. Retrieved from: http://www.stf.jus.br/arquivo/cms/noticiaNoticiaStf/anexo/ADPF54.pdf.
20. The procedure for public hearings at the STF had been established in 1999, by Law 9.868, but it had not been implemented by the Court.
21. Internal regulations of the STF establish that one of the justices (*Ministro Relator*, Justice-Rapporteur) should be in charge of organising and directing the process in a case. It is a competence of the Justice-Rapporteur to convene public hearings with expert actors in cases of institutional and public relevance, as well as to accept amicus curiae briefs (see the STF's internal procedural regulations (*Regimento Interno*) retrieved from: http://www.stf.jus.br/arquivo/cms/legislacaoregimentointerno/anexo/ristf_120anos.pdf).

References

Andersen, E. (2005). *Out of the closets and into the courts: Legal opportunity structure and gay rights litigation*. Ann Arbor: The University of Michigan Press.
Bagenstos, S. (2009). *Law and the contradictions of the disability rights movement*. New Haven, CT: Yale University Press.
Barroso, L. R. (2004, August 15). Conheça os bastidores da discussão sobre anencefalia. *Revista Consultor Jurídico*.
Barroso, L. R. (2012, June 4). Direito e política: A tênue fronteira. *Revista Época*, pp. 78–81.
Botelho, E. (2003). Brazil: The road of conflict bound for total justice. In L. Friedman & R. Perez-Perdomo (Eds.), *Legal culture in the age of globalization: Latin America and Latin Europe* (pp. 64–107). Stanford: Stanford University Press.
Cleary, E. (1997). The Brazilian catholic church and church–state relations: Nation building. *Journal of Church and State*, 39(2), 253–272.
Corrêa, S. (2005). Abortion and human rights. In A. Ruibal (Ed.), *Seminário Direitos Sexuais e Direitos Reprodutivos na Perspectiva dos Direitos Humanos* (pp. 208–220). Rio de Janeiro: Anais-Advocacy.
Diniz, D. (2004). *Anencefalia e Supremo Tribunal Federal*. Brasilia: Letras Livres.
Diniz, D., & Costa Ribeiro, D. (2003). *Aborto por anomalia fetal*. Brasilia: Letras Livres.

Epp, C. (1998). *The rights revolution. Lawyers, activists, and supreme courts in comparative perspective.* Chicago, IL: The University of Chicago Press.

Ferraz, O. (2011). Brazil: Health inequalities, rights, and courts: The social impact of the judicialization of health. In A. Yamin & S. Gloppen (Eds.), *Litigating health rights: Can courts bring more justice to health?* (pp. 76–101). Cambridge: Harvard University Press.

Ferree, M. (2003). Resonance and radicalism: Feminist framing in the abortion debates of the United States and Germany. *American Journal of Sociology, 109*(2), 304–344.

Gebara, I. (1995). The abortion debate in Brazil: A report from an ecofeminist philosopher under siege. *Journal of Feminist Studies in Religion, 11*(2), 129–135.

Godinho, T. (2009). Legalização do aborto: Enraizar o debate. In S. Fleischer (Ed.), *Vozes Latino-americanas pela legalização do aborto* (pp. 61–67). Brasilia: CFEMEA.

Hilson, C. (2002). New social movements: The role of legal opportunity. *Journal of European Public Policy, 9*(2), 238–255.

Hoffman, F., & Bentes, F. (2008). Accountability for social and economic rights in Brazil. In V. Gauri & D. Brinks (Eds.), *Courting social justice: Judicial enforcement of social and economic rights in the developing world* (pp. 100–145). Cambridge: Cambridge University Press.

Kapiszewski, D. (2011). Power broker, policymaker, or rights protector? The Brazilian Supremo Tribunal Federal in transition. In G. Helmke & J. Ríos-Figueroa (Eds.), *Courts in Latin America* (pp. 154–185). New York, NY: Cambridge University Press.

Lamas, M. (2008). El aborto en la agenda del desarrollo en América Latina. *Perfiles Latinoamericanos, 31,* 65–93.

Marshall, A.-M. (2003). Injustice frames, legality, and the everyday construction of sexual harassment. *Law & Social Inquiry, 28*(3), 659–689.

Martins, L. (2009). Justiça constitucional dos direitos fundamentais no Brasil: Report 2009/10. In B. Víctor & N. Claudio (Eds.), *Justicia Constitucional y Derechos Fundamentales* (pp. 43–54). Montevideo, MN: Fundación Konrad Adenauer.

Navia, P., & Ríos-Figueroa, J. (2005). The constitutional adjudication mosaic of Latin America. *Comparative Political Studies, 38*(2), 189–217.

Roa, M., & Klugman, B. (2014). Considering strategic litigation as an advocacy tool: A case study of the defence of reproductive rights in Colombia. *Reproductive Health Matters, 22*(44), 31–41.

Siegel, R. (2001). Text in contest: Gender and the constitution from a social movement perspective. *University of Pennsylvania Law Review, 150,* 297–351.

Siegel, R. (2004, June). *The jurisgenerative role of social movements in United States Constitutional Law.* Presented at SELA, Oaxaca, Mexico.

Siegel, R. (2006). Constitutional culture, social movement conflict and constitutional change: The case of the de facto ERA. *California Law Review, 94,* 1323–1419.

Vanhala, L. (2011). Social movements lashing back: Law, social change and intra-social movement backlash in Canada. *Studies in Law, Politics, and Society, 54,* 113–140.

Wilson, B., & Cordero, J. (2006). Legal opportunity structures and social movements: The effects of institutional change on Costa Rican politics. *Comparative Political Studies, 39,* 325–351.

Interviews

Davis Mattar, L. (2012, August 31). Program manager, Conectas Human Rights; member of Global Doctors for Choice/Brazil. Author interview, São Paulo.

Gonçalves, T. (2012, August 16). Coordinator of CLADEM/Brazil. Author interview, Latin American and Caribbean Committee for the Defense of Women's Rights, Brasilia.

Negrão, T. (2012, August 8). Former Executive Secretary of the National Feminist Network for Sexual and Reproductive Health and Rights (2006–2012). Author telephone interview, Porto Alegre.

Paranhos, F. (2012, August 14). Member of ANIS. Author interview, Institute of Bioethics, Human Rights, and Gender, Brasília.

Rodrigues, K. (2012, August 13). Member of CFEMEA. Author interview, Feminist Centre for Studies and Advisory Services, Brasilia.

Sarmento, D. (2012, August 9). Federal Public Prosecutor. Author interview, Rio de Janeiro.

Soares, R. (2012, August 27). Sociologist; Member of Catholics for Choice Brazil. Author interview, São Paulo.

Vieira Villela, W. (2012, August 9). Professor, Member of the Research Group on Women's Health and Gender Relations. Author interview, Universidade Federal de São Paulo, Rio de Janeiro.

Pollution, Institutions and Street Protests in Urban China

Yang Zhong and Wonjae Hwang

ABSTRACT

Street protests have become commonplace in China. Utilizing extensive survey data, this study attempts to shed light on the nature of environmental street protests in China. The key question to be answered in the article is: why, facing the same issue, do some people choose the option of participating in street protests while others do not? Multivariate analytical findings indicate that Chinese urban residents' willingness to participate in street protests over a hypothetical pollution issue in China is significantly related to their attitudes toward institutions in China. What motivates people to participate in street protests has a lot to do with their trust and support of the political system in China and their perceived government transparency. In other words, these protests are not just what Lewis Coser calls 'realistic conflicts' which primarily involve specific issues and solutions. One implication from this study is that street protests in China may not be as benign and non-regime threatening as some scholars might think.

Introduction

Looking from outside, the Chinese government has been stable and is described as 'resilient'[1] despite the third wave of democratization and, recently, the Arab Spring. However, the picture is not so rosy inside China. In fact, street protests [or *quntixing shijian*], one form of contentious politics,[2] have become commonplace in China. The most cited official figure of social protests in China was 87,000 that occurred in 2005.[3] According to a *Wall Street Journal* report, the figure reached 180,000 in 2010.[4] Due to the frequent occurrences of street protests the Chinese government has made maintaining stability [*weiwen*] a top priority for all levels of government in China. It is reported that China currently spends more on domestic security than on its military.[5] What is the nature of these street protests? Do these activities pose a potential threat to destabilize the political regime in China? Answering these questions is critical for understanding contentious politics in China and assessing the prospect of change in the country.

---

[1] Andrew Nathan, 'Authoritarian resilience', *Journal of Democracy* 14, (2003), pp. 6–17.

[2] On contentious politics, see Doug McAdam, Sidney Tarrow and Charles Tilly, *Dynamics of Contention* (New York: Cambridge University Press, 2001).

[3] Zhao Peng *et al.*, 'The warning signal of "typical social protests"', *Outlook Weekly*, (8 September 2008), p. 36. For whatever reason, the Chinese government stopped publishing statistics with regard to street protests after 2006.

[4] Tom Orlik, 'Unrest grows as economy booms', *Wall Street Journal*, (26 September 2011), available at: http://online.wsj.com/news/articles/SB10001424053111903703604576587070600504108?mg=reno64wsj&url=http%3A%2F%2Fonline.wsj.com%2Farticle%2FSB10001424053111903703604576587070600504108.html (accessed 26 September 2011).

[5] Ben Blanchard and John Ruwitch, 'China hikes defense budget, to spend more on internal security', *Reuters*, (5 March 2013), available at: http://www.reuters.com/article/2013/03/05/us-china-parliament-defence-idUSBRE92403620130305 (accessed 11 January 2014).

There are different assessments among China scholars on the nature of street protests in China. Some believe that social protests pose serious threat to social stability in China and may lead to significant political changes.[6] Others argue that social protests in China are primarily issue-driven and, therefore, they do not undermine the fundamental structure of the existing political system.[7] Elizabeth Perry, an influential scholar on contentious politics in China, even argues that social protests have become a normal form of political participation for ordinary Chinese in Chinese politics and these activities actually contribute to social stability in China because protesters use these occasions to vent their anger and have their demands met.[8]

One way to shed light on the nature of street protests in China is to study what motivates people to participate in likely street protests. A key question in this debate involves whether these street protests are purely issue-driven or are also motivated by other factors, especially institutional factors? Why, facing the same issue, do some people decide to participate in street protests while others do not? If institution-related factors significantly affect street protest participation, these social activities can be perceived as a challenge to the stability of the authoritarian regime. A missing piece in assessing the danger of street protests in China is the type of street protest. Common causes for most street protests in China in the last two decades fall into the following categories: inadequate compensation for land-related disputes in both rural and urban areas of China; abuse of power by local Chinese officials; China's one-child policy; labor disputes; environmental pollution; and religious and secessionist movements.[9] Some of the street protests, such as land- and labor-related conflicts, involve small groups of people and are clearly narrow and specific-issue-driven. However, some other contentious conflicts are more general in nature. Most environment-related street protests are such conflicts because the environmental issues involved in the conflicts may carry potentially long-term detrimental health effects and affect a relatively large number of people. As such, people may have less incentive to participate in street protests over these issues (free ride problem). Therefore, this article picks environmental protests as the focus of study. The authors believe that environment-related street protests are better cases to test the effect of institutional factors in motivating people to participate in street protest activities in China.

Environment-related protests, which have experienced an annual increase of close to 30% since the mid-1990s in China,[10] have attracted scholars' attention in recent years.[11] This type of conflict is worthy of our attention for the following additional reasons. First, unlike land or labor dispute issues which only concern a small specific group of people, environmental pollution and degradation are of wide concern to the general population and can arouse widespread societal reaction due to the fact

[6]Li Zhu, 'Analysis of China's social risk: the social conflict nature of mass protests', *Xuehai* 1, (2009), pp. 69–78; Kevin O'Brien and Lianjiang Li, *Rightful Resistance in Rural China* (Cambridge: Cambridge University Press, 2006); Merle Goldman, *From Comrade to Citizen: The Struggle for Political Rights in China* (Cambridge, MA: Harvard University Press, 2005).

[7]Yu Jianrong, 'Categories and main features of China's current mass protests', *Zhongguo zhengfa daxue xuebao* 6, (2009), pp. 114–160; Elizabeth Perry, 'Chinese conceptions of "rights": from Mencius to Mao—and now', *Perspectives on Politics* 6, (2008), pp. 37–50.

[8]Elizabeth Perry, *Challenge the Mandate of Heaven: Social Protest and State Power in China* (Armonk, NY: M. E. Sharpe, 2002).

[9]Peter Ho, 'Who owns China's land', *The China Quarterly* 166, (2001), pp. 394–442; Xiaolin Guo, 'Land expropriation and rural conflict in China', *The China Quarterly* 166, (2001), pp. 422–439; Tyrene White, 'Domination, resistance and accommodation in China's one-child campaign', in Elizabeth Perry and Mark Selden, eds, *Chinese Society: Change, Conflict and Resistance* (London: Routledge, 2000), pp. 171–196; Jun Jing, 'Environmental protests in rural China', in Perry and Selden, eds, *Chinese Society*, pp. 297–214; David Zweig, 'To the courts or to the barricades: can new political institutions manage rural conflict?', in Perry and Selden, eds, *Chinese Society*, pp. 123–147; Ching Kwan Lee, 'Pathways of labor insurgency', in Perry and Selden, eds, *Chinese Society*, pp. 57–79; William Hurst, 'Understanding contentious collective action by Chinese laid-off workers: the importance of regional political economy', *Studies in Comparative International Development* 39, (2004), pp. 94–120; Feng Chen, 'Subsistence crises, managerial corruption and labor protests in China', *The China Journal* 44, (2000), pp. 41–63; Jae Ho Chung, Hongyi Lai and Ming Xia, 'Mounting challenges to governance in China; surveying collective protestors, religious sects and criminal organizations', *The China Journal* 56, (2006), pp. 1–32.

[10]'China experiences 23% annual increase in environment-related protests and the Chinese court refuses to litigate these cases due to their sensitivity', *News*, (28 October 2012), available at: http://news.163.com/12/1028/02/8ESBJE2B00014AED.html (accessed 28 October 2012).

[11]Fengshi Wu, 'Environmental politics in China: an issue area in review', in Sujian Guo, ed., *Political Science and Chinese Political Studies: The State of the Field* (London: Springer, 2013), pp. 103–124.

that environmental problems are getting worse every day in China and they affect people's health and livelihood directly. According to an official report by China's Ministry of Environmental Protection, 57.3% of groundwater in 198 Chinese cities was described as 'bad' or 'extremely bad', 30% of the country's major rivers were polluted or seriously polluted, and over 85% of Chinese key cities did not meet air quality standards in 2012.[12] The survey in this article found that 72.4% of our surveyed urban residents said that the city they lived in was polluted or seriously polluted and 68% of them believed that pollution in their city affected their health. Environmental problems have drawn by far the largest crowds of protesters in China since Tiananmen. Planned construction of polluting chemical and power plants in Xiamen in 2007, Dalian in 2011 and Kuming in 2013 drew tens of thousands of urban protesters to the streets. Second, unlike rural land conflicts and urban labor disputes, environmental movements and campaigns particularly attract urban middle-class participants who have been understudied.[13] The urban environmental movement is probably the most vigorous civil society force in China.[14] One scholar claims that the urban environmental movement is the style of the new citizen activism in China.[15] Third, environmental protests seem to be more successful in achieving their goals due to the large number of participants (resulted partly from the use of new technologies in mobilization) and the wide appeal to the general population. A number of high-profile environmental protests have led to either the shutdown of existing polluting factories or the cancellation of proposed environmentally hazardous facilities.[16]

Despite the importance of the question, there have been few empirical studies focusing on street protests in China. This study, based on a large-scale random survey conducted in 34 Chinese cities, attempts to shed some light on the factors that contribute to Chinese people's willingness to participate in street protests and, therefore, the nature of street protests in China. Specifically, this article tests two models concerning Chinese urban residents' propensity to participate in environment-related street protests: the issue-oriented model vs. the institutional model. These two models are not necessarily mutually exclusive, since all protests are issue-driven to some extent. Nevertheless, if it is issue or grievance-relevant factors that solely drive people's willingness to participate in this form of public demonstration, it can be said that street protests may not pose a serious threat to the stability of the political regime. On the other hand, if it is also their distrust or dissatisfaction with the government that mobilizes people in a country where many open forms of political activities are discouraged or forbidden, the growing street protests can be a serious threat to the Chinese authorities and a destabilizing factor of the authoritarian regime. The findings of this article lend support to the institutional model.

This article makes several contributions to the current literature on contentious politics in China. First, unlike some other studies which explain the dramatic rise of social protests or the success or failure of popular protests,[17] this article focuses exclusively on the motivational factors, both issue-related and institutional, explaining people's willingness to participate in street demonstrations in urban China. Second, this article chooses environmental pollution as the protesting issue for the study. Environmental pollution has no doubt become a significantly serious challenge in China's economic development. Since pollution affects people's livelihood directly, it has also become a new focus for street protests in China, and, therefore, a serious social and political issue for the Chinese government. In addition, environmental protests involve post-material values.[18] Yet, studies of street protests over environmental

---

[12]'China's environmental problems are grim, admits ministry report', *The Guardian*, (7 June 2013), available at: http://www.theguardian.com/environment/chinas-choice/2013/jun/07/chinas-environmental-problems-grim-ministry-report (accessed 25 January 2014).

[13]Kevin O'Brien, 'Introduction: studying contentious politics in contemporary China', in Kevin J. O'Brien, ed., *Popular Protest in China* (Cambridge, MA: Harvard University Press, 2008), pp. 11–25.

[14]Yanfei Sun and Dingxin Zhao, 'Environmental campaigns', in O'Brien, ed., *Popular Protest in China*, pp. 144–162.

[15]Guobin Yang, *The Power of the Internet in China: Citizen Activism Online* (New York: Columbia University Press, 2009).

[16]The most well-known cases were the cancellation of a planned PX chemical factory in Xiamen in 2007 and the shutdown of a PX chemical factory in Dalian in 2011 due to large-scale popular street protests.

[17]Xi Chen, *Social Protest and Contentious Authoritarianism in China* (Cambridge: Cambridge University Press, 2012); Yongshun Cai, *Collective Resistance in China: Why Popular Protests Succeed or Fail* (Stanford, CA: Stanford University Press, 2010).

[18]O'Brien, 'Introduction', pp. 21–22.

issues have not been sufficient. Third, differing from other research that focuses on contentious politics in rural China,[19] the focus of this article is exclusively on Chinese urban residents for the important role that cities and urban residents play in Chinese politics and political development.[20] The number of urban residents, for the first time in Chinese history, has surpassed that of rural residents.[21] Urban residents tend to be better educated and many of them are elites in various fields of Chinese society. They live in political, economic and social centers in China. Their trust and support are indispensable for the current regime in China. The 1989 protest events that shook up Chinese politics occurred primarily in China's urban areas. The final contribution is that this article adopts an empirical survey research technique in understanding why some people choose street protests as their first option with regard to the issue of environmental pollution. This article draws from large-scale updated cross-regional survey data from 34 Chinese cities, which is unprecedented in the literature of contentious politics in China. To analyze both individual and city-level factors, the authors employ a multilevel modeling with a Bayesian simulation method.

Understanding contentious politics in China

Contentious politics is not new in contemporary China. In fact, contemporary Chinese history is filled with revolutions, revolts, insurgencies and protests. The most serious and memorable mass protests in the reform era were the Tiananmen events that occurred in China in the summer of 1989.[22] There is no question that popular contentions with authorities have been on a dramatic rise in China since the 1990s even though official figures for popular collective social actions in China are hard to find.[23] According to Xi Chen, participants of collective petitioning per million increased by 13.59 times and 4.16 times in Hunan and Henan provinces respectively between 1991 and 2000 (p. 29).[24] According to another study, between 2000 and 2013 there were 871 street protests in China that involved over 100 participants. About 200 of them occurred in 2012 alone.[25]

Contentious politics in China has to be understood from a broader theoretical framework. There is extensive literature on why people decide to be involved in street protests. Classical theories explaining people's participation in protests are the grievance theories that contribute people's protesting activities to relative deprivation, frustration and perceived injustice.[26] Grievance theories, however, are not sufficient to explain why, among people who have the same or similar grievances, some people participate in protest activities while others do not. As a result, other theories have been developed focusing on resources, efficacy, opportunities, organization and personal traits such as emotion to explain people's engagement in protests.[27]

---

[19] O'Brien and Li, *Rightful Resistance in Rural China*.

[20] Urban residents in our survey include both permanent residents as well as temporary residents in the surveyed cities.

[21] According to China's National Bureau of Statistics, 51.27% of Chinese citizens lived in cities and towns by the end of 2011, as published on 17 January 2012, available at: http://www.nytimes.com/2012/01/18/world/asia/majority-of-chinese-now-live-in-cities.html (accessed 11 July 2015).

[22] Two book-length studies provide excellent analysis of the Tiananmen events in 1989. See Dengxin Zhao, *The Power of Tiananmen* (Chicago, IL: The University of Chicago Press, 2001); and Jeffrey N. Wasserstrom and Elizabeth Perry, eds, *Popular Protest and Political Culture in Modern China* (Boulder, CO: Westview Press, 1994).

[23] Cai, *Collective Resistance in China*, pp. 22–25.

[24] Xi Chen, *Social Protest and Contentious Authoritarianism in China*, p. 24.

[25] Lin Li and Tian He, *Zhongguo fazhif fazhan baogao 2014* (Beijing: Shehui kexue chubanshe, 2014), pp. 272–273.

[26] Walter G. Runciman, *Relative Deprivation and Social Justice* (London: Routledge, 1966); Ted Gurr, *Why Men Rebel* (Princeton, NJ: Princeton University Press, 1970); Leonard Berkowitz, 'Frustrations, comparisons, and other sources of emotion aroused as contributors to social unrest', *Journal of Social Issues* 28(1), (1972), pp. 77–91; Allen Lind and Tom Tyler, *The Social Psychology of Procedural Justice* (New York: Plenum Press, 1988).

[27] Bert Klandermans, 'Mobilization and participation: social–psychological expansions of resource mobilization theory', *American Sociological Review* 49(5), (1984), pp. 583–600; Doug McAdam, *Political Process and the Development of Black Insurgency, 1930–1970* (Chicago, IL: The University of Chicago Press, 1982); John D. McCarthy and Mayer N. Zeld, 'Resource mobilization and social movements: a partial theory', *American Journal of Sociology* 82(6), (1977), pp. 1212–1241; Martijn Van Zomeren, Russell Spears, Agneta Fischer and Colin W. Leach, 'Put your money where your mouth is! Explaining collective action tendencies through group-based anger and group efficacy', *Journal of Personality and Social Psychology* 87(5), (2004), pp. 649–664.

One scholar's work on social conflict is particularly useful for this study. Unsatisfied with both Marxism which puts too much emphasis on revolutions and Tarcott Parsons's general theory of social action that puts a great value on equilibrium, Lewis Coser in his seminal work, *The Functions of Social Conflict,* argues that social conflict is, first of all, the norm of every society and is not necessarily dysfunctional. He further argues that social conflict serves a number of positive functions, not the least of which is the function of a safety-valve in a given society.[28] Coser distinguishes two different types of internal social conflicts: realistic conflicts and unrealistic conflicts. Realistic conflicts involve specific objects and demands, while unrealistic conflicts are targeted at the fundamental values or interests of the existing structure or system.[29] While the former may stabilize the system and re-establish unity by releasing tension between antagonistic parties, the latter is likely to disrupt the existing structure and threaten the legitimacy of the social system. The key for a social system to prevent realistic conflicts from becoming unrealistic conflicts, according to Coser, is to reduce rigidity of the system to allow for conflict resolution in a tolerant fashion.[30]

Are street protests in China realistic or unrealistic social conflicts? Elizabeth Perry's analysis of Chinese protest activities is particularly enlightening. Perry traces Chinese conceptions of people's 'rights' from ancient Chinese philosopher Mencius to contemporary Chinese revolutionary leader Mao, and argues that the Chinese understanding of 'rights' is significantly different from that of the Anglo-American cultural tradition.[31] In the discourse of traditional Chinese philosophers and political leaders, according to Perry, the emphasis of 'rights' is on collective socioeconomic justice, while 'rights' from the Anglo-American perspective is more about individual rights and civil liberties. Chinese 'rights consciousness' is more concerned with livelihood issues than fundamental and abstract moral principles surrounding human rights. Perry believes that Chinese protesters are actually more 'rule conscious' than 'right conscious'.[32] In other words, people protest in China because their perceived rules are broken or policies are not properly carried out, not because they want to secure 'their naturally endowed protections against state intrusion'.[33] As a result, Perry concludes, 'widespread popular protest in China points neither to an indigenous moral vacuum nor toward an epochal clash with state authority'.[34] Differing from some other studies, Perry's analysis puts popular protests in China into the category of what Coser calls 'realistic social conflicts' and, therefore, they are not regime threatening.

Most studies on Chinese contentious politics seem to argue that Chinese contentious political activities are primarily issue-driven and, therefore, are not a serious threat to the current political regime in China. Following traditional approaches toward social movements that are under 'the assumption that social movement operated outside of politics, attacked political institutions, and followed different mechanisms and processes than did institutional groups',[35] however, the authors argue that what motivates people to participate in environment-related protests in China has to be broader than specific issues themselves and that institution-related factors such as support of the political regime and trust of the government are important factors in understanding why people choose to participate in environmental protests in China. In other words, the authors believe that people in China, as people elsewhere in the situation of a street protest, tend to perceive growing social issues such as pollution to be linked to institutional deficiencies such as lack of government transparency or lack of trust in government. People who are willing to participate in environmental protests may very well have institutional issues on their mind. As a result, environmental protests in China may be more regime threatening than some people think.

---

[28]This is a viewpoint that was initially proposed by German Sociologist Georg Simmel.
[29]Lewis Coser, *The Functions of Social Conflict* (Glencoe, IL: The Free Press, 1956), pp. 151–152, 156.
[30]*Ibid.*, p. 80.
[31]Perry, 'Chinese conceptions of "rights"'.
[32]Elizabeth Perry, 'Studying Chinese politics: farewell to revolution?', *China Journal* 51, (2007), pp. 1–22.
[33]Perry, 'Chinese conceptions of "rights"', p. 46.
[34]*Ibid.*, p. 47.
[35]Sidney Tarrow, 'Prologue: the new contentious politics in China: poor and blank or rich and complex', in O'Brien, ed., *Popular Protest in China*, p. 9.

Research design and data

This research is not a comprehensive study of why people participate in street protest in China. Rather it tests two hypotheses on likely participants of street protests over a potential environmental issue in urban China. Even though there have been a number of studies on protest activities in China, few have approached the issue of motivations for people's participation in street protest activities in a systematically empirical fashion. The main reason for the lack of such empirical studies rests in the difficulties with data collection. It is not feasible to conduct extensive interviews or surveys among protest participants while the protest is still going on. Even if it can be done, the interviews or survey would not include non-participants who face the same protesting issue but decide not to participate in the protest. It is also difficult to conduct surveys among participants and non-participants after the protest is over since it is almost impossible to identify the protest participants who would be reluctant to come forward for fear of reprisal. A substitute or proxy for surveying actual protest participants is an experimental survey study of likely protest participants and compares them with people who are less likely to participate in street protests. The main assumption in this article is that people who say they would choose to participate in street protest are more likely to do so, while those who say they would not opt for participating in street protests are unlikely to take part in such activities.

Data for this research were collected in a random telephone survey covering 34 large cities throughout China, most of which are provincial capital cities.[36] The cities represent different regions and different levels of economic development. The survey was carried out between April and May of 2013 by the Center for Public Opinion Research of Shanghai Jiao Tong University. The sample size for each city is 100 people, totaling 3,400 from all 34 cities. The sampling frame includes both landline and cell phone numbers in these cities. The Computer Assisted Telephone Interview (CATI) system generated random telephone numbers. Trained graduate and undergraduate students at Shanghai Jiao Tong University and several other surrounding universities in Shanghai conducted the anonymous survey. The dataset is truly unique in the sense that these kinds of large cross-regional scientific random surveys with political questions are not often carried out in mainland China.

Surveyees' responses can be influenced by city-level factors such as the level of economic development or the actual air pollution level as well as individual-level factors. To address this hierarchical structure of our data and explain variation across cities, this article employs a multilevel logit model with varying intercepts.

A related issue in this survey analysis is the potential social desirability bias. That is whether respondents in these types of surveys may freely express themselves in an authoritarian country like China. Survey experience in China tells us that if the questions are too sensitive in the Chinese context, it is problematic to judge whether Chinese respondents do indeed give truthful answers. However, the authors do not believe that our survey questions are too sensitive to be asked in the current political atmosphere in China. Moreover, the survey was conducted over the telephone (instead of face-to-face) in an anonymous fashion to ensure that respondents gave truthful answers. In addition, since this bias is associated with under-reporting of respondents' willingness to participate in street protests, we are likely to fail to find significant relationships between issue/institution-related factors and a respondent's probability of participating in street protest, not the other way around. Nevertheless, as the results show in the following sections, there are some institutional variables that reveal a strong positive impact on street protest, which implies that the real impact of these variables on the probability of street protest could be bigger than we observe in the results, if the social desirability bias exists. Therefore, even if this bias exists, the survey analysis still provides us with valuable information about contentious politics in China.[37]

---

[36]The following is the list of the surveyed cities: Beijing, Shanghai, Tianjin, Chongqing, Changchun, Changsha, Chengdu, Dalian, Fuzhou, Guangzhou, Guizhou, Harbin, Haikou, Hangzhou, Hefei, Huhhot, Jinan, Kunming, Lanzhou, Nanchang, Nanjing, Nanning, Ningbo, Qingdao, Shenyang, Shenzhen, Shijiazhuang, Taiyuan, Wuhan, Xian, Xining, Xiamen, Yinchuan and Zhengzhou.

[37]On survey research in China, see Melanie Manion, 'A survey of survey research on Chinese politics: what have we learned?', in Allen Carlson, Mary Gallagher, Kenneth Lieberthal and Melanie Manion, eds, *Contemporary Chinese Politics: New Sources, Methods and Field Strategies* (New York: Cambridge University Press, 2010), pp. 181–200.

Table 1. Willingness to participate in street protests (%).

	Do nothing	Contacting local people's congress deputies	Contacting local government officials	Mobilizing neighbors to contact local government officials	Participating in street protests	Other options
If a polluting accident happens in your area, what would be your first choice of action?	4.1	4.9	16.3	48.3	19.8	6.6

Note: N=3,400.

Willingness to take to the streets in environmental protests

The survey asks a straightforward question on people's willingness to take to the streets in protest: 'If a polluting accident happens in your living area, what would be your first choice of action to get the problem solved?'. The respondents were asked to choose one of the following six options: (1) no action; (2) personally contacting local people's congress representatives; (3) personally contacting local government officials; (4) mobilizing neighbors to contact local government officials; (5) participating directly in street protest to get the problem solved; or (6) other options. The authors fully realize that people in reality may pursue multiple venues and tactics to solve this problem. However, the central concern in this study is to find out how willing people are to participate in street protests. The authors feel that this question, in which our respondents were forced to choose just one option, can best capture their propensity or willingness to take part in street protests.

The survey finds that close to 20% of the respondents chose street protest as their first option while the rest preferred other options in dealing with a hypothetical polluting incident (see Table 1). Obviously it does not mean that people who say they would participate in street protests will actually do so in reality. However, it is logical to assume that those who say they would take part in street protests are more likely to do so in reality than those who do not choose street protests as their first option. Even though most people in our survey did not choose street protests as their first option to deal with a pollution problem, it is still significant that one fifth of our surveyed urban residents did. For a mega city like Shanghai with over 20 million residents, this means that 4 million of them are willing or have the propensity to participate in street protests. Even if a small fraction of those people do actually participate in real street demonstrations, the impact or consequence can be significant. It should be noted that, even though most street protests are tolerated by the Chinese authorities,[38] this form of contentious political activity is still considered unconventional and carries some political risk in China. For example, participants in street protests may be black-listed as 'trouble makers', which will affect their career, especially for those who work in the state sectors (government, universities, hospitals, state-owned enterprises, etc.). In addition, it is still possible that participants in street protests may be detained or arrested if the authorities decide to crackdown on the demonstration, especially when the protest turns less civil or even violent. Local government, which handles most street protests, is less tolerant than the central government in China.[39] Moreover, it is much harder for people in authoritarian countries to organize protest activities.[40] The sheer percentage of people who expressed their willingness to protest on the streets indicates that there is deep dissatisfaction with the official channels of interest articulation among Chinese urban residents. Willingness to participate in street protests

[38]Shaohua Lei, *Contentious Politics and Political Stability in China: An Institutional Explanation,* unpublished Ph.D. dissertation, The University of Utah, 2013, p. 155.

[39]Cai, *Collective Resistance in China*, p. 32.

[40]Ruth Kricheli, Yair Livne and Beatriz Magaloni, 'Taking to the streets: theory and evidence on protests under authoritarianism', paper presented at the annual meeting of the American Political Science Association, 2–5 September 2010, available at: http://ssrn.com/abstract=1642040 (accessed 12 July 2015).

Figure 1. Subjective evaluation of city pollution level (%).

as the first option in dealing with a hypothetical pollution problem is used as the binary dependent variable in our multilevel logit analysis in this study.

Multivariate analysis

The central question to be answered in this study is why, facing the same or similar issues, some people choose street protests as their preferred option while others do not? Specifically, the authors are interested in the motivating factors behind people's intention to participate in environment-related street protests. This article designed three models to test the hypotheses. The first model consists of variables at the individual level, such as age, gender, education, communist party membership, personal wellbeing and level of political interest. The second model includes an additional cluster of environment-related issues. In the survey people were asked a number of questions concerning urban residents' feelings about environmental pollution and issues. First, the survey asked respondents to grade the pollution level in their city (from 0 to 10). More than half of Chinese urban residents in our surveyed cities graded the pollution level in their city above five (see Figure 1). When asked how pollution in their city affects their personal health, 16.6% believe the pollution in their city brings serious harm to their health, 51.4% claim it brings some harm, 28% say there is not much harm or no harm, and 4.1% do not know.

The survey next wanted to know how much knowledge our respondents have about environmental pollution. The authors presume that if people are concerned with the environment, they would like to know more about what leads to environmental pollution. Particular matters, especially particles less than 2.5 micrometers in diameter ($PM_{2.5}$), are extremely harmful to one's health.[41] Many Chinese cities have been plagued by $PM_{2.5}$ in recent years. When asked how familiar they are about $PM_{2.5}$, our respondents' answers are split in the middle. About half of them claimed they know a lot (2.2%) or some (42.9%) about $PM_{2.5}$, and the rest had basically no idea (45.1%) or absolutely no idea (4.2%) about it. More people in our survey claim that they know some or a lot about the general causes of pollution (78.1% and 5.5%, respectively).

The authors also believe that if one cares about the environment enough, he or she is willing to sacrifice material gains, time and money to protect and improve the environment. Development and environmental protection are often pitted against each other. China's double-digit economic growth in the last 30 years comes with a high cost in environmental degradation. Deng Xiaoping's famous saying 'development is the hard truth' is the central policy of the Chinese government in the reform era. How do Chinese urban residents feel about the trade-off between economic development and protection

---

[41]On the harmful effects of $PM_{2.5}$ see information provided by the US Environmental Protection Agency, available at: http://www.epa.gov/ttn/naaqs/pm/pm25_index.html (accessed 28 January 2014).

Table 2. Willingness to protect the environment (%).

	Very willing	Willing	Unwilling	Very unwilling	Hard to say
Willingness to sort garbage	15.5	76.9	3.7	0.3	3.6
Willingness to bring shopping bags to supermarket	16.1	71.0	8.6	0.3	4.0
Willingness to donate to environmental groups	2.7	60.8	18.2	1.3	17.0
Willingness to volunteer for environmental groups	4.5	72.8	13.3	0.4	9.2

Note: $N=3,400$.

of the environment? When asked what is more important: economic development or environmental protection, only 11.2% chose the former, while 77.2% preferred the latter, and the rest did not know how to answer the question. In the survey people were also asked about their willingness to help with the environment with some specific actions. Most of our respondents do express their willingness to protect the environment. The four items concerning willingness to improve the environment (see Table 2) are combined to form an additive index as the variable of environmental participation in the multivariate analysis.

If environment-related street protests in China are purely or mostly issue-driven, it would have to be assumed that people who are more concerned with pollution and the harm that pollution causes, who are more knowledgeable about pollution issues, who put environmental protection ahead of economic development and who are more willing to help in the endeavor to improve the environment, are more likely to participate in an environmental protest.

The third model adds some institutional factors. Traditional studies on why people participate in protests have focused on institution-related factors, such as lack of social justice and fairness, relative deprivation and distrust of authorities.[42] It is believed that, even though a protest activity may be triggered by an incident over a non-political issue, people who tend to participate in the protest are partially motivated by their feelings about the governing authorities and institutions. Specifically, this article hypothesizes that support for the political regime, trust of government, perceived governmental transparency and support for democracy are positively associated with Chinese urban residents' willingness to participate in street protests over an environmental issue.

This article measures urban residents' regime support by asking them a straightforward question on their attitudes toward system change. Respondents in the survey were provided with three general statements and were asked to choose one to describe their attitude toward the existing system in China. The three statements are: (1) We have many serious problems in our country, and we must fundamentally reform the current system; (2) We indeed have some problems in our country, and we should adopt gradual reform measures to improve the current system; and (3) Our country is basically good, and we should maintain the status quo so that destructive forces cannot harm the current system.

The authors believe that these three carefully designed statements can detect our Chinese urban residents' true attitudes and feelings toward the current political regime in China.[43] Around a quarter (25.6%) of respondents chose the first statement, indicating that they prefer fundamental change and lack of support for the current system in China. A plurality majority (43.7%) of respondents favored the second statement, indicating that they are moderates and prefer non-revolutionary change to the current system. A fraction (1.4%) of the surveyed opted for the *status quo* while the rest (29.2%) chose 'hard to say'. The authors coded preference for fundamental system change as '0' and coded all other responses as '1' for the *regime support* variable.

Another institutional factor used in the multivariate analysis is the trust of government. A number of surveys done in China over the last two decades have shown that levels of political trust among

[42]Tom R. Tyler and H. J. Smith, 'Social justice and social movements', in Daniel Gilbert, Susan Fiske and Gardner Lindzey, eds, *Handbook of Social Psychology* (New York: McGraw-Hill, 1998), pp. 595–629; Robert Folger, 'Rethinking equity theory: a referent cognitions model', in Hans Werner Bierhoff, Ronald Cohen and Jerald Greenberg, eds, *Justice in Social Relations* (New York: Plenum, 1986), pp. 145–162; Gurr, *Why Men Rebel*; Berkowitz, 'Frustrations, comparisons, and other sources of emotion aroused as contributors to social unrest', pp. 77–92.
[43]Yand Zhong and Yongguo Chen, 'Regime support in urban China', *Asian Survey* 53, (2013), pp. 369–392.

Table 3. Levels of political trust among Chinese urban residents (%).

	Strongly disagree	Disagree	Neutral	Agree	Strongly agree	Hard to say	N
The central government always tries to do the right things for the people	0.3	7.5	11.7	62.9	10.3	7.2	3,400
The municipal government in your city always tries to do the right things for the people	0.7	13.0	16.0	53.2	6.6	10.5	3,400

Chinese citizens toward the Chinese government and institutions are actually relatively high even though the questions asked in the surveys concerning political trust were phrased differently.[44] A survey conducted as far back as in 1993 shows that 70% of Chinese citizens trusted decisions made by their central government.[45] In fact, the World Value Survey shows that trust of political institutions among Chinese citizens is higher than the world averages.[46] However, anecdotal evidence seems to suggest that lack of trust on local government is a major factor in environmental protests in China. This article measures political trust of both the central government and local government among Chinese urban residents by asking them to agree or disagree with the following statements: 'The central government always tries to do the right things for the people' and 'The municipal government in your city always tries to do the right things for the people'. It is believed that these statements, which are based on a political trust question asked in the US National Election Studies (NES) survey,[47] are sufficient to capture the essence of political trust of the central government and the local government among Chinese urbanites. The majority of respondents agree that they trusted the central and local governments to do the right things for the people, even though the trust level of the central government is higher than that of the local government (see Table 3).

A third institutional factor is popular support for electoral democracy among Chinese urban residents. China currently is not a Western-style democracy and its national leaders are not directly elected by the population. Chinese intellectuals have long debated whether Chinese culture is suited for democracy, given China's long history of authoritarian tradition. Do Chinese people, especially the urban dwellers, support democracy? The survey examined respondents' attitudes toward democracy by asking them to agree or disagree with the statement regarding whether Chinese top leaders should be democratically elected directly by the people. More than half of our Chinese urban respondents either strongly favored (9.0%) or favored (47.7%) the direct election of Chinese top leaders, 17.2% were opposed to it, while the remaining 26.2% remained neutral.

The last institutional factor concerns perceived governmental transparency on environmental issues. Transparency in governmental affairs is believed to be associated with people's trust in government.[48] Lack of government transparency also seems to be a central theme in several large-scale environmental street protests in the last several years in China.[49] This article measured perceived governmental

[44]Lianjiang Li, 'The object and substance of trust in central leaders: preliminary evidence from a pilot survey', paper presented at the Annual Meeting of the American Political Science Association, Seattle, Washington, 1–4 September 2011.
[45]Tianjian Shi, 'Cultural values and political trust: a comparison of the People's Republic of China and Taiwan', *Comparative Politics* 33(3), (2001), pp. 401–419.
[46]Yang Qing and Wenfang Tang, 'Exploring the sources of institutional trust in China: culture, mobilization, or performance?', *Asian Politics and Policy* 2(3), (2010), pp. 415–436.
[47]The question asked in the National Election Studies survey is: 'How much of the time do you think you can trust the government in Washington to do what is right?' See Gabriela Catterberg and Alejandro Moreno, 'The individual bases of political trust: trends in new and established democracies', *International Journal of Public Opinion Research* 18(1), (2005), pp. 31–48.
[48]Yang Zhong, 'Do Chinese people trust their local government and why? An empirical study of political trust in urban China', *Problems of Post-Communism* 61(3), (2014), pp. 31–44.
[49]Lack of governmental transparency was a major cause for the large protests against the proposed and existing polluting chemical and power plants in Xiamen, Dalian and Kunming.

transparency by asking our respondents to assess whether the government is transparent with environmental issues and policies. The survey reveals that 31.3% of Chinese urban respondents did not think the government is transparent with regard to environmental issues, 31.4% remained neutral on this issue, and the remaining 37.4% did believe that the government is forthcoming with issues related to the environment.

Finally, this article included two control variables at the city level. One is level of economic development as represented by Gross Domestic Product per capita for the 34 cities included in our study.[50] It is anticipated that, since economic development fosters post-modern values such as concern with the environment,[51] people living in more economically developed cities are more likely to participate in environment-related street protests. Another city-level variable is the level of air pollution in the 34 cities between January and April before the survey was conducted.[52] It is logical to assume that a higher air pollution level is positively related to people's willingness to take part in environmental protests.

To perform a multilevel analysis with the binary dependent variable, this article employs a multilevel logit model. The multilevel logit model can be written in the general form $\pi_{ij} = f(X_{ij}\beta_j)$, where π_{ij} is the probability that the i-th individual in the j-th city is associated with willingness to participate in street protest; f is a nonlinear function (logit link function) of the linear predictor $X_{ij}\beta_j$. It is needed to specify a distribution for the observed response $Y_{ij}|\pi_{ij}$ The Y_{ij} are the observed (0,1) responses with the standard assumption that they are binomially distributed $y_{ij} \sim Binomial(n_{ij}, \pi_{ij})$ where n_{ij} is the denominator for the probability π_{ij}. It is also assumed that $var(y_{ij}|\pi_{ij}) = \pi_{ij}(1 - \pi_{ij})/n_{ij}$. The model including individual-level variations can be written as $y_{ij} = \pi_{ij} + \varepsilon_{ij}x_0$, where x_0 is used to specify the variation at the first level. With the assumptions that the n_{ij} are all equal to 1 and x_0 is also equal to 1, the variance of individual level random term ε_{ij} is $\pi_{ij}(1 - \pi_{ij})$. Full details can be found in the works by Goldstein, Rodriguez and Goldman, and Rasbash et al.[53]

In the two-level logit model, the probability π_{ij} is defined as a function of the intercept and a series of individual-level predictors:

$$\text{logit}(\pi_{ij}) = \beta_{oj} + \beta_1 * Trust_{ij} + ... + \varepsilon_{ij} \tag{1}$$

Additionally, the intercept is a function of city-level predictors, GDP per capita and Air pollution variables:

$$\beta_{oj} = \gamma_0 + \gamma_1 * GDPPC_j + \gamma_2 * AirPollution_j + \mu_{0j}. \tag{2}$$

This specification allows the intercept term, β_{0j}, to be a function of the city-level variables. That is, GDP per capita and the air pollution level measured in each city are assumed to affect the baseline probability of willingness to participate in street protests in different cities. To simplify the model, Equation (2) is substituted into Equation (1):

$$\text{logit}(\pi_{ij}) = \gamma_o + \beta_1 * Trust_{ij} + ... + \gamma_1 * GDPPC_j + \gamma_2 * AirPollution_j + \mu_{0j} + \varepsilon_{ij}. \tag{3}$$

In this equation, γ_0 denotes the intercept. The multilevel disturbance term is composed of the two different components: μ_{0j} the city-level disturbance and ε_{ij} the individual-level disturbance. As a result, the multilevel disturbance term does not have constant variance. By testing whether μ_{0j} is statistically different from zero, which means that there are no remaining variances to be explained at the city level, it can be checked whether city-level predictors are good measures of explaining causal heterogeneity.

---

[50]Specifically, this variable is the annual GDP per capita of the 34 cities in 2012, obtained from the government websites of the 34 cities.

[51]Ronald Inglehart, *Modernization and Postmodernization: Cultural, Economic, and Political Change in 43 Societies* (Princeton, NJ: Princeton University Press, 1997).

[52]Data for this variable come from China National Environmental Monitor Center, available at: http://www.cnemc.cn/ (accessed 28 October 2013).

[53] Harvey Goldstein, *Multilevel Statistical Models* (New York: The Americas by Halsted Press, 1995); German Rodríguez and Noreen Goldman, 'An assessment of estimation procedures for multilevel models with binary responses', *Journal of Royal Statistical Society* 158(1), (1995), pp. 73–89; Jon Rasbash, William Browne, Harvey Goldstein, Min Yang, Ian Plewis, Michael Healy, Geoff Woodhouse, David Draper, Ian Langford and Toby Lewis, *A User's Guide to MLwiN* (Centre for Multilevel Modelling, Institute of Education, London: University of London, 2002).

Table 4. Pollution, institutions and street protestation in urban China (34 cities).

DV: street protestation	Model 1 (Individual-related)	Model 2 (Issue-related)	Model 3 (Institution-related)
Fixed effects			
Individual level			
Political interest	−0.063 (0.041)	−0.068 (0.058)	−0.058 (0.059)
Personal wellbeing	−0.184 (0.054)***	−0.167 (0.055)***	−0.113 (0.057)**
Male	0.127 (0.090)	0.119 (0.094)	0.097 (0.096)
Age	−0.063 (0.041)	−0.067 (0.043)	−0.060 (0.043)
Education	0.048 (0.074)	0.027 (0.077)	−0.029 (0.075)
Party membership	−0.110 (0.127)	−0.104 (0.128)	−0.086 (0.127)
Perceived pollution level		0.034 (0.018)*	0.019 (0.018)
Harm to personal health		0.061 (0.058)	0.025 (0.058)
Knowledge of causes of pollution		−0.016 (0.085)	−0.039 (0.086)
Knowledge of PM 2.5		0.039 (0.070)	0.010 (0.071)
Environmental protection over economic development		0.141 (0.106)	0.142 (0.110)
Environmental participation		−0.068 (0.047)	−0.058 (0.049)
Government transparency			−0.265 (0.052)***
Trust in the central government			−0.117 (0.067)*
Trust in the local government			−0.145 (0.064)***
Support for the system			−0.274 (0.097)***
Support for democracy			0.115 (0.121)
City level			
Constant	−0.867 (0.423)**	−1.055** (0.453)	0.940 (0.552)*
GDP per capita	0.050 (0.024)**	0.044 (0.023)**	0.037 (0.024)
Air pollution	−0.0005 (0.030)	−0.015 (0.030)	−0.002 (0.030)
Random effects			
City level	0.034 (0.028)	0.030 (0.027)	0.031 (0.027)
N	3,400	3,400	3,400
DIC	3,372.02	3,374.87	3,324.48

Notes: Multilevel analysis with MCMC estimation (50,000 iterations, 10,000 burn-in period). Standard errors are in parentheses. Significant credibility intervals: *** 99%, ** 95%, * 90%.

The individual-level disturbance variance is given as one, which means the model is fitted to have a binomial error distribution. To identify the multilevel model, this article assumes zero covariance between individual and city-level disturbances.

Estimation

Since the likelihood of the observed data in a binary dependent variable model does not have a closed-form expression in general, it is necessary to use approximate methods of estimation. Also, since quasi-likelihood methods tend to produce biased estimates, this article employs a Bayesian simulation method (i.e. Markov chain Monte Carlo estimation).[54] Specifically, the model is fit by the second-order penalized quasi-likelihood (PQL) procedure to obtain estimates. Then, using these estimates as starting values and vague prior distributional assumptions for the model parameters, this article simulates and generates parameter estimates with a burn-in period of 10,000 iterations followed by 50,000 iterations for the estimates. The *MLwiN* statistical package and its associated *Stata* program are used to obtain these estimates.[55]

Results

Table 4 reports test results in three different models in which different sets of variables at the individual level are included along with two city-level variables. In Model 1, this article includes only

[54]George Leckie and Chris Charlton, 'Runmlwin: a program to run the MLwiN multilevel modeling software from within Stata', *Journal of Statistical Software* 52(11), (2012), pp. 1–40.
[55]Rasbash *et al.*, *A User's Guide to MLwiN*; Leckie and Charlton, 'Runmlwin'.

individual-related variables, while pollution-related variables and institution-related variables are added to Model 2 and Model 3, respectively. With respect to individual-related variables, only *personal wellbeing* is statistically significant in all three models. As people feel happier, they are less likely to participate in street protests. Other than this variable, all other individual and issue-related variables (except for one) are not statistically significant at the 5% significance level. In the first two models, the GDP per capital variable is statistically significant. That is, as the level of economic development increases, cities have higher baseline chances to face pollution-related street protests. This result implies that people tend to pay more attention to the pollution issue when economic development becomes a less salient issue in the city.

The theoretical claim centers on the relationship between perceptions of institutions and willingness to participate in street protest. In Model 3, *transparency, trust in the central government, trust in the local government* and *support for the system* are all statistically significant and have their expected signs. However, *support for democracy* is not significantly related to people's propensity in taking part in street protests. As the perceived governmental transparency, trust in both local and central governments or regime support declines, people are more likely to participate in street protests. To measure the impact of these variables on willingness to participate in street protests, this article estimates predicted probabilities of street protestation at different levels of perceived government transparency, trust in both central and local governments, and regime support. To this end, the authors fix all other variables at their means (continuous or ordinal variables) or mode (binary variables) except *education* at three (two or four year college education) and *age* at three (30–39 years old).

This article reports four figures to effectively demonstrate the overall effects of these government-related variables on the predicted probability of people's participating in street protests. Figure 2 shows the predicted probabilities that those who trust in their local governments and support the current system are likely to participate in street protests at different levels of government transparency. Figure 3 shows the predicted probabilities that those who do not trust in their local government and do not

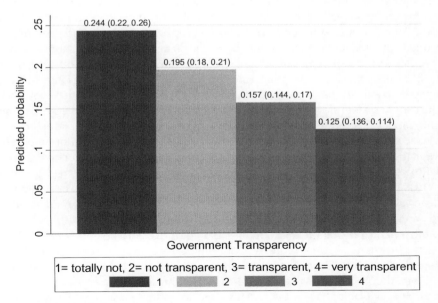

Figure 2. Predicted probabilities of street participation conditional on government transparency (individuals who trust the local government and support the system).
Notes: To estimate the predicted probabilities, we fix all other variables at their means or modes except 'Trust in the local government' at five (i.e. great trust) and 'Support for the system' at one (i.e. support the system); 95% CI in parentheses.

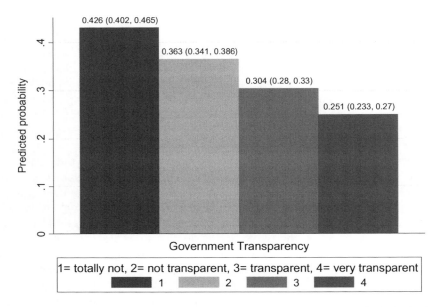

Figure 3. Predicted probabilities of street participation conditional on government transparency (individuals who do not trust the local government at all and do not support the system).
Notes: To estimate the predicted probabilities, we fix all other variables at their means or modes except 'Trust in the local governments' at one (i.e. do not trust at all) and 'Support for the system' at zero (i.e. do not support the system); 95% CI in parentheses.

support the current system are likely to participate in street protests at different levels of government transparency.

As seen in these figures, the difference is striking. When those who trust in their local government and support the current system perceive their government to be transparent, holding their trust in the central government at its mean value, the predicted probability of participation in a street protest is only about 12% in Figure 2. However, this probability increases up to 24% when the transparency level of the local government is minimal. Moreover, when those who do not trust in their local government and do not support the current system perceive their government to be not transparent at all, the predicted probability of participating in a street protest increases up to 42%, as shown in Figure 3. Figure 4 shows the predicted probabilities that those who strongly trust in both local and central governments and support the current system are likely to participate in street protests at different levels of government transparency (about 11% at the highest level of government transparency), while Figure 5 shows the same predicted probabilities for those who trust in neither government and do not support the system (about 51% at the lowest level of government transparency).[56] Between supporters and non-supporters of the political regime, there is about 4.5% difference in their probabilities of street protestation participation (19% and 23.5% for each group), holding trust in the local and central government variables at their mean values. Overall, these results highlight the importance of institution-related variables in explaining people's willingness to participate in street protests.

On the other hand, pollution-related variables did not turn out to be good predictors of people's willingness to participate in street protests in our multivariate analysis. *Perceived pollution level* has its expected positive sign and is only weakly statistically significant in Model 2 but very insignificant in Model 3. Even though perceived harm to personal health, favoring environmental protection and knowledge of $PM_{2.5}$ variables have positive signs, they do not have a statistically meaningful impact on willingness to participate in street protests. These results imply that it is not necessarily the actual

---

[56]It is likely that trust in the central government is highly correlated with trust in local governments. To see whether multicollinearity affects performance of these variables, the authors re-estimated Model 3 by including each variable separately as a robustness test. The results remain the same.

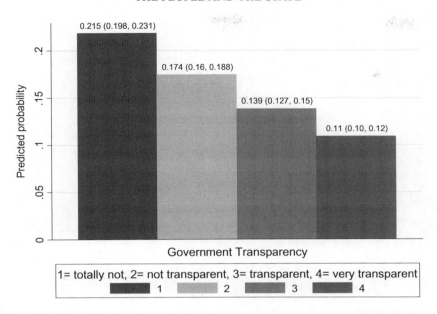

Figure 4. Predicted probabilities of street participation conditional on government transparency (individuals who trust both local and central governments and support the system).
Notes: To estimate the predicted probabilities, we fix all other variables at their means or modes except 'Trust in the central government' and 'Trust in the local government' at 5 (i.e. great trust) and 'Support for the system' at one (i.e. support the system); 95% CI in parentheses.

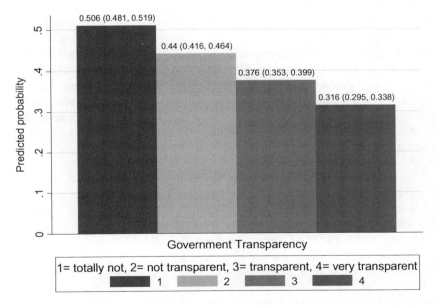

Figure 5. Predicted probabilities of street participation conditional on government transparency (individuals who do not trust the local and central governments at all and do not support the system).
Notes: To estimate the predicted probabilities, we fix all other variables at their means or modes except 'Trust in the central government' and 'Trust in the local government' at one (i.e. do not trust at all) and 'Support for the system' at zero (i.e. do not support the system); 95% CI in parentheses.

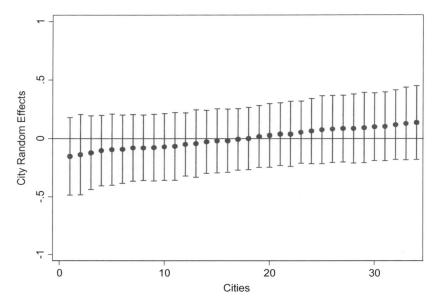

Figure 6. City random effects.
Note: This caterpillar plot shows 34 city level residuals (random effects), one for each city in the dataset. These residuals represent city departures from the overall average line predicted by the fixed parameters. Since the 95% credibility intervals for all residuals include zero, this means that all cities do not differ significantly from the average lines.

pollution issues or people's understanding of these issues that are associated with people's willingness to participate in street protests over pollution. Rather, it is their trust of the government, (dis)satisfaction with (or support for) the current system, and perceived government transparency that mostly explain their decision to take to the streets.

In all three models, random effects at the city level are not statistically significant. This implies that there is no remaining variance to be explained at the city level. To examine how random effects in each city differ significantly from the average city random effects, this article reports a caterpillar plot that shows 34 city-level residuals (random effects) using Model 3 (see Figure 6). These residuals represent city departures from the overall average line predicted by the fixed parameters. Since the 95% credibility intervals for all residuals include zero, this means that all the cities in this study do not differ significantly from the average lines, and also that the two-level model has a good fit to the data.

Conclusion

Contentious political activities have been on a dramatic rise in China. However, scholars differ on the nature of these activities. Some argue that these protesting activities are serious threats to stability in China, while others believe that these protests are primarily issue-driven and do not pose any serious threat to the Chinese political system. Unlike studies which try to explain the increase of protest activities in China, this article focuses on what motivates people to participate in street protest. In this study the authors try to differentiate between environmental street protests and other types of street protests that center on land issues or labor disputes. Using survey data from 34 Chinese cities, this article tries to explain why, facing environmental problems, some people choose to participate in street protests while others opt otherwise or who are more likely to participate in street protests in dealing with the same environmental issue.

Descriptive findings reveal that about 20% of surveyed urban residents choose street protests as their first option to deal with a hypothetical environmental problem in their area. This is not a comforting number for the Chinese government because it shows that a sizable portion of the Chinese urban population are potential street demonstrators or tend to use street protests to voice their concern. More importantly, findings from multilevel analysis show that institutional factors play a more important role in explaining the willingness of Chinese urban residents to take part in street protests. Specifically, people who prefer more fundamental change of the Chinese system, have less trust in the government and are more dissatisfied with government transparency, are more willing to take to the streets in protestation. In contrast, environment-related factors such as general concern with environmental degradation, knowledge of environmental problems and preference for environmental protection over economic development are not positively related to people's willingness to participate in a street protest in a hypothetical environmental accident.

Such multivariate analytical findings indicate that street protests in China are not purely issue-driven and they are related to institutional settings. What motivates people to participate in street protests has a lot to do with their feelings about the political system. In other words, these protests are not just what Coser calls 'realistic conflicts' which primarily involve specific issues and solutions. One implication from our study is that street protests in China may not be benign and as non-regime threatening as some scholars think. Since this study examines environmental issues only and their impact on street protests, there is a limitation in generalizing findings in this research into all different types of issues and protests. At the same time, however, it is also noticeable that, even though protest events are more often triggered by a specific issue or incident, they have the potential to spill over to other more general issues to become protestation against the regime if protesting participants are motivated by institutional factors. This may be particularly true for large-scale environmental protests. We should not forget that the massive demonstrations against the authoritarian regime in Tunisia in January 2011 were triggered by a small incident involving a policeman mistreating a young street vendor. This article also finds that people's willingness to participate in street protests is not associated with people's democratic value or preference for a democratic system, suggesting that social conflicts in China may not have become 'unrealistic conflicts' that involve fundamental ideological beliefs and values..

Political activists' frames in times of post-politics: evidence from Kirchnerism in Argentina and Podemos in Spain

Iban Diaz-Parra, Beltran Roca and Silvina Romano

This article studies the transformation of the frames of political activists who come from autonomous social movements in Argentina and Spain. The cases of Kirchnerism in Argentina and Podemos and the local electoral coalitions in Spain, despite all their contextual and historical differences, follow the same pattern of politicisation. They took place within a general social tendency towards post-politics, understood as the reduction of politics to technical management, without questioning the existing capitalist order. In both cases, the model of politicisation starts within an exceptional political event: the social protests of 2001 in Argentina and the mobilisations of the 15M or *indignados* in Spain in 2011. Drawing on participant observation and semi-structured interviews, the article examines how social actors re-adjust their frames by managing the contradictions between their previous autonomous logic of action and their new institutional roles, according to the changing economic and political context. It concludes that there has been a clear process of politicisation, materialised in the rise of new generations of political activists, but to some extent the post-political situation remains both in the exceptional political moment and in the electoral coalitions, as the core of the economic system remains unquestioned.

Introduction

In March 2015 the Kirchnerist government organised the International Forum 'Emancipation and Equality' at the Cervantes Theatre of Buenos Aires. Dozens of leftists and progressive intellectuals, social scientists and politicians from Latin America and Europe were invited to speak at the event. One of the most anticipated invited speakers was Íñigo Errejón, Secretary of Policy of Podemos (We Can), who explained that his political party was an attempt to create an electoral expression of the demands of the Spanish *indignados* (outraged) or 15M. Another speaker was Alex Kicillof, who was then the Ministry of Economy and Public Finances of Argentina. He gave a personal account of his own evolution, from having an autonomist perspective – during his participation in the student movement and in the protests during the 2001 economic crisis – to joining the Kirchnerist party. Kicillof portrayed autonomist practices as an expression of neo-liberal hegemony:

> This [neoliberal] idea, that the State is useless, came to be assumed by us. We thought it was an enemy, an enemy of mobilisation (…) And we, who were part of these autonomist ideas, Zapatistas, Chiapas, understood that they were forms of resistance. They were not so much about direct and clear advancement as about resistance. But we understood after 2003 that the State can also be, must be, an instrument for emancipation.[1]

The similarities between the narratives of Errejón and Kicillof were not accidental. Their organisations – Frente para la Victoria (Front for Victory, directed by Kirchner's couple) and Podemos – are political coalitions which seek to channel the demands of spontaneous protest movements which, paradoxically, are characterised by strong hostility towards political parties, professional politics, and even any kind of institutionalised political organisation.

Despite the historical and contextual differences, there is a strong link between Spain and Argentina's recent historical political processes. In a frame of neoliberal economic political hegemony, financial crisis have led to a crisis of political representation. In both cases, the first anti-neoliberal response came from strong autonomist and anti-institutional protest. However, in both cases, in a short period, trust in political and state institutions was recomposed through the creation of new political parties or coalitions, which, to some extent, raised some of the anti-neoliberal critics and demands of the previous protests. These elements connect not only these two countries but the processes in many Latin-American countries in the first decade of the twenty-first century and European peripheral countries affected by 2008 financial crisis, as some others have discerned (e.g. Levey, Ozarow, & Wylde, 2016). In any case, Spain and Argentina share some further elements which make them especially interesting for illustrating these processes, mainly the implementation of what has been interpreted as a populist strategy which would overcome previous post-political situation created by neoliberal hegemony (Errejón, 2015; Errejón & Mouffe, 2015; Laclau, 2005).

The recent political history of Argentina and Spain can be characterised by reference to the shift from the typical post-political situation (Wilson & Swyngedouw, 2015) towards the strong politicisation of society at different levels. In both countries, this development was mediated by the crash of their respective national economies and the wide discrediting of the political elite. Our perspective here is that the Argentinean and Spanish cases, despite all their contextual and historical differences, follow the same pattern of politicisation. This process is structured through two moments: first, an exceptional political moment (an historical moment or event which opens the possibility for a partial re-foundation of the basis of society), and second, a subsequent moment in which some features of this extraordinary political moment are extended to everyday politics (Echeverría, 1998). To what extent are both political moments part of the same political movement? How can we explain the contradictions between the activists' political practices in both moments? To what extent does this movement entail a real politicisation of society or even the overcoming of the post-political situation? The hypothesis of the article is that the post-political characteristics remaining in 2001 and 2011 protests forced a radical turn in the anti-neoliberal activists towards more pragmatic relationships with state institutions and more concrete goals. That is (partially) the result of a change in political activist's frames, understanding them as the activist's interpretation of the conditions of possibility for political action and social change in a particular context. The lack of political expectations of change in the scale of nation-state drove to the logic of anti-neoliberal autonomous social movements, focused in the realisation of local micro-utopias, which remain in the first years after the exceptional political moment (2001 and 2011). However, a new scenario is open by the economic crisis and subsequent crisis of political representation, leading to a new frame of anti-neoliberal activist's interpretation of the political possibilities and subsequently to the logic of participation in state institutions.

Ultimately, the transformation of political and economic context leads towards the transformation of activist's frames, and subsequently, towards the transformation of the shape of political struggle against neoliberalism. The article studies to what extent this shift from different logics and different frames of interpretation of the conditions of possibility of political change leads to overcome the neoliberal post-political situation. For this purpose, it pays attention to how social actors re-adjust their frames and manage the contradictions they experience in shifting political and economic context.

This article is divided into four sections. First, it frames its hypothesis in the theoretical discussion of 'the political' and post-politics. Second, it explains the methodology followed by the researchers. Third, it contextualises the analysis through a discussion of the national and state crises experienced by Argentina and Spain, describing the rise of social movements and new electoral coalitions related to the demands of the protest movements. Fourth, it focuses on the changing political frames of the political activists. It concludes that there has been a certain process of politicisation, materialised in the rise of new generations of political activists, but at a certain level the post-political situation remains both in the exceptional political moment and in the electoral coalitions, as the core of the economic system remains unquestioned.

State fetish, post-politics and re-politicisation

Echeverría (1998) defines the political as the capacity to influence, found or transform human sociability, which, in capitalist society, tends to be monopolised by politics. This reduction of the political to pragmatic political management in the area of institutions, to professional politics, Echeverria calls the fetish of the State. The fetish of the State hides other levels of the political, which tend to emerge anyway as an impure and peripheral exercise. Besides, Echeverria speaks about two different moments of the political. Firstly, an extraordinary moment of foundation or re-foundation of society: war, civil war or/and revolution, the political par excellence. Secondly, the political in everyday social life, prolonging the extraordinary moment, which completes the transformative action and consists of the apolitical work that serves the events of the extraordinary moment. In Žižek's (2011) words, the gap between the political act and the administration of really existing social relations is that the first 'changes the very frame which determines how things work' (p. 216).

The fetish of the State, a substantial tendency in capitalism for Echeverría (1998), leads to a kind of post-political situation. Thus, the context of neoliberal success raises the contemporary debate concerning post-politics. This has been defined as a situation in which the political is reduced to politics, to technocratic mechanisms and consensual procedures that operate within an unquestioned framework of representative democracy, free market economy and cosmopolitan liberalism (Wilson & Swyngedouw, 2015, p. 6).

The expansion of neoliberal capitalism from the seventies onwards, until it achieved a virtual post-political situation in the nineties, has been challenged through different political projects: from projects tied to the radical and pluralistic democracy of new social movements (NSM) to the more recent projects tied to Laclau's populist hypothesis. First, one of the political manifestations of the political shift in the seventies was the emergence of the so-called NSM. The actions of these NSMs favoured the rise of a New Left, which included in its discourse ideas related to ecology, sexual rights, gender equality, displacing issues related with trade unionism and social classes (Melucci, 1999). This also coincides with the rise of political autonomism (as a model of internal organising principles based on horizontal structures), from German squatters movements to the Zapatista movement in México. Secondly, in the context of the emergence of NSM, Laclau and Mouffe (2004) developed a critique of the supposed Marxist essentialism and the primordial role assigned to the class struggle. They proposed a redefinition of the socialist project in terms of a radicalisation of democracy. Democracy should work in this project by articulating the irreducible multiplicity of struggles against different forms of subordination. So the new task of the left was not to fight the liberal democratic ideology but the opposite, to deepen and to expand it in the direction of a radicalised and plural democracy. Thirdly, also in the context of the NSM emergence, Kitschelt (1989) proposed the concept 'party-movement' to refer to those new political parties that were promoted by left-libertarian and ecologist groups in Western Europe during the 1980s. In contrast to the traditional communist parties, these parties were defined by their attempt to preserve some of the characteristics of social movements (horizontal organisational structure and so on) (Kitschelt, 2006). The political cycle opened by the economic crisis of 2008 have driven some authors to rescue the concept of 'party-movement' in order to explain the rise of new political formations born or invigorated by NSM, such as Syriza in Greece, Podemos in Spain, Movimento 5 Stelle in Italy and Bloco de Esquerda in Portugal (Martín, 2015; Subirats, 2015).

Later on, Laclau (2005) moved from radical democracy to his particular definition of populism. For Laclau, populism is not a specific political movement, but the political at its purest, a neutral matrix of an open struggle whose content and stakes are themselves defined by the contingent struggle for hegemony. What characterises populism is the emergence of the people as a political subject, and all different particular struggles and antagonism appear as part of the struggle between the people and the Other (this content of us and them is not prescribed, but what is at stake is the struggle for hegemony). In a context where hegemonic power cannot incorporate a series of popular demands, an antagonistic force would struggle for some empty signifiers (democracy, justice, decency), which can incorporate the multiple particular and unsatisfied demands of the people. This thesis has been highly influential on Podemos and was partially based on the analysis of the Argentina's political tradition.

Diverse criticisms have been raised against the project of multiple identities and radical politics, as well as against Laclau's populist proposal. To begin with, for Žižek (2011, pp. 226–228) as well as for Dean (2015), the postmodern identity politics, related to particular life styles, fits very well with the idea of a de-politicised society. The recent proliferation of cultural groups and life styles is only possible and thinkable in the context of capitalist globalisation. The only link that connects all these multiple identities is the capitalist market, always eager to satisfy its clients. Moreover, Žižek (2008, p. 95) criticises Laclau and Mouffe's defence of the 'democratic invention' since in the very definition of political democracy there is a tendency to exclude the non-political, the (liberal) sphere of politics as separated from private life and the economy (the fetish of the State, in Echeverria's words). On the other hand, Swyngedouw (2015, p. 177) blames particularistic and local protests for representing a colonisation of the political by the social, rather than politicising the outer flanks of the political dimension, substituting the political by a proliferation of identity-based and fragmented communities.

The other key topic is the abandonment of criticism of capitalism. Postmodernism has politicised aspects previously considered apolitical o private, but it has contributed to the de-politicisation of the economy and the naturalisation of capitalism. For Žižek (2008, p. 178) and Dean (2016, p. 54), the escape from Marxist essentialism drove Laclau and Mouffe to the acceptance of capitalism and the renunciation of any real attempt to overcome the existing social order. In a similar way, due to the necessary externalisation of the enemy into an intruder or obstacle, from a populist perspective the cause of one's troubles is ultimately never the system as such, but the intruder who corrupted it (financial manipulators and not capitalists as such). In addition, Žižek dismisses the current polarisation between the post-political administration and the populist politicisation. Both can coexist even in the same political force, replacing tolerance for multiculturalism as an ideological supplement with post-political administration (Žižek, 2006). Thus, for Žižek and Dean, politicisation in the current neoliberal context seems to unavoidably entail the politicisation of the economy.

Methods

The cases of Argentina and Spain have been selected for illustrating what we propose as a possible model of politicisation, understood as an overcoming of the post-political (neoliberal) situation. This process is analysed in political activists, active mainly in two concrete political organisations, as a change in their political frames and strategies, according to changes in the wider political and economic context. Qualitative methods are especially suitable for the study of political frames. This article is based on participant observation and 15 semi-structured interviews conducted in 2015 and the first quarter of 2016 and with political activists belonging to Podemos and local electoral coalitions in Spain as well as to *Nuevo Encuentro* (New Encounter-NE), which is part of the Kirchnerist coalition *Frente para la Victoria*, in Argentina. In order to select the informants the researchers have attempted to cover different levels of personal engagement in social protest and/or electoral struggle; so different viewpoints on political action could be reflected. The interviews were conducted in Buenos Aires, Seville and Cádiz.

The participant observation took place in assemblies, demonstrations and meetings of committees of local branches of these parties and coalitions. These observations were complemented by an analysis of documents pertaining to these political groups. The sample has followed the criterion of theoretical saturation. The researchers have stopped collecting data as new research did not provide additional information on the research questions.

The interviews and document analysis focused on the changing frames of the activists in relation to: the identification of enemies or those responsible for social problems, the existence of general strategies and the changing perception about the plausibility and desirability of the relationship with state institutions, alliances with different actors and goals, concrete measures and proposed alternatives.

These research techniques will be used in order to study the transformations of the frames of the political activists, which experienced the transition from participating in spontaneous and/or autonomous protests to being actively involved with political parties. The seminal work of Snow, Burke Rochford, Worden, and Benford (1986) introduced the concept of frame alignment to the study of social movements. Frame alignment takes place when the individuals reinterpret their biographies and life experiences according to the discursive contexts of the movement – producing new identities and becoming persons who can be mobilised and whose self-interest coincides with the goals of the movement. In this article, we will use the concept of 'frame transformation' (Snow et al., 1986, p. 473) in order to explain the shift of social protest and opposition to neoliberalism. Frame transformation is a type of frame alignment that takes place when the proposed frames, or logics of action, of the activists appear contradictory to the frames, rituals, practices and routines of the population and the institutions in which they are participating. In order to maintain and acquire social support and members, and to manage their new institutions and organisations, activists must propose new discourses, meanings and values. It must be added, however, that framing processes do not take place in a socio-economic and political vacuum; they are powerfully conditioned by political opportunities and the socio-economic context (McAdam, McCarthy, & Zald, 1996, pp. 2–6).

Context: from post-politics to the political?

Social crisis and 'populism' in Argentina

From the last military dictatorship, Argentina has been one of the many laboratories of neoliberal politics. In the nineties, the democratic government of Menem was responsible for a high financiarisation of the economy, privatisation of public companies and high rates of public indebtedness (Lozano, 2001). The key policy of this period was the convertibility (a fixed exchange relation between the Argentinian peso and American dollar), which generated an effect of perceived enrichment in the population which contributed to the consensus on neoliberal model (Levey et al., 2016). Starting in 1998, Argentina suffered from a recession, the unemployment rate rose to 20%, and in the end the whole national financial system collapsed in 2001. As a result, the government blocked the bank deposits to prevent the flight of capital.

The period prior to the 2001 protests is usually characterised as one of low political unrest, low participation in protests and the fragmentation of demands. However, the outbreak of unrest in December 2001 involved street protests, shop looting and violent riots for weeks, mainly in Buenos Aires. The declaration of a state of emergency and around 39 people being killed in confrontations with police did not stop the protests. The popular claim *Que se vayan todos* (All of them must go!), directed against the political parties and policy professionals, gathered strength. Four presidents resigned in one week and there was a long period of political instability all through 2002. Argentina's 2001 protests are quite famous because of the innovation witnessed in its repertories of action and the influence of autonomist tendencies. The *piqueteros'* (picketers') movement, fragmented in a multitude of Trotskyist and autonomist organisations, introduced the 'cut the road and assembly' formula of protest, consisting in the blockade of the main roads of access to the city. These actions were organised by unemployed lower-class protesters using direct democracy and involved some kind of 'deinstitutionalisation' (Carrera & Cotarelo, 2002). On the other hand, the Popular Assemblies emerged in 2001 as an urban and middle-class form of horizontal organisation for protesting. This form of organisation is opposed to hierarchic and vertical structures typical of the State and traditional political parties. Besides, multiple initiatives of barter networks without official money were developed in the context of economic collapse. Finally, around 250 ruined companies were taken over by the workers and run through cooperatives. So, horizontal organisations and new political subjects were mobilised in this context (Almeyra Casares, 2005).

After a long period of political unrest, the left-wing Peronist Nestor Kirchner won the presidential election in 2003. Kirchner's popularity was the result of several factors (Boron, 2004), including the earlier low profile of the new president, being unconnected to prior governments, his personalist political style (populist to his detractors), his confrontation with the IMF, the World Bank and the US, his policy of purging agents involved in the military dictatorship and the reparations to victims of the dictatorship. For Muñoz and Retamozo (2008), Kirchner's government managed to spread the idea of taking back politics and the state for the people.

On the other hand, in relation to the economy, although there was not a radical change, following Wylde (2012, 2014), there was a notable shift from the previous neoliberal political economy. Néstor Kirchner and Cristina Fernández (the Kirchner governments) have managed an interventionist political economy in industry and social welfare. These governments developed a coherent political economy from 2003 to 2015, in the opinion of Vilas (2016), articulating with more or less success the particular interest of different social classes and factions with a nationalist discourse. Kirchnerism tried (successfully for a period) to combine the maintaining of the privileges of national elite with the assistance and the improving of living conditions of the working and lower classes.

Kirchnerism was widely supported by popular classes and brought practices and discourses from the radical left (e.g. promoting working coops). However, the Argentina's left-wing parties and many academics blame Kirchner governments for neutralising social movements and normalising capitalism and bourgeois state after the strong crisis of 2001 (Dinerstein, 2014; Katz, 2013 or Vega, 2015). During this period, popular assemblies were gradually broken up (with exceptions) and the public relevance of the *piqueteros* declined dramatically as result of the economic growth and the reduction in unemployment. In addition, there were significant processes of co-optation performed by the Kirchner governments, getting close to radical unions (such as the Central de Trabajadores de la Argentina, Argentine Workers' Central Union) as well as to *piqueteros* organisations. In general terms, the bulk of the *piqueteros* organisations became dependent on state subsidies (Almeyra Casares, 2005).

From financial crisis to political renewal in Spain

Spain had a period of enormous economic growth from the second half of the eighties, with an economy progressively deregulated, based on the tourist sector and on highly speculative real-estate and financial bubbles (Diaz-Parra & Solanas, 2015). The outbreak of the financial crisis in 2008 had a great impact on the Spanish economy. The first symptoms could be seen in the labour market indicators, particularly the unemployment rate. The income per capita of the country declined, unemployment and poverty started to grow, rising to alarming rates among the youth population and home evictions became widespread. The way the crisis was managed after 2011, with severe cutbacks in public services and investments being imposed and the labour market being deregulated, in response to the demands of the 'Troika' (European Commission, International Monetary Fund and European Central Bank), worsened the situation. As a result of these policies, some public services, including education and health, experienced significant drops in budget resources. There were also significant cuts in pensions, unemployment benefits and social services.

The political management of the crisis, together with the numerous corruption scandals, turned the economic crisis into a crisis of representation. It was in this context of the political sphere having been discredited that the protests of the *indignados* or 15M movement in 2011 emerged, which became the most prominent social movement in contemporary Spanish history. Public square occupations, protest camps, networks, assemblies, work commissions and protests were extended throughout the country, building a new movement characterised by horizontalism and the use of new information and communication technologies (Castells, 2013). In the next years, there were two general strikes and they were raised strong and influential movements of housing and against cutback in public services. However, by the middle of 2013 the movement showed clear signs of withering away, mostly due to the difficulties it was having in generating an effective and stable organisational structure and in achieving any of its goals (Roca & Diaz-Parra, 2016).

The closeness of the political institutions to the social movement's demands and the frustration of many activists led a group of militants of the anti-capitalist left, a small Trotskyist-oriented party and several university lecturers to create a new political party in order to give institutional expression to the demands of the social forces unleashed by the 15M (Iglesias, 2015). They founded the party, which they named Podemos – inspired by Obama's campaign – in 2014 and participated in the elections for the European parliament in May of that year. The skilful communication strategy of the party and its leader, Pablo Iglesias, succeeded in attracting the attention of the mass media, and Podemos gained five seats in the European Parliament and 1.2 million votes (Errejón, 2015). After that, there was a transfer of militancy from the 15M and other social movements and political groups to Podemos. The new party set up its organisational structure to a great extent following the model of the networks formed by the 15M assemblies

(Romanos & Sádaba, 2015); however, institutional participation demanded a greater level of centralisation.

With the municipal elections on 24 May 2015 on the horizon, activists launched hundreds of municipal candidatures throughout the Spanish territory, most of them supported by Podemos and, in some cases, by other leftist political forces. These candidatures, which included in their programs many of the demands of the 15M and other social movements, seized power in the two most important cities, Madrid and Barcelona, but also in many other relevant cities such as A Coruña, Cádiz or Zaragoza. In other cities they gained hundreds of seats on city councils. Notoriously, some of the first measures adopted by the new governments of these cities were related to demands of the housing movement.

As time went by the media campaign against Podemos intensified, eroding the public image of its leaders and its social support. Nevertheless, in the general elections of December 2015 and June 2016, the coalition of Podemos with other leftist forces (En Comú Podem, Compromis and En Marea) received the third most votes. Anyway, electoral results in Argentina and Spain have made evident the differences from a social and territorial perspective. While Kirchnerism has wide support in the poorest regions and in the poorest areas of the big cities (provinces in the north of Argentina and Province of Buenos Aires), Podemos has got its support from the richest regions in the north of Spain (Catalonia and Basque Country) and its biggest support comes from young people with higher education. The old social-democrat party (Partido Socialista Obrero Español [PSOE]) keep being hegemonic in the poorest regions of the country (Andalusia and Extremadura) and among non-educated people ('Elecciones Congreso', 2015; 'Resultados electorales del balotaje', 2015).

Analysis of the frames of political activists

In this epigraph we check critically the proposition of a change from a post-political frame towards a populist-politicised frame through the analysis of fieldwork empirical material (Figure 1).

Post-political frame

In Argentina, prior to 2003, the enemy for left-wing activists as well as for a good part of the population were (professional) politicians, who were seen as being corrupt burglars. Politicians were blamed for the enormous problems of unemployment and poverty, which led to the political instability of 2001–2002. Today this is admitted but criticised by NE militants, some of whom

	Post-political frame	*Populist frame*
Enemies and allies	Professional politicians Activism as a marginal phenomenon	National economic elite and foreign institutions. Class alliance (nationalist populism)
Relationship with state institutions	Absence of relations with state institutions. Professional politics separated from society	Focus on institutional and party politics.
Proposed alternatives for political and social change	Cultural and social focus. Prefigurative politics. Local micro-utopias	Change through state institutions.

Figure 1. Changing frames.

were already left-wing activists but also by many others who were not (despite the age difference, the discourse of the militants about this period is quite homogeneous). The 'All of them must go!' slogan is interpreted by NE activists as a sign of impotence. All NE informants suggested that the time prior to 2001 was characterised by left activism being isolated, reduced to 'ghettoes' and separated from 'real people', with young Argentineans being completely de-politicised. They explain this fact by the abundance of consumer goods, thanks to the dollarisation of the Argentinean economy. One of the activists spoke about trade unions as an important political reference in these times, but, according to his point of view, their scope was very limited due to the left's lack of involvement in 'real' politics. Two of the interviewees told the researchers that in the 1990s politicians were not people they looked up to. In those times, political and/or youth rebelliousness was supposed to be sublimated in music icons and rock counter-culture. The autonomous rise of 2001 seems to have reversed this tendency only partially:

[...] before the rebellion was in rock music, in culture. I identified myself with *Los Redondos* (an Argentinean rock band). Young people followed these type of referents. Today this has changed. Young people identify themselves with politicians rather than with rock stars, because the rebellion they saw in musicians can be found nowadays in politicians. And politicians are no more these persons separated from society without any relation with you. You can humanize them. (Basteiro, interviewed in Buenos Aires, February 2016)

For NE activists, there was an emergence of left-wing activism, characterised by the relative absence of relations with state institutions and focused on prefigurative politics. NE activists show some disdain for prefigurative politics. Distance from state institutions is perceived as distance from the political itself.

In Argentina, an intensive autonomist and far left-wing activism, with multitude of small anti-capitals projects, has characterised the post-2001 period. Nowadays, it is easy to find popular markets, cooperatives and autonomous assemblies, which, paradoxically, are usually linked to some kind of state sponsorship, at least prior to the 2015 elections.

Political activism in Spain in the eighties and nineties was to a large extent focused on prefigurative politics (with small counter-cultural groups acting in the ambits such as squatting and anti-militarism). The strong movements at the end of the 1970s began to decline as the labour organisations came to be institutionalised and the left-wing parties were included in the governmental institutions. In this context the tendencies and campaigns characteristic of the European NSMs were introduced in Spain: feminism, environmentalism, squatters and so on. Within these, the criticism of the institutionalisation of the parties and trade unions was a central issue.

The 15M slogan *No nos representan* (They do not represent us) reflected the initial disaffection of the protesters (and a significant part of the population) towards political elites and the management of the economic crisis. It also illustrates the ambiguity of the discourse of the movement, which favoured the identification of people from very different backgrounds. Veteran activists from the radical left, trade unions and civil society organisations mobilised together with young people, leading to some internal conflicts. According to some interviewees, the new generations of activists liked long assemblies where they could speak freely and express their feelings, while veteran activists attempted to introduce more dynamism into the decision-making.

Another widespread slogan – 'It's not the left against the right, it's the bottom against the top' – manifested that the discontent was directed towards both the conservative Partido Popular and the socialist PSOE, which implemented austerity measures and were involved in corruption scandals. María, today a member of an electoral coalition, illustrated this tendency when she explained that before 2014 she did not vote. Her interest in politics came out of participating in the anti-austerity movement:

I voted when I was 18 years old for the United Left. After that I never voted. Not because I was not interested in politics, in fact I was very interested in it, but because I didn't feel represented by anyone.

The 15M assemblies were critical moments of political learning and awareness for a young generation: 'the people who were there and who were very politicised, used to think one thing one week and a different thing the following week, because the discourses enriched us and we were learning'.

The autonomist organisation and initiatives raised by the economic and political crisis have a continuity with previous trends in extreme left-wing political organisation (Diaz-Parra & Candon, 2014; Dinerstein, 2014). These leads to interpret that the frame of political possibilities previous to the political representation crisis remained in the first years after 2001 and 2011, in contradiction with the new context leading to further changes in militants frames.

A new populist-politicised frame?

In comparison with the pre-Kirchnerist period, NE militants say that Argentinean people today speak in the streets about politics. People discuss and fight about politics and the political economy in the shops and in their own houses. From Laclau's sympathetic perspective, Kirchner's government succeed in displacing the empty signifier 'people', previously used in the opposition towards the state as a whole and professional politicians, towards the traditional antagonism in Peronist politics – 'the national-popular' against the oligarchy and foreign interests, under the guise of 'neoliberalism', as has been pointed out by Muñoz y Retamozo (2008).

Sometimes, NE members speak about capitalists as the enemy, but they usually spare national or nationalist capitalists, little entrepreneurs and so on. The class alliance is part of the discourse of the militants. This is one of the main criticisms from the left towards Kirchnerism, which they relate to the resignation of the capitalist frame as unavoidable.

For one NE militant the enemy is 'the enemy of the people', for another 'the ones who don't want to be the people'. Defining people, however, is not an easy task. NE militants, as well as Peronists in general, are strongly nationalist, Argentinean nationalist and (for those more left wing) Latin-American nationalist, what they understand as opposed to USA imperialism. The main references of NE militants are Argentinean nationalist leaders, from Kirchner to Peron and Evita and many others, but also Latin-Americans: Che Guevara, Chávez, Fidel Castro and the *Movimento dos Sem Terra* of Brazil. On the other hand, every NE militant identifies the political with the intervention of state institutional politics. The state is no longer the enemy of the people by nature, it depends on who is in control of the state and its bureaucracy. Even if they accept other means of political participation (through religious congregations, NGOs and others) these are not seen as completely political.

The interviewee's impression (supported by the ethnographic fieldwork of the researchers) is that NE militants are young middle-class city dwellers, which, in the previous frame, would be identified with an anti-political perspective. This contrasts with their militancy in a party that they define as a 'cadres in formation' party, which is organised according to principles of democratic centralism, and with an evident hierarchy of leadership that is highly accepted by the disciplined militants. This is a classical Marxist-Leninist organisation, but with a nationalist discourse and a neutral citizenship aesthetic. Centralised leadership runs through Peronism, Cristina Fernández de Kirchner and its past leaders (Evita and Perón). The current leadership of Cristina Fernández is a typical charismatic strong leadership. One of the interviewees spoke about Nestor and Cristina as her parents. Even if all the militants have the 2001 demonstrations as their reference point and identify with this event, most of them began to change course after

Nestor Kirchner's death. They refer Nestor's funeral as the main event that nudged them to take an active part in national politics.

Beyond the national meaning, the term 'people' has an evident class component. The people are also the lower-class (the working class) as main reference of Kirchnerism. Redistributive politics, social aids to the poorest, the creation of a national social security system and the promotion of the national industry have been some of the main banners of Kirchnerism. In contrast with Peronism, which it is undoubtedly a floating signifier, Kirchnerism is a newly created identity ascribed to the left-wing, even if there are strong criticism and opposition from left-wing positions.

Podemos clearly has tried to give a populist electoral expression to the frame created in the 15M (Errejón, 2015) – using the dichotomy of us (those from below) against them (those from the top), and connecting individual narratives and fragmented social problems into a common discourse. It has also developed a strong charismatic leadership. It made possible a turn in the frames of many activists. For example, in relation to the state, one interviewee stated, representing the point of view of many of them, that:

> I think now that the state can be a tool for defending the popular classes. I now have a different point of view on this. […] It is one of the few cushions that the working class has in the context of neoliberalism, in which multinational companies and non-democratic institutions rule.

Thus, the state is seen as a counter to neoliberal politics and a means for social democratisation. Moreover, there has been a concession to other apparatuses of the state, such as the army or the police. For example, they have included an Army officer as candidate for the elections, something that has provoked strong criticism from left-wing positions.

In Argentina, in some sense the pre-Kirchnerist frame was as post-political as the subsequent one. Right-wing anti-Kirchnerist discourse has been against the political and politicisation. Kirchnerism has been blamed for politicising society, polarising it as result. It is a common place in Argentina to speak about the creation of a political gap or breach between those who are Kirchnerist and those who are anti-Kirchnerist. In contrast, the right-wing coalition, winner of the 2015 national elections, used a paradigmatic post-political discourse. An interview with the current president Mauricio Macri in *El Pais* (Cué, 2016), soon after winning the election, is a good example of this, as he speaks about a 'return to normality', after a period of internal and external confrontation, and where he says that the 'right-left' political axis is something of the past. A good example of the quick destruction of political symbols by the new government are the new bills. Whereas in the Kirchnerist government the bills were marked with the face of Evita Peron or the Mothers of the May Square (a group symbol of the resistance against military dictatorship), the new bills show pictures of animals and natural landscapes.

On the other hand, the reaction of Kirchnerism to the defeat in 2015 has been to adopt, in some way, a post-political strategy. A militant said that the message of Cristina Fernández is 'to do politics from non-political spaces' as 'citizens'. The NE militants have a consensus in the analysis of the defeat. They think they worked too much for the popular classes and not enough for the growing middle classes. 'We haven't grown with the middle class'. So the new orientation is to abandon the gap, the polarisation.

The Spanish political formations are at a different stage. They have just entered into several public bodies (at European, state, regional and local levels) and are governing in some important cities. However, the aggressive reaction of the mass media and some old professional politicians from different parties has a point in common with the social polarisation around the Kirchnerist government. The participation in state institutions, and particularly the experience of municipal governments, has raised important expectations in many activists. They aimed at 'breaking the dynamics which have prevailed up until now'. The first change, says Iliana, is an aesthetic one: 'We are governed by ordinary people, with a closer language. We are achieving many things.'

Nonetheless, the electoral success has also generated critical challenges. As Ernesto pointed out in relation to the local government,

> I miss that the representatives reiterate certain messages strongly. They should insist more publicly in four or five issues that we [the coalition] understand as essential. Not being carried along by the bureaucracy. I miss certain moments of insubordination from within.

To many Spanish political activists and leaders, the priority at the short term is to win the general elections. However, other activists highlight the limits of institutional politics and defend a combination of mobilisation and electoral dispute. The problem, according to Ernesto, is that today, 'Only a few people are giving more importance to the street [mobilisation].'

The internal debates (and conflicts) within Podemos during 2015 confronted a view of the party as a movement, to some extent with strong fidelity to 15M practice and discourses, and a more pragmatic view oriented strategically to wining the general elections, focusing on the short term. The victory of the second perspective has driven political activism to focus on the electoral arena, abandoning street protest. Thus, the discourses about radical economic and political change have been supplanted to some extent by the focus on the critique of political corruption.

Conclusion

The frame of activists in a post-political situation is characterised by low expectations of big scale political changes and, especially, mistrust with political parties, formal politics and participation in state institutions. Political activism becomes a marginal phenomenon and takes on the form of union struggles, prefigurative politics and counter-culture.

In contrast to the post-political situation, the exceptional political moment and the posterior everyday political management can be understood as forms of politicisation. The events of 2001 and 2011, as well as the continued work of some electoral coalitions have raised problems that question the neoliberal post-political discourse, raising economic topics on class antagonism, financial deregulation abuse and/or elite's privilege. Thus, negation of the existing order and positive action to change it through old or new political mechanisms can be seen as two necessary moments for the political transformation of the society. The exceptional moment means the introduction of a street revolt and the crowd comes to represent an expression of opposition to the status quo (Dean, 2016). Everyday political management means the politicisation of institutional (and post-politicised) politics, and represents a possibility of practically challenging neoliberalism. In this regard, the cases have shown how neoliberalism is not about dismantling the state but about de-politicising it (something that party-movements attempt at least partially to counter).

The Kirchnerist populism is not so far from the politicisation of the economy in Žižek's terms. It has risen as a new frame in which class issues, resistance against neoliberalism and alternative economic policies (redistributive policies) are central to its militants. It permeates their political identity and the state project. In Argentina, as well as in Spain, political activists are aware of the strong limitations of prefigurative politics and the impotence of anti-political street protests. They have been driven to embrace the seemingly opposite frame, based on the acceptance of a centralised organisation and political pragmatism (although with certain reluctance or even fierce opposition among some left-wing activists and organisations).

This frame transformation brings us to the post-political elements that are present in both political moments. In the exceptional political events of 2001 and 2011, post-politics was reflected in the central slogans *Que se vayan todos* and *No nos representan*, and in the lack of a strategy with respect to the political economy and state power. The autonomous rebellions, and further local utopian projects, seem to be post-political as far as they exclude a basic dimension of the political in the current context: the state, inverting the Echeverria's fetish of the State. In the following moment, the politicisation of economy seems more evident in the Argentinian case than in the Spanish one, where it is still too soon to draw any conclusions. However, both Kirchnerism and Podemos have post-political elements: the consensus about the capitalist development inside the country and the apparent state fetishism in the interpretation of the political by the militants. Some of the results of the electoral coalitions could be interpreted even as a contribution to the naturalisation of capitalism and liberal democracy. Consequently, who reflects a greater post-political character, the radical movements which refuse to participate in political institutions or the political parties which translate political disagreement to policy?

The recent evolution of Podemos and Kirchnerism seems to draw them gradually closer to post-political discourses, focusing on short-term strategy and pragmatism. This post-political component is much more notorious in the Spanish case and this can be a consequence of the extreme contextual differences between both cases. The immersion of Spain in a central region and an economic power bloc such as the European Union made the economic crisis much less radical; so the failure of neoliberalism has been less evident. In addition, in Argentina there has been a prolonged experience of Kirchnerist government. As a partial result, in Argentina's case at least there has been a clear politicisation of the economy through micro utopian projects as well as through reformist state politics.

Nonetheless, the post-political discourse is more evident among the right-wing rivals of both political coalitions since the post-political situation begins with the acceptance of the neoliberal economic consensus. Post-political elements are likely to be present in any political movement that aspires to create a great consensus on its proposed social order, or even a new understanding of what is regarded as common sense. Ultimately, the post-political situation emerges from the success of a particular ideology – that of neoliberalism.

Funding
This work was supported by the Ministry of Economy and Competitiveness of Spain under [grant number HAR2012-38837].

Disclosure statement
No potential conflict of interest was reported by the authors.

Note
1. The full speech can be seen in Spanish at: https://www.youtube.com/watch?v=J7zY3J0EGP0.

References

Almeyra Casares, G. (2005). Los movimientos sociales en Argentina, 1990–2005. *Argumentos*, *48/49*, 43–67.

Boron, A. (2004). Reflexiones en torno al gobierno de Néstor Kirchner. *Revista SAAP*, *2*(1), 187–205.

Carrera, N. I., & Cotarelo, M. C. (2002). La insurrección espontánea. Argentina. Diciembre de 2001. In F. Herrero (Ed.), *Ensayos sobre las protestas sociales en la Argentina* (pp. 111–132). Lanús: UNLa.

Castells, M. (2013). *Redes de indignación y esperanza*. Madrid: Alianza.

Cué, C. (2016). Macri: La corrupción se instaló en la sociedad argentina en su conjunto. *El País* 20 de Enero.

Dean, J. (2015). After post-politics: occupation and the return of communism. In J. Wilson & E. Swyngedouw (Eds.), *The post-political and its discontents. Spaces of depoliticisation, spectres of radical politics* (pp. 261–278). Edinburgh: Edinburgh University Press.

Dean, J. (2016). *Crowds and party*. New York, NY: Verso.

Diaz-Parra, I., & Candon, J. (2014). Espacio geográfico y Ciberespacio en el movimiento 15M. *Scripta Nova*, *470*(18). Retrieved from http://www.ub.edu/geocrit/sn/sn-470.htm

Diaz-Parra, I., & Solanas, M. (2015). De aquel cemento estos lodos. Vivienda, desahucios y okupación en la crisis española. *Servicios sociales y política social*, *108*(32), 101–120.

Dinerstein, A. C. (2014). Disagreement and hope: The hidden transcripts in the grammar of political recovery in post-crisis Argentina. In C. Levey, D. Ozarow, & C. Wylde (Eds.), *Argentina since the 2001: Recovering the past, reclaiming the future* (pp. 115–133). London: Palgrave Macmillan.

Echeverría, B. (1998). *Valor de uso y utopía*. México, DF: Siglo XXI.

Elecciones Congreso [Results of the general elections]. (2015). *Eldiario.es*. Retrieved from http://elecciones.eldiario.es/congreso/diciembre-2015/?refresh_ce

Errejón, I. (2015). We the people. El 15M: ¿Un populismo indignado? *ACME: An International E-Journal for Critical Geographies*, *14*(1), 124–156.

Errejón, I., & Mouffe, C. (2015). *Construir pueblo. Hegemonía y radicalización de la democracia*. Barcelona: Icaria.

Iglesias, P. (2015). Understanding Podemos. *New Left Review*, 93, 7–22.

Katz, C. (2013). Anatomía del Kirchnerismo. *Rebelión.org*. Retrieved from http://www.rebelion.org/noticia.php?id=162376

Kitschelt, H. (1989). *The logics of party formation: Ecological politics in Belgium and west Germany*. Ithaca, NY: Cornell University Press.

Kitschelt, H. (2006). Movement parties. In R. Katz & W. Crotty (Eds.), *Handbook of party politics* (pp. 278–290). London: Sage.

Laclau, E. (2005). *La razón populista*. México, DF: Fondo de Cultura Económica.

Laclau, E., & Mouffe, C. (2004). *Hegemonía y estrategia socialista. Hacia una radicalización de la democracia*. México: Fondo de Cultura Económica.

Levey, C., Ozarow, D., & Wylde, C. (Comp.) (2016). *De la crisis de 2001 al kirchnerismo. Cambios y continuidades*. Buenos Aires: Prometeo.

Lozano, C. (2001). Contexto económico y político de la protesta social de la Argentina contemporánea. *Observatorio Social de América Latina (CLACSO)*, *5*, 5–10.

Martín, I. (2015). Podemos y otros modelos de partido-movimiento. *Revista Española de Sociología*, *24*, 107–114.

McAdam, D., McCarthy, J., & Zald, M. (Eds.). (1996). *Comparative perspectives on social movements: Political opportunities, mobilizing structures, and cultural framings*. Cambridge: Cambridge University Press.

Melucci, A. (1999). *Acción Colectiva, Vida Cotidiana y Democracia*. México: El Colegio de México.

Muñoz, M. A., & Retamozo, M. (2008). Hegemonía y discurso en la Argentina contemporánea. Efectos políticos de los usos de *pueblo* en la retórica de Néstor Kirchner. *Perfiles Latinoamericanos*, *21*, 121–149.

Resultados electorales del balotaje [Results of the general elections]. (2015). *La Nación*. Retrieved from http://www.lanacion.com.ar/elecciones-2015-t50499

Roca, B., & Diaz-Parra, I. (2016). Blurring the borders between old and new social movements: The M15 movement and the radical unions in Spain. *Mediterranean Politics*, *21*(3), 1–20. doi:10.1080/13629395. 2016.1151138

Romanos, E., & Sádaba, I. (2015). La evolución de los marcos (tecno) discursivos del movimiento 15M y sus consecuencias. *Empiria*, *32*, 15–36. doi:empiria.32.2015.15307

Snow, D. A., Burke Rochford, Jr., R., Worden, K., & Benford, R. D. (1986). Frame alignment processes, micromobilization, and movement participation. *American Sociological Review*, *51*, 464–481.

Subirats, J. (2015). Todo se mueve. Acción colectiva, acción conectiva. Movimientos, partidos e instituciones. *Revista Española de Sociología*, *24*, 123–131.

Swyngedouw, E. (2015). Insurgent architects, radical cities and the promise of the political. In J. Wilson & E. Swyngedouw (Eds.), *The post-political and its discontents. Spaces of depoliticisation, spectres of radical politics* (pp. 169–188). Edinburgh: Edinburgh University Press.

Vega, R. (2015). *Neodesarrollismo. Acumulación de capital y clases dominantes en el capitalismo latinoamericano actual*. Tesis de Maestría del Programa de Posgrado en Estudios Latinoamericanos, Facultad de Ciencias Políticas y Sociales de la Universidad Nacional Autónoma de México.

Vilas, C. (2016). *Política, estado y clases en el kirchnerismo: una interpretación* (Working-paper). University of Lanus. Retrieved from http://cmvilas.com.ar/index.php/rppp/7-novedades/136-politica-estado-y-clases-en-el-kirchnerismo-una-interpretacion

Wilson, J., & Swyngedouw, E. (Eds.). (2015). *The post-political and its discontents. Spaces of depoliticisation, spectres of radical politics*. Edinburgh: Edinburgh University Press.

Wylde, C. (2012). ¿Continuidad o cambio? Política económica argentina posterior a la crisis y el gobierno de Néstor Kirchner, 2003–2007. *Iconos, Revista de Ciencias Sociales*, *43*, 109–133.

Wylde, C. (2014, July 23–25). *The IPE of postneoliberalism: Cristina Fernandez de Kirchner in Argentina*. ISA-FLACSO annual conference, Buenos Aires.

Žižek, S. (2006). Against the populist temptation. *Critical Inquiry*, *32*(3), 551–574.

Žižek, S. (2008). Multiculturalismo o la lógica cultural del capitalismo multinacional. In F. Jameson & S. Žižek (Eds.), *Estudios culturales. Reflexiones sobre el multiculturalismo* (pp. 137–188). Buenos Aires: Paidos.

Žižek, S. (2011). *El espinoso sujeto. El centro ausente de la ontología política*. Buenos Aires: Paidos.

Protest in South Africa: motives and meanings

Tom Lodge and Shauna Mottiar

South Africa is experiencing record levels of protest. Interpretations of protest fall into two groups. First, there is the argument that protests represent only limited rebellion and that though unruly, they are a mechanism for political re-engagement. A second understanding links "new social movements" that address general grievances to wider hegemonic challenges. This article addresses the issue of whether these upsurges in militant mobilization threaten or complement democratic procedures. The article draws from a study of two protest "hotspots" in Durban.

Protest in South Africa: popular participation or a counter-hegemonic movement?

Commentators note that the frequency of South African protest is high; many times the levels elsewhere.[1] In one widely used data set, the number of protests peaked in 2012 at 470 events. Here researchers distinguish between peaceful, disruptive, and violent protest: the latter two categories have been rising since 2009.[2] The rising trend of violent protests may reflect the increasing propensity of the police using violence, though.[3]

Understandings of the beliefs shaping this tumult vary. First, there is the argument that protests represent very limited kinds of rebellion and that though unruly they help the ruling party re-engage with its base. Susan Booysen has argued that today's riotous protests are only ostensibly insurrectionary. Their resemblance to the township insurrections of the 1970s is misleading, because they are not anti-systemic. They occur mostly, she suggests, in vicinities in which the record for government's "delivery" has been above-average. Moreover, she maintains, protests "work". They elicit quick responses, including dismissals of local scapegoats, and better facilities. Protests work the other way, too. Ward-level voting trends indicate that protest communities continue to vote for the African National Congress (ANC), with high turnouts.[4]

Peter Alexander is less certain about these protests' limitations. He is explicitly critical of Booysen's argument that rioting and voting for the ANC represent "dual repertoires". He draws his analysis from interviews with activists in two local eruptions, in Balfour and Piet Retief in 2009. Yes, it was true that visits and promises from national ANC leaders could still restore calm and public anger remained primarily directed at local politicians. But both protestors' tactics *and* the police response were "reminiscent of the apartheid era". Local leaders belong to a new activist generation: young, unemployed, and often well educated. In such settings government might retain legitimacy for a while, by removing unpopular councillors and promising better services, but in Alexander's view, the resources needed to address local needs are not there. The insurrectionary character of still-localized protests allow for the possibility one day of a more interconnected and even revolutionary "rebellion of the poor".[5]

For several observers, those interconnections that make protest more fundamentally challenging are already present. Here research is focussed upon specific clusters of activists engaged in building "new social movements", who in addressing particular grievances link these to wider systemic concerns. Kelly Rosenthal[6] perceives the Soweto Electricity Crisis Committee as a key site where alternatives to "dominant hegemony" are emerging. In a South African setting, such movements are "new" because they can be critical of the ANC and also, because their own activists call them this. Read in this way, then, contemporary protest assembles fresh configurations of actors seeking radical changes. Here South African movements respond to similar changes in the political economy that affect comparable groups elsewhere, at times consciously so, inspired by externally derived ideas.[7]

None of these assessments of protest address whether predispositions to engage in confrontational protest affect support for democratic values. Booysen's argument suggests that protest does not weaken the appeal of formal democratic channels, but it does not tell us about the ways in which procedural channels are understood by those who engage in protest. The implication in her argument might be that in as much as protest elicits reactions that then serve to maintain government legitimacy, democratic procedures are being conserved. In this vein, Mottiar and Bond also view protest as a form of political participation in which citizens find alternatives to elusive formal channels of access through "inventing" their own spaces and eliciting "highly visible" redress from senior politicians.[8] Similar conclusions arise from analysis of environmental protests in Durban: here, too, "protest is a component of, rather than an alternative to politics".[9]

But if protest signifies a trajectory in which poor communities finally abandon the ANC and instead embrace groups that lead them into "counter hegemonic terrain", does this not imply rejection of liberal democratic procedures? This seemed likely to early observers. In 1997, South African surveys suggested that "citizens [did] not feel yet a widespread attitudinal commitment to democracy"[10] and that the extent to which they supported it was a consequence of "instrumental" calculations of the material benefits rather than because of a more "intrinsic" attachment to its essential principles. In such settings, Bratton and Mattes proposed, in which commitment to constitutional values is uncertain, for citizens democracy may not be "the only game in town". In studies of democratic consolidation, democracy becomes the only game in town when no significant political groups attempt to overthrow the democratic regime and when, even in adversity, the overwhelming majority of people believe that change must emerge from within the parameters of democratic formulas.[11] This begs the question, though, of how such formulas are publically understood. In Balfour and Piet Retief, Peter Alexander discerned "disappointment with the fruits of democracy".[12] But such disappointments may be prompted by more than just the government's failure to deliver material goods. If popular expectations of democracy are grounded upon notions of active citizenship in which elected officials are perceived as accountable delegates,[13] then existing representative democracy may well undergo challenge.

In this article our concern will be whether these militant upsurges threaten or complement existing democratic procedures. We will explore the understandings of the purposes of protest among residents in two vicinities in Durban with very high levels of protest as well as their engagement with democratic procedures. By 2004 "struggle politics" in South Africa had become characterized by a tide of localized so-called "service delivery" protest. Situated mostly in poor neighbourhoods, protesters framed their grievances as material demands for water, sewage systems, street lighting, roads, housing, as well as jobs. Analysts are critical of the term "service delivery" protest, pointing to calls for rights to participatory democracy.[14] For aside from "service delivery" grievances, protests often cite lack of accountability and misbehaviour of local government officials.

It is in this context that we consider two case studies of protest "hotspots" in Durban. "Hotspots" is the term used by the Municipal IQ Monitor, an agency that assesses performance of local governments. As noted above, our general concern here will be to explore local levels of commitment to democracy. We do so in light of Juan Linz and Alfred Stepan's[15] understanding of a "consolidated" democracy being "the only game in town".

Methodological considerations

This study is based on interviews with 20 households in Durban in September and October of 2013. Ten of them took place in Ward 30 in Cato Manor. Of these, five were drawn from Masxha where there are Reconstruction and Development Programme (RDP) houses and services such as electricity and water. The other five were drawn from Greenland, a nearby informal settlement where water is accessed from standpipes and electricity through illegal connections. The remaining ten interviews took place in Ward 68 in South Durban. Five were in Merebank amongst a flatted community and the other five, also conducted in apartments, in

Wentworth. In these two communities, living on either side of a main road, house-holds have access to services. Sampling employed snowballing rather than random selection, because interviews took place during the day when people were often away from home. A range of demographic variables made up the sample with both male and female householders represented as well as a variety of age and race groups (all the Cato Respondents were black, the five Merebank respondents were Indian, and of the five Wentworth respondents four were "coloured" and one black). Despite interviewing taking place in daytime, several respondents indicated that they were employed.

The choice of the two vicinities as field sites, Cato Manor and South Durban, reflected several considerations. Both are areas that have accommodated well-sup-ported protest movements. In Cato Manor, though, ANC electoral support as well as its organizational presence appear pervasive. In South Durban, the ANC has for-midable electoral rivals. Moreover, in Merebank and Wentworth, a "new social movement", the South Durban Community Environmental Alliance (SDCEA) plays a conspicuous role in mobilizing protest. SDCEA views issue-based asser-tions as a means through which "a bottom up unity of the people" can be fostered, in which "interlinking struggles" in time will constitute hegemonic challenges to the "current model of economic and corporate globalisation" – this language is from its website. Both locations, for different reasons, then, seem promising places to explore the extent to which militant street action may reflect generally shared political disaffection.

Interviewing took place anonymously in order to encourage respondents to speak freely. Cato Manor, Merebank and Wentworth were visited with local acti-vists as guides. This study acknowledges the limitations arising from political orientations and network relations held by these activists. This was controlled as much as possible through employing a snowballing technique relying upon input from respondents, not guides. The three activists were also interviewed, as were two of their colleagues in Cato Manor and Merebank. Our guides were local residents in a setting where people tend to know their neighbours. This may have affected people's responses to us, positively in the sense that they may have been reassured about our credentials as researchers, and negatively in that they would have been aware of the guides' political orientations. None of the guides hold any office on any local political organization, though: they would not be seen as potentially politically threatening. We also spoke later with other Durban-based activists.

Cato Manor: "It's our democratic right to protest"

Cato Manor is seven kilometers from Durban's centre and has a population of 90,000. Named at the time of the 1845 land grant to Durban's mayor, George Cato, the area first developed as market gardens bought up by ex-indentured Indian labourers. By the 1930s, Indian landlords were renting out plots to African shanty dwellers and Cato Manor had 30,000 residents. Freedom from officials as well as its size and density supplied economic opportunities for the growth of petty trading and a base for cultural activity. Cato Manor's historians have argued that such resources helped to build "a sense of unity and community spirit".[16] The expulsion of Indian landlords during the 1949 riots, locally perceived as a "victory" for shack dwellers, reinforced local consciousness of "agency".[17] Through the 1950s Cato Manor supplied the ANC with one of its most important bases in which organizers claimed to have constructed a street-level structure on the basis of its M-Plan.[18] ANC recruitment in Cato Manor expanded in 1957 through the agency of "shebeen queens" and "shack lords", who with the help of the ANC began mobilizing opposition to city plans to resettle African residents in more distant townships. The removal of Africans from Cato Manor was completed in 1964 but in the 1980s once again the area had become resettled by Africans, with both Inkatha and ANC-aligned groups organizing their own territorial enclaves.[19]

Today, Cato Manor's residents include some of the poorest people in Durban and it is the target of ambitious municipal planning. It is a conspicuous "hotspot" for protest. *Abahlali*, very much a Durban-based shack-dwellers movement, claiming a signed-up membership of 10,000, is active in Cato Manor, though not in our fieldwork vicinity. In Ward 30, which includes the district in Cato Manor in which we conducted our research, the ANC has yet to encounter any serious electoral competition.

Judging from our interviews, predispositions to actively participate in protest are generalized. Six out of the ten residents suggested they were willing to join protest actions. In their view such action was animated by two concerns. On the one hand, protests were prompted by poor services. This was particularly a concern for Greenland respondents who lived in informal dwellings and accessed water from standpipes and electricity through illegal connections. Their demands centred on formal housing to replace their shanties and access to water, sanitation, and electricity. Second, though, protest was a way for local residents to make their voices heard outside Cato Manor and to compel politicians to be more responsive. Indeed, the main grievance in Masxha was the local councillor, who was seen to be unaccountable. Hence protest " ... is about service delivery but also we feel ignored and disrespected by the ANC" (Respondent 1, Cato Manor). As one of our guides informed us, "We want the ANC to visit us, they must come to the grass roots and hear our voices" (Activist 1, Cato Manor). Protest was undertaken as "a last resort" (Respondent 1, Cato Manor) when residents' "formal" engagements were not taken seriously.

In Ward 30, "last resort" action was because of the inattentive local ward councillor. As one of the Greenland residents observed, "We also want a new councillor, this one is lazy" (Respondent 6, Cato Manor). "Our councillor who's been on office since 2011 has not called a single meeting. She's not visible, she's not active" (Respondent 1, Cato Manor). Also, many residents, we were told, did not consider the councillor legitimate as she was not originally from the area, she was a "non-struggle" person and had been "imposed" on them by the ANC − "They've being doing this since 1994" (Respondent 4, Cato Manor). Following this imposition they had felt marginalized from formal or "invited" participatory spaces such as the ward committee.

> There are two camps in this ward. One supports the ward councillor (they are the minority) and we are the other (the majority) who support another candidate. So we don't go to ward meetings. We do attend ANC regional and province meetings, though. (Respondent 1, Cato Manor)

Interpreting this sort of testimony needs care. As we shall see, at least two of our respondents were still attending ward meetings and evidently had not given up on the councillor. The predecessor to the present councillor was also the target of dissatisfaction, because she was believed to be involved in venal housing allocations.[20] The reference to "two camps" might indicate a local politics configured around patrimonial factions. This certainly exists elsewhere in Cato Manor. In those parts of Cato Manor in which new housing is being constructed, the stakes involved in such factionalism can be high. In September 2013, police shot an activist during an eviction in Cato Crest in an occupation known as "Marikana" where people set up makeshift homes after their shacks had been destroyed to make room for new housing. The development did not promise to benefit the occupiers as they could not afford to pay bribes for the new houses nor did they have connections to local party structures.[21] In Ward 30, though, there was no promise yet of new housing, perhaps one reason why the ward councillor is perceived as ineffectual. Significantly, one Masxha resident attributed the councillor's unpopularity to her failure to "give out all the tenders she promised" (Respondent 4, Cato Manor). The ward councillor's outsider status, notwithstanding her local residency, helps explain her failure to make herself visible. Imposed on the ward by the regional party leaders, it is likely that for her the essential accountability requirements are upwards, towards her patrons.

Even so, not everyone agreed that institutionalized channels were useless. As one of the Masxha residents (Respondent 2, Cato Manor) explained, " ... we need to follow the correct processes to influence government – we must engage properly and then persevere". In general, she insisted, attending ward meetings was quite likely to engender helpful responses, though she did concede that "protest has its value such as just before the election". This view was echoed by Greenland shack-dwellers. One maintained that " ... following the political procedure is much better than protest" (Respondent 7, Cato Manor) while the other even suggested that "The ward councillor is a good option too" (Respondent 8, Cato Manor). Rather strikingly, though, even their more militant co-residents were emphatic that protests followed a predictable sequence: "We call meetings to discuss the issue, we usually write letters ... then we wait ... set a date ... delegate people to collect tyres" (Activists 2 and 3, Cato Manor). But though protest could be forceful and even reproduce the tactics used in the insurrectionary rebellions against apartheid, both residents and activists insisted that its repertoire should be constrained.

So, what kinds of action were off limits? Here our respondents diverged. Three were against burning houses or offices. Most did not view burning tyres as especially confrontational, though. Barricades of burning tyres are used to make protests visible, they insisted, and have no intended resonances with the struggles of the 1980s. Residents were ambivalent about the use of arson: "I used to support burning down houses and offices because it sent a message, even though I don't support damaging property. I don't support assassinations. I support camping (occupying) but I don't support intimidation" (Respondent 2, Cato Manor). Especially older respondents had personal reservations about burning things down, but " . . . burning goes with what the majority want" (Respondent 8, Cato Manor). In any case, "burning" is not seen as violent: "When we burned the councillor's office (a container) it was 10.30 at night and there was no one there who could be harmed" (Activists 2, Cato Manor).

The variety of views does not suggest generally agreed limitations. Arguably tyre burning and camping may be disruptive rather than violent, to borrow Alexander, Runciman, and Ngwane's distinction.[22] Burning down the councillors' office, even though undertaken at night with no risk to life, is surely different. That the councillor herself deploys security guards outside her house suggests she believes she is under threat. Most of the people we spoke to were uneasy about attacks on property, but the observation that "burning goes with what the majority want" is telling for it suggests that the choice of tactics is a matter of collective determination. And, as noted above, whilst protestors may embargo actions that risk death or injury, police responses to disruptive protest can be lethal.

In these vicinities, protest events are not mobilized through specially organized networks nor do they feature engagement with externally-led social movements. For example, the shack-dwellers' movement, *Abahlali*, had no visible following in Masxha or Greenland, though parts of its core membership are located elsewhere in Cato Manor. What was a really striking feature of the way in which residents spoke about protest activity was the impression of agency and ownership they conveyed: "It's led by us . . . " ; "Our protesting" (Respondent 9, Cato Manor); "We also link with other communities"; "We are the ones that start it – we take the initiative" (Respondent 3, Cato Manor).

Residents disagreed about whether protest really worked better than procedural channels. Two of the respondents believed that " . . . protest is far more effective" whereas " . . . in meetings just a lot of promises are made" (Respondent 1, Cato Manor), but others were more sceptical. Certainly, "Protest shows them that we are angry". However " . . . it doesn't really work either. It's like you are popcorn in a pot. You just pop, pop, pop and no one takes you seriously" (Respondent 4, Cato Manor). But, at least " . . . they notice us", we were told (Respondent 1, Cato Manor), and sometimes, even, " . . . they investigate the cause and if necessary, heads roll" (Respondent 2, Cato Manor). Winning "notice" might be the limit of any redress, though: "They respond. First by the councillor then by the regional office and the provincial chair – but nothing is done" (Respondent 4, Cato Manor).

In any case, the aim of protest is not just to obtain incremental improvements. Only one of our respondents believed that "Once there's development there'll be no need for protest" (Respondent 9, Cato Manor). Repeatedly our informants suggested that *through* protest communities became more democratically engaged. Even in a better world protest would still happen, because: " ... it's about solidarity about the problems we have in common – it's not just this single issue of the councillor, it's about all things that affect us – it doesn't stop at an RDP house" (Activists 2 and 3, Cato Manor). Protest is perceived as a democratic entitlement. Protesters argue that it has possibilities for both empowerment and transformation, because " ... you make people (protesters) see the light and it encourages them to act like citizens and ask for their rights" (Activists 2, Cato Manor). "It's our democratic right to protest" (Respondent 3, Cato Manor).

The key victories were those in which action elicited civility. As one of the Masxha residents recalled,

> Once during a protest, though, we didn't run. We said to the police "stones down" and "guns down". We moved towards them, near enough to talk and told them why we are protesting. They understood our grievances and allowed us to stay instead of chasing us away. (Respondent 1, Cato Manor)

On another occasion, " ... after one of our protests the ANC PEC and NEC came to a meeting where they listened to us. Now, Ward 30 meetings are never peaceful, there's always security and rotten fruit, but this meeting was good". It was good " ... because there was no one dictating and there was mutual respect with the ANC listening to us and hearing our problems. It left them with a new impression of us, that we are civil people" (Activists 2 and 3, Cato Manor).

In Cato Manor does protest presage real challenge to the ANC's political leadership? All the evidence from the testimony we collected might indicate not. Cato Manor protesters were emphatic their actions were not intended to displace the ANC from power. As they reminded us "We mobilise under the banner of the ANC despite protesting ANC" (Respondent 1, Cato Manor). Remember, Cato Manor is heartland ANC territory: "We live the ANC, we were born ANC" (Respondent 4, Cato Manor). Protests were about making leaders more responsive: "We don't hate the ANC, but they must listen to us – they mustn't hide" (Respondent 4, Cato Manor). In Masxha, all the residents we interviewed were party members and three regularly attended meetings. Activists who led protests were adamant: "We are working inside the system, asserting a democratic right" and, moreover, "We belong to the ANC and we hope they will always lead us" (Activist 1, Cato Manor). However deep were the local discontents that prompt popular tumult, "There's no challenge to the ANC. We don't for example want the Democratic Alliance (DA) in power. We were born and bred ANC. We don't want another home, but change is needed" (Activist 2, Cato Manor).

Maybe, though, on careful reading, there is more ambiguity in this sort of testimony than is ostensibly evident. "We don't hate the ANC, but they must listen to us", we were told. In such professions, who is "we" and who are "they"? Here, the "we" appears to be not quite "living" in the ANC. The phraseology in the statement that "We belong to the ANC and we hope they will always lead us" may be expressing a degree of conditionality. In Cato Manor, replacing the ANC with its main parliamentary opponent is implausible: for residents democracy is not about party choice, not when party support is so inextricably bound up with "born and bred" identity. Democracy is as much about what happens within the ANC as it is about the state's formal channels of political participation. Indeed, when residents seek redress, they might first summon the ward councillor, and failing that they will turn to the "regional office and then the provincial chair": party structures rather than those of elected government. But if redress is not forthcoming, then there will have to be change. Memories of replacing an aloof party leader with a "listener" are still fresh, especially in the province that supplied Jacob Zuma with his core support.

Even insurrectionary-seeming protest is hardly anti-systemic, respondents insisted. "We work in the system" the Cato Manor activists insisted, "Protest is our right. We are not at all anti-system" (Activists 2 and 3, Cato Manor). Nor did Cato Manor protestors frame their activism with ideas drawn from an external source and they did not perceive that their actions were part of a wider international movement: "I've seen the Occupy Wall Street on TV but it doesn't help me – that's American" (Respondent 3, Cato Manor). Did their activism signal disenchantment with democracy? All the residents said that they voted in all elections and all but one would vote in future. Voting was a moral obligation, they felt, "It's like a religion, we are forced to stay involved" (Respondent 3, Cato Manor). Indeed, " . . . it's our right, not like the days of apartheid when we couldn't" (Respondent 1, Cato Manor). "Yes, it's protocol" (Respondent 2, Cato Manor). More specifically, "We want to re-elect the councillor for ward 30, because the councillor was elected unfairly, the count was done all wrong, there was disrespect for the majority" (Respondent 1, Cato Manor). Protest did not replace procedural politics: "Protest is a democratic expression and it's not the same as anti-apartheid protest. It's just politics" (Respondent 2, Cato Manor). Indeed, "We are about sober politics – we want equality" (Respondent 1, Cato Manor).

Again, though, beliefs and intentions may be more complicated then these professions suggest. Protest may not be anti-systemic in the sense of offering explicit challenges to the "dominant hegemony" of liberal capitalism, but in Cato Manor the changes our informants want are profound. Their conception of democracy is of an order in which direct accountability and shared obligations are the critical norms. The fulfillment achieved on the occasions when officials were ready to discuss their grievances suggest their willingness to reach decisions through a process of deliberation and argument. To be sure, liberal democracy can accommodate a much greater range and frequency of citizen participation than its institutions allow conventionally,[23] but representative democracy in South Africa is organized in ways that limit assertive citizenry. In this setting the equating of "sober politics" with "equality" has radical implications.

Merebank and Wentworth: "democracy has not sunk in"

Merebank and Wentworth are located in the South Durban Basin. The basin is home to two large petrochemical refineries as well as 22,000 households. During the 1950s "coloured" and Indian communities were moved here despite the proximity of heavy industry. Merebank is a historic area of Indian settlement, inhabited first in the 1870s by ex-indentured labourers. By 1914 the village accommodated a middle class with a well-organized social life: for example a Literary and Debating Society.[24] Wentworth was established as a designated "coloured" township in the 1950s directly adjacent to the oil refinery, housing communities forcibly removed through the Group Areas Act. Merebank's population expanded in the 1960s with the arrival of relocated Indian shack dwellers who were accommodated in newly constructed breezeblock dwellings they were allowed to buy over ten years. Both neighbourhoods provide settings for "a sedimented network of civic and community based organisations".[25] The Merebank Residents Association (MRA) is led by "homeowners", including veteran activists from the 1970s.[26] However these civic bodies do not function through routine neighbourhood engagement or local membership structures. Studies of the functioning of the MRA and other local bodies in the environmental protests over the last decade stress their "poor network[ing]" and the way that "mistrust undermines collective action".[27] Such mistrust is likely to be especially entrenched in parts of Wentworth in which multigenerational gangs conduct territorial feuds over drug sales. Wentworth is especially overcrowded and has unusually high levels of youth unemployment.[28] Despite a heritage of local political activism, propensities for communally-based collective protest are clearly weaker than in Cato Manor.

Merebank and Wentworth are heavily affected by the pollution hazards associated with the petrochemical industry. This area in South Durban has been the site of lively opposition in the face of these challenges. Examples include the 2011 march by Merebank and Wentworth residents to the gates of the Engen refinery following an explosion which sent out a shower of crude oil. School children were admitted to hospital with breathing difficulties and skin irritations.[29] More recently, protest has centred on proposed port expansion, which threatens to relocate communities. Various organizations are active in the South Durban area. Among them are Earth-life Africa and the South Durban Community Environmental Alliance (SDECA). Local elections indicate majority support for the DA in 2000 and 2011 – in 2006 an independent candidate won the ward seat.

In Cato Manor a majority of our informants were frequent participants in protest, but in South Durban only two of the residents had engaged in any protest and only one was still willing to do so. In Wentworth, though, three out of the five residents we interviewed believed that "protest is effective", whereas all the Merebank residents perceived protest as unrewarding or pointless.

Merebank residents tended to think that activism was unlikely to win concessions. Engen was too big a giant to battle: "I used to protest, but I don't anymore, because Engen does nothing" (Respondent 1, Merebank). "We can protest, but you think we can shut Engen down? They'll shut us down!" (Respondent 5, Mere-bank). Respondents were also sceptical about the ANC's propensity to address their concerns given that Merebank was mainly an Indian community: "No, it's not worth protesting. It never comes right. If you don't have a Zulu name – nothing for you!" (Respondent 4, Merebank). Uncertainty about tenure was another inhibiting consideration. As the one former protestor we encountered in Merebank observed: "They want us to go and live with the black community in KwaMashu, but this is our community here. And they want to pay us half the value of our flats" (Respondent 1, Merebank). Merebank residents believed that the municipal authorities favoured the South Durban port expansion and would prefer the residents in the vicinity to leave: "They want for things to get very bad. They want to chase us out so they can build a harbour" (Respondent 4, Merebank).

Their reluctance to protest also reflected perceptions about the absence of soli-darity. As one resident explained, large numbers demonstrated in 2011 when an oil spill damaged apartment walls and spoiled laundry on washing lines. But then many of these same people later denied having taken part in the protest. This was because Engen had compensated them with R3000 vouchers (Respondent 5, Merebank). In any case, Engen's gesture appeared to have won residents over: "Those who did were paid out by Engen though so they do take responsibility when things happen" (Respondent 2, Merebank). "So now they are 'for' Engen. There's no unity" (Respondent 5, Merebank). This point was elaborated on by a Wentworth resident. Residents, he maintained, are content to remain passive citi-zens. "We are not a very progressive community. Democracy has not sunk in. People in this community are still just looking for hand outs" (Respondent 2, Went-worth). Activists suggested that assertive kinds of citizenship were especially unli-kely in Merebank: "Merebank folk are inward and introverted. They don't want us to get out there and fight the 'bad' or 'hopeless' causes".

Merebank residents agreed that their neighbours across the road had more appetite for protest. After all, they lived nearer the refinery and they were more likely to be affected by "all the trucks, the smell and all that". "We don't protest. It's mostly the 'coloureds' in Wentworth who protest. They are led by Des D'Sa [the SDCEA's leader]. He never comes here, though, except to meetings to which we don't go to, because everyone talks nonsense" (Respondent 5, Mer-ebank). Indeed, Wentworth residents did appear to be more predisposed to mili-tancy: three out of the five we interviewed opined that "protest is effective" (Wentworth Respondent 4). In their community, the Wentworth residents believed, protest had yielded dividends: "Protest at times is better – they listen to you. In meetings they just talk" (Respondent 1, Wentworth). When asked whether it could be empowering they agreed that protest might strengthen the community, but here respondents mainly repeated the phraseology in the question. Evidently, for them, the 2011 protest against Engen had represented a high point of mobilization and they referred to it several times: "Young and old came, men and women" (Respondent 6, Wentworth). But the impetus for the Engen protest was external – the leadership was supplied by the SDCEA. "We've never really had a community protest. It's all issue related – like anti-drugs etc." (Respondent 7, Wentworth). All the respondents that retained faith in the efficacy of protest agreed about tactical limits, though. Protest should never be violent, they stressed, and their notions of what was violent would have included much of the protest repertoire in Cato Manor. "We don't burn", the activists insisted.

The disinclination towards protest among South Durban residents was mirrored in low levels of participation in formal political events. Only one respondent, a Wentworth resident, could report he attended gatherings called by the ward councillor. In Merebank, we were told, the old councillor used to be a local resident and he was "more accommodating" when he met residents. Only one of the residents we interviewed had joined a political party. This was our first Wentworth respondent, by his own account a "heavy member" of a political party and also an enthusiastic protestor and the one resident out of the ten who attended ward meetings. As with this respondent, the two activists guiding our interviewing felt that "You should work in both, inside and outside the system". Seven out of the ten residents were habitual voters, though. Merebank residents, we were told, " ... support the ANC but they just don't hear us. They once came here and listened to what we had to say – but they said they would come back to us but never did" (Respondent 1, Merebank); "The ANC representative doesn't ever come round and check on us" (Respondent 4, Merebank). Political disaffection was most likely to result in disengagement, not active opposition to the ANC. On this point, commentary from Wentworth residents was illuminating: "No, there's no anti-ANC sentiment. Protest is just a way for people to be heard. You don't listen – let's punish you, that's why we protest" (Respondent 6, Wentworth); "The ANC has no opposition – people are just apolitically protesting" (Respondent 7, Wentworth).

Organized social movements had a discernable presence in these neighbourhoods. The residents intermittently referred to Des D'Sa. Most of them were evidently familiar with his record of environmental activism. One activist told us there would be no protest in South Durban without SDCEA because people simply would not understand the issues and do not possess the resources. Certainly SDCEA attracts externally derived resources. It mobilizes with loud hailers. It has a list of email contacts. It can supply transport to protests in more distant locations. It prints and distributes T-shirts. It applies to the authorities for the relevant permit required for demonstrations and in general undertakes "all the logistics of protest" (Activist 1, South Durban). In contrast to the tried and tested repertoires employed by Cato Manor protestors, the methods used in SDCEA-orchestrated events were innovative and elaborate: for example, 300 SDCEA volunteers held up traffic at the port entrance by lying down across the road. In Cato Manor, activists indicated that their struggles were born within affected communities and directed by residents themselves using whatever resources were available (Activists 2 and 3, Cato Manor). In South Durban, though, SDCEA worked closely with local residents' associations, the environmental activists were obviously driving the protest. The activists conceded that SDCEA protests focussed on the "broader" issues, but there were "finer" locally specific concerns that fell outside their remit that "communities need to take up themselves". Notwithstanding, then, the relative success SDCEA enjoyed with respect to mobilization of significant numbers of protestors and in eliciting concessions, its example has not served as a catalyst, igniting self-directed modes of citizen participation around locally specific issues that directly affect residents.

So, what can we learn from this testimony from South Durban? Compared to Cato Manor residents, the respondents in Merebank especially were more sceptical about the possibility that protest might engender any kind of positive response from politicians. The main difference, though, was the absence of the kinds of everyday "civicness" that we encountered in Cato Manor. In Wentworth, residents were more inclined to perceive protest as efficacious, than those in Merebank, but even so, the most important actions were led by outsiders and they "had never really had a *community* protests" (our italics). The language used to refer to the behaviour of politicians suggests particular presumptions about the location of power. A good councillor was an individual who was "accommodating", and neglectful ANC representatives failed to "check on us". In this phraseology, elected political officials seem to be expected to be socially distant. Residents here were much less inclined than the people we interviewed in Cato Manor to believe that politicians *should* be locally "visible". And, in the absence of vigorously engaged local political leaders there is indeed space for non-governmental organizations (NGOs) to mobilize support for protest around very particular grievances. The SDCEA's successes, though, seemed to have been mainly attributable to its command of resources from outside and these for a while can sustain protest without the sorts of networked community life that is so deeply entrenched in Cato Manor. But in the end, its victories simply result in another set of "hand-outs".

Conclusion: the political trajectories of protest

As we have seen, the Cato Manor residents we interviewed were much more predisposed to participate in confrontational kinds of protest than the people in South Durban. The Merebank residents were especially disinclined to become actively engaged in protest not least because they were worried about the consequences of attracting official attention. After all, the South Durban neighbourhoods are under threat because of proposals for industrial expansion.

Cato Manor residents in protesting seemed to be mobilized through informal networks rather than from prompts by externally-based NGOs – these appeared to be the main agencies in inspiring demonstrations in South Durban. The extent to which the residents themselves felt a sense of political efficacy was very striking in Cato Manor; much less so in South Durban. Most of the people we spoke to in both locations were habitual voters, though in Cato Manor residents were more likely to attend meetings and use any other procedural channels for political participation as well as being susceptible to direct action through protest. In contrast to most of the residents we interviewed in South Durban, Cato Manor residents felt a strong emotional loyalty to the ANC, even though they were critical of its local leadership.

How do we explain these differences between our findings from our two research sites? Cato Manor's "action preparedness" may be a reflection of the empathies that are fostered by a particular pattern of settlement. Distinctions between public and private space are looser in densely built RDP settlements as well as the shanty neighbourhoods of Cato Manor, and public spaces are important sites of sociability. Our respondents in South Durban lived in two-storey apartment blocks, located in fenced compounds. Common spaces existed for parking and for hanging out washing, but residents seemed much more likely to spend time at home, behind closed doors. This, together with the social distinctions and divisions that are the effect of a more complex local class structure in the South Durban neighbourhoods, as well as the fears arising from territorial gangsterism in Wentworth, might inhibit the kinds of confidently assertive communal identity evident in Cato Manor.

The most obvious difference, though, between Cato Manor and South Durban, likely to influence local political behaviour, is the presence of street-level political organization in the one and not in the other. In Cato Manor the ANC's day-to-day presence was very evident from residents' habitual attendance at branch meetings and their consideration of themselves as active members of the organization. This was especially the case in Masxha, the RDP settlement. In Merebank, political parties did not seem to have assertive local networks and ANC representatives, in the experience of our informants, were visitors not neighbours, and infrequent ones at that. As noted above, in any case, election results suggest that in this vicinity of South Durban, electoral support for the ANC is as patchy as other localities in KwaZulu Natal in which most residents are Indian or "coloured". Presence or absence of localized membership-based political organization is probably the key variable that explains the degree of confidence residents have in their ability to initiate action that will engender helpful responses. As noted by Cato Manor's historians, this widespread public confidence in communal "agency" has existed for a long time; this confidence is absent in the South Durban neighbourhoods.

How likely is it that our case studies are typical and generalizable? Remember these findings are drawn from very small groups of informants; they have to be tentative. One of our field sites was a particularly strong area of support for the ANC – as our Cato Manor respondents told us, they were "born and bred" adherents. As we've noted, the ANC's history in this locality stretches back decades. The party loyalty these residents profess may be unusually intense even among the ANC's "core" supporters. It may not be shared by all Cato Manor residents, though. The shack-dwellers' movement *Abahlali* has no obvious following in Masxha – itself constituted by built, formal housing – nor in the Greenland shanty settlement, but is very active elsewhere in Cato Manor. *Abahlali* leaders are careful to describe their movement as politically neutral, not anti-ANC, but the movement originated in 2005 in a shack-dwellers protest which the local ANC councillor denounced as "criminal". The arrest and trial of the shack-dwellers' leaders was followed by the rejection of local ANC-affiliated SANCO groups and their replacement with committees that then constituted themselves into *Abahlali*.[30] In the 2006 local elections, *Abahlali* called on its supporters to boycott the poll. One *Abahlali* leader that we interviewed for this study told us that she did not want "to do politics" – she "joined Abahlali ... because its neutrality appealed to me". Some of *Abahlali*'s members, though, she reported "feel that we should in elections remove the ANC just to show them that they are not bigger than the people".

So, even around Durban, where ANC support amongst "Africans" is comparatively strong, propensity to protest might not always coincide with maintained ANC adherence. Shortly before polling in 2014, *Abahlali* offered its endorsement to the DA. Overall, in Durban, the ANC vote held up well. In Cato Manor results are available for one of the voting districts (43371413, Ekuphileni Clinic) in which our Masxha informants lived. Here the ANC's share of the vote went down, but only slightly, from 87.58% to 80.38% but this was in a context in which turnout was higher and the absolute numbers voting for the ANC increased. Cross-checking with other Cato Manor districts confirms that on the whole loyalty to the ANC held, that only a few heeded *Abahlali*'s call, and that Cato Manor residents are generally more inclined to vote today than they were five years ago.

Certainly, with respect to the Cato Manor residents that we spoke to, protest was part of the routine of political participation. It did not imply disengagement with formal procedural channels nor did it signal disaffection with the ANC. In Masxha and Greenland, militant street action, it seems, continues to help the ruling party to reconnect with its base. It can still generate opportunities for the creation of "mutual respect" between residents and officials "with the ANC listening to us and hearing our problems". But, in their expectations of the way democracy should function, residents evidently have expectations which are shaped by notions of active citizenry and delegative democracy that would challenge a much more accountable system of representation than South Africa's. In the less organized communities of South Durban, militant protest is possible, but so far it has failed to instil a culture of local self-generating activism let alone any counter-hegemonic challenge. As the comparison between Cato Manor and Merebank/Wentworth in this article suggests, it is the domains in which the ANC more or less functions as a "single party democracy" in which one is most likely to encounter assertive citizenship. Collective street actions by these citizens are not anti-systemic, not yet, but they do signal dissatisfaction with the way existing South African democracy actually functions. Increasingly, though, police action treats them as if they were the rebellions or "hegemonic" confrontations that they may develop into.

Even in those areas where it is strong, the ANC's inclination to use demonstrations as opportunities for re-engagement through conciliatory response is not a given. After all, *Abahlali*'s emergence was after ANC councillors and more senior officials had condemned protestors as criminal. This reaction may reflect perceptions that have become more widespread in senior ANC echelons. At the beginning of 2013, the ANC's secretary general announced that the ANC's

executive was directing "the state to find ways ... to deal with the twin phenomenon of violent strikes and violent community protests". Ngoako Ramatlhodi subsequently explained that what was needed was an "iron fist" to deal with the "seas
of anarchy" generated by service delivery protests.[31]

In the last few years protests have increased and the numbers of such protests
perceived to be violent by the authorities have also risen while the frequency of
violent public order policing has also increased: in January 2014, nine demonstrators were shot dead by the police. Authoritarian perceptions of violence are now
shaped by an increasingly comprehensive framework of regulation, which in
Durban underwent fresh codification in by-laws about behaviour in public space
before the World Cup in 2010.[32] Note that the "middle class" environmental activists in South Durban are careful to apply for the relevant permits needed to make
demonstrations legal and, hence, less vulnerable to armed police suppression. The
absence of anecdotal references to the police in the testimony from Merebank and
Wentworth was rather striking, though other research in Wentworth has elicited
widespread perceptions of local police as "corrupt, incompetent and disinterested".
Here, in poorer neighbourhoods, policing takes the form of incursions in which
police "zoom in with their vans, create a stir, and then leave again".[33] Though
more violent public order policing might be a consequence of more aggressive
protest, it is also likely to reflect an official policy since 2010 of police "remilitar-
isation" and the deployment of larger numbers of poorly trained officers following
a 50% increase in the force between 2003 and 2012.[34] In short, the likelihood of
protestors engendering the kind of "listening" reaction experienced by our Cato
Manor informants might be lessening. If this is so, then the predisposition of
ANC supporters "to alternate the brick (protest) and the pro-ANC ballot"[35] may
reduce. If this happens, one key mechanism through which the ANC renews its
authority will weaken. If repression of protest becomes more frequent and ANC
leaders become more inclined to follow the course suggested by Ramatlhodi,
then it is possible that the citizens of Cato Manor may become more disengaged.
Or they might become more inclined to consider alternative political parties or even
the more radical choices posed by new social movements.

In general, the evidence emerging from the testimony reported in this article
does not suggest that participants in very confrontational kinds of protest lack commitment to democratic values and procedures. In particular, our Cato Manor informants evidently placed a high value on civility: a protest was deemed successful if
it opened opportunities for discursive exchanges with officials. Protest enabled
people "to act like citizens" and was itself a "democratic expression", it was
intended to realize already conceded "rights". And most importantly, the more
assertive protestors we interviewed were emphatic about their obligations to
vote, this was "protocol". Significantly, the strongest advocacy for using procedural channels was among the militant Cato Manor residents rather than
among less protest-predisposed South Durbanites: this is one of the most significant findings from the comparison of the data from the two field sites. The
norms cited most often in our interviews were "fairness", "respect", "equality",

and responsiveness. Here popular understandings of democracy – "sober politics" – are so firmly grounded in an ethic of accountability. This sort of testimony does indicate strong "intrinsic" attachment to certain democratic principles, not just simply instrumental cost–benefit calculations about the material goods that might accumulate from democratic operations. Our evidence is limited, but, at least with respect to the people we encountered in our Durban fieldwork, their conception of democracy remained the only game in town.

Acknowledgements

We are extremely grateful to Olwethu Silangwe, Jabu Wanda, and Dimple Deonath as well as to all the residents we interviewed in Masxha, Greenland, Merebank, and Wentworth.

Disclosure statement

No potential conflict of interest was reported by the authors.

Notes

1. Alexander, "Rebellion of the Poor," 27.
2. Alexander, Runciman, and Ngwane, *Media Briefing*.
3. Duncan, "The Politics of Counting Protests."
4. Booysen, "The African national Congress," 138.
5. Alexander, "Rebellion of the Poor," 37.
6. Rosenthal, "New Social Movements."
7. Seddon and Zeilig, "Class and Protest," 23.
8. Mottiar and Bond, "Discontent and Social Protest," 18.
9. Leonard and Pelling, "Mobilisation and Protest," 139.
10. Bratton and Mattes, "Democratic and Market Reforms," 458.
11. Linz and Stepan, *Problems of Democratic Transition*, 5.
12. Alexander, "Rebellion of the Poor," 37.
13. Held, "Democracy," 18.
14. Friedman, "People are Demanding Public Service"; Pithouse, "The Service Delivery Myth."
15. Linz and Stepan, *Problems of Democratic Transition*.
16. Edwards, "Swing the Assegai Peacefully," 84.
17. Popke, "Modernity's Abject Space," 745.
18. Suttner, *The ANC Underground*, 29.
19. Edwards, "Swing the Assegai Peacefully"
20. Meth, "Committees, Witchdoctors and the Mother-Body," 273.
21. Pithouse, "There Will be Blood."
22. Alexander, Runciman, and Ngwane, *Media Briefing*.
23. Beetham, "Liberal Democracy."
24. Bhana, *Gandhi's Legacy*, 114.
25. Barnett and Scott, "Space of Opposition," 2621.
26. Freund, "Brown and Green," 730.
27. Leonard and Pelling, "Civil Society Response."
28. Anderson, "I'm Not So Into Gangs Anymore," 57–58.
29. Naidoo, "Crude Oil."

30. Pithouse, "A Politics of the Poor."
31. Burger, "Between a Rock and a Hard Place."
32. Roberts, "Durban's Future," 1490.
33. Marks and Wood, "The South African Policing Nexus," 146.
34. Smith, "South African Police Brutality."
35. Booysen, "The African National Congress," 485.

Bibliography

Alexander, Peter. "Rebellion of the Poor: South Africa's Service Delivery Protests – A Preliminary Analysis." *Review of African Political Economy* 37, no. 123 (2010): 25–40.

Alexander, Peter, Carin Runciman, and Trevor Ngwane. *Media Briefing: Community Protests 2004–2013*. Social Change Research Unit, University of Johannesburg, February 12, 2013.

Anderson, Bronwyn. "'I'm Not So Into Gangs Anymore': Coloured Boys Resisting Masculinity." *Agenda* 23, no. 80 (2011): 55–67.

Barnett, Clive, and Dianne Scott. "Space of Opposition: Activism and Deliberation in Post-apartheid Environmental Politics." *Environment and Planning* 39, no. 11 (2001): 2612–2631.

Beetham, David. "Liberal Democracy and the Limits of Democratization." *Political Studies* XL (1992): 10–39.

Bhana, Surendra. *Gandhi's Legacy: The Natal Indian Congress, 1894–1994*. Pietermaritzburg: University of Natal Press, 1997.

Booysen, Susan. *The African National Congress and the Regeneration of Political Power*. Johannesburg: Witwatersrand University Press, 2011.

Bratton, Michael, and Robert Mattes. Democratic and Market Reforms in Africa. *Afrobarometer Paper* No. 5. Cape Town, South Africa: Institute for Democracy in South Africa, 2000.

Burger, Johann. "Between a Rock and a Hard Place – Policing Public Violence in South Africa." *ISS Today*, February 14, 2013. http://www.issafrica.org/iss-today. Institute of Security Studies, Pretoria.

Duncan, Jane. "The Politics of Counting Protests." *Mail and Guardian*, April 17, 2014.

Edwards, Iain. "Swing the Assegai Peacefully." In *Holding Their Ground*, edited by P. Bonner, I. Hofmeyr, D. James, and T. Lodge. Johannesburg: Ravan Press, 1989.

Freund, Bill. "Brown and Green in Durban: The Evolution of Environmental Policy in a Post-apartheid City." *International Journal of Urban and Regional Research* 25, no. 4 (2001): 717–739.

Friedman, Steven. "People are Demanding Public Service not Service Delivery." *Business Day*, August 6, 2012. http://www.bdlive.co.za/articles/2009/07/29/people-are-demanding-public-service-not-service-delivery

Held, David. "Democracy: From City-states to a Cosmopolitan Order." *Political Studies* XL (1992): 10–39.

Leonard, Llewellyn, and Mark Pelling. "Civil Society Response to Industrial Contamination of Groundwater in Durban, South Africa." *Environment and Urbanization* 22, no. 2 (2010): 579–595.

Leonard, Llewellyn, and Mark Pelling. "Mobilisation and Protest: Environmental Justice in Durban South Africa." *Local Environment: The International Journal of Justice and Sustainability* 15, no. 2 (2010): 137–151.

Linz, Juan, and Alfred Stepan. *Problems of Democratic Transition and Consolidation.* Baltimore, MD: Johns Hopkins University Press, 1996.

Marks, Monique, and Jennifer Wood. "The South African Policing Nexus: Charting the Policing Landscape in Durban." *South African Review of Sociology* 38, no. 2 (2007): 134–160.

Maylam, Paul. "The Black Belt: African Squatters in Durban, 1935–1950." *Canadian Journal of African Studies* 17 (1983): 413–428.

Meth, Paula. "Committees, Witchdoctors and the Mother-body: Everyday Politics in the Township of Cato Manor, South Africa." *Habitat International* 39 (2013): 269–277.

Mottiar, Shauna, and Patrick Bond. "Discontent and Social Protest in Durban." *Politikon* 39, no. 3 (2012): 1–23.

Naidoo, Pralini. "Crude Oil Haunts Durban Community." *Green Times*, November 17, 2011. Accessed August 10, 2014. http://www.thegreentimes.co.za/stories/action/item/871-crude-oil-haunts-durban-community

Pithouse, Richard. "A Politics of the Poor: Shack Dwellers' Struggles in Durban." *Journal of Asian and African Studies* 43 (2008): 63–94.

Pithouse, Richard. "The Service Delivery Myth." *Dispatch Online, February 3, 2011, Pambazuka News 110209.*

Pithouse, Richard. "There Will be Blood." *Daily Maverick*, September 27, 2013.

Popke, E. Jeffrey. "Modernity's Abject Space: The Rise and Fall of Durban's Cato Manor." *Environment and Planning* 33 (2001): 737–752.

Roberts, David. "Durban's Future? Rebranding Through the Production/Policing of Event-specific Spaces at the 2010 World Cup." *Sport in Society: Cultures, Commerce, Media, Politics* 13, no. 10 (2010): 1486–1497.

Rosenthal, Kelly. "New Social Movements as Civil Society: The Case of Past and Present Soweto." In *Popular Politics and Resistance Movements in South Africa*, edited by William Beinart and Marcelle Dawson. Johannesburg: Witwatersrand University Press, 2010.

Seddon, David, and Leo Zeilig. "Class and Protest in Africa: New Waves." *Review of African Political Economy* 32, no. 103 (2007): 9–27.

Smith, David. "South African Reports of Police Brutality More Than Tripled in the Last Decade." *The Guardian*, August 22, 2013.

Suttner, Raymond. *The ANC Underground in South Africa, 1950–1976.* Boulder, CO: First Forum, 2009.

Intellectual radicals challenging the state: the case of Hizb ut-Tahrir in the west

Elisa Orofino

Within the broad panorama of twenty-first-century protest movements, this paper focuses on the activity of the Islamist group Hizb ut-Tahrir (HT) in the West. Founded in Palestine in 1952, HT stands out today as one of the most controversial groups on the global scene and is active in more than 45 countries. HT's 'war of ideas', based on a strong anti-integration agenda, an open rejection of democracy, personal freedom and Western foreign policy, has fostered a negative image of HT and it is seen as potentially dangerous. This paper explores how HT challenges Western states with its 'Shock, Demolish, and Rebuild' strategy, and places particular emphasis on the political and social fields. Through an attentive content analysis, interviews with current HT members and observation conducted during the author's fieldwork in London and Sydney, this paper contributes to the debate on protest movements, exploring an innovative form of dissent against the state based on the exaltation of the Caliphate.

Introduction

Hizb ut-Tahrir (HT) literally means 'Liberation Party'. The focus on liberation, as highlighted by the name, stresses the core aim of the group, that is, to set Muslims free from their oppressors all over the world. HT emerged in 1952 in Jerusalem as a protest-for-justice group engaging in an intellectual fight for the rights of Muslims (Taji-Farouki, 1996). The founder, Sheikh Mohammed Taqiuddin an-Nabhani, was an Islamic scholar and judge whose ideas were strongly anti-capitalist and anti-liberal. His writings, today constituting the literature of the group, show an-Nabhani's idea of the West, as a political, social and economic system extremely exploitative of other civilisations, especially of Muslims. This conviction is still a central pillar of the group's ideology, which considers the West as the enemy to be challenged in every area.

Just like the Muslim Brotherhood and Hamas, HT stood out as a protest movement against the occupation of Palestinian territories, referring back to the Caliphate (Islamic State or *Khilafah*) as the only adequate setting to assure stability, citizens' protection, and bringing the *ummah* (community of Muslim believers) back to their *deen* (Islamic way of life).[1] The name 'party' highlights HT's desire to engage with politics, challenging authorities mostly 'at an intellectual level through innovative concepts' (Abdullah, HT Australia, personal communication, 5 March 2016).[2] Given that HT's struggle against the West is, at the moment, a powerful 'war of ideas' (Baran, 2005), the author will focus on two main fields where this war occurs: the political and the social one. Data used in this research were collected through an accurate content analysis of HT's main informative material and literature, along with the fieldwork conducted in the UK and Australia. In particular, the author spent six months in London and Sydney, HT's headquarters in the two Western countries, interviewing current members of the group and its leaders. Furthermore, the author attended HT lectures, events and conferences observing HT's functioning from within. In situ data collection and first-hand contact with HT's members led to significant findings; HT challenges the West by winning acolytes through a three-step process here defined as 'Shock, Demolish and Rebuild'. They are able to alter an individual's beliefs in favour of new HT-framed ones, assuring long-term and stable membership.

Theoretical premises for challenging the west: HT as a new social movement

Theoretically speaking, HT falls under the umbrella of new social movements (NSMs) (Sutton & Vertigans, 2006). Adopting a different line from that of their predecessors, NSMs started in the 1960s and were characterised by post-materialistic values, middle-class activism, a flexible structure, and the creation of new identities. This description perfectly portrays HT, where a set of grievances was the starting point for its activity. As stressed by Melucci (Melucci & Bimbi, 1986), NSMs represent a new era where conflicts around specific themes (such as pollution, gender equality and war) give birth to new forms of aggregation that mobilise parts of society. Hizb ut-Tahrir, just like the feminist, the ecology/green, and the anti-war/peace movements, was founded with a specific aim (re-establishing the Caliphate) associated with a particular situation (a new form of Western colonialism and an on-going alleged persecution of Muslims).

As highlighted by the literature recognising Islamist movements as NSMs (Adkins, 2008; Berna, 2008; Hamid, 2007, 2016; Karagiannis & Mccauley, 2006; Sutton & Vertigans, 2006; Wiktorowicz, 2005), they can be better explored by taking into consideration three variables: the Political Opportunity System (POS), resource mobilisation and framing. POS is a mixture of different elements embracing accessibility to alliances, government level of control over the activities performed by the group and the legitimacy of the state (Samarov, 2008). Over the decades, Hizb ut-Tahrir has proved its ability to interact with several POSs, managing to survive and carry out its activities even where it is banned (such as Germany, Turkey and Russia). In countries such as the UK and Denmark, where the group enjoys greater freedom of action, HT has never denied its anti-integration agenda, energetically challenging the legitimacy of the liberal-capitalistic model. Like feminist groups, conventionally accepted by the literature as NSMs (Maber, 2016; Offe, 1985; O'Brien, 2016; Roy, 2004; Zulver, 2016), HT promotes a negative image of the institutional environment it operates within, defining it as oppressive of the social group it advocates, in this case, Muslims.

Resource Mobilization Theory (RMT), within NSMs Theory, gives a clear insight into how new forms of collective action assemble, organise, and use their resources. Charles Tilly defines mobilisation as a 'procedure through which a movement collects resources and then puts them under common control to be used in order to achieve a collective aim through a joint action' (Tilly, 1978, p. 78). Resources of any kind are essential to empower a movement, to strengthen it against its rivals, and to increase its influence on the political, economic and social scene. For this reason, HT takes very good care of its resources, especially of the human ones. As with feminist groups and NSMs in general, HT has created a system of non-material incentives to mobilise its human resources, referring in particular to solidary incentives (personal fulfilment and a sense of belonging deriving from participation), purposive incentives (the noble cause the individuals fight for and their higher purpose), and lastly the concept of *tarbiya*, or restoring and promoting proper Islamic beliefs and practices (Adkins, 2008).

The third variable with which to analyse a movement is framing. Frames are 'interpretive schemes that provide a cognitive structure to understand and interpret the reality in which an individual lives' (Wiktorowicz, 2005, p. 16). Moreover, they define the boundaries between 'us' as members of the group and 'them' who are not part of it (Tarrow, 1998). Ideology here plays a fundamental role since it shapes the frames that make a movement a 'network of shared meanings and a basis for common identity' (Wiktorowicz, 2005, p. 17). As NSMs do, HT is engaged in a framing process for three main reasons (Benford & Snow, 2000): (i) to identify a problem and the people to be blamed for it; (ii), to present an effective solution to the problem; (iii) to introduce valid motivations to encourage collective action. Just as feminist groups do in liberal, but also in repressive political contexts (Maber, 2016; Zulver, 2016), HT highlights the terrible conditions under which its target group lives (i.e. persecuted Muslims in the West living in Islamophobic societies), it identifies the responsible actors (i.e. Western governments as former colonial powers who still want to dominate Muslims), and proposes a solution in the form of the re-establishment of the Caliphate as the only effective political, social and economic system. These frames encourage a common understanding of the world among the group's members, who share the same motivations for action, the same goals and the same priorities.

Ideological premises for challenging the west

The framing process is deeply intertwined with the ideology a movement promotes. HT strongly believes that the West – as a system of political, social, economic and religious values and practices – is not compatible with Islam. This is clearly stated in the book 'The Clash of Civilizations', in which HT defines civilisation as 'a collection of concepts about life' (Hizb ut-Tahrir, 2002, p. 5). Western civilisation is depicted as praising man-made concepts instead of God, and also of having opposite goals to those of Islam. In fact, while Western societies' ultimate aims are mostly related to profit and power, a genuine Islamic society should be focused on the afterlife and on works that please Allah (Ahmed & Stuart, 2010). This argument highlights the post-materialistic views of the group. In line with Inglehart's (1977) vision of NSMs focused on post-materialistic values, HT is not concerned with food security or other primary needs; instead, its main focuses are spiritual purity, protection of the *ummah,* and a renovation of Muslim minds through the familiarisation with 'right' concepts.

HT links post-materialist goals with a spiritual and intellectual dimension, stressing the importance of holding onto the 'true Islam' by resisting any form of Western new colonialism, such as music, fashion or cuisine (Hizb ut-Tahrir, 1996). As highlighted by Roy (2004) in his 'Globalized Islam: The Search for a New Ummah', Muslims in the West are re-Islamising their world in order to resist assimilation to the West. In order to preserve their Muslim identity, Roy argues that Muslims are going back to their symbols and traditions, linking themselves more to the de-territorialised *ummah* rather than to the country they live in Roy (2004). This is a perfect environment for Islamist groups to flourish and gain supporters. In fact, movements such as HT advocate for the rights of Muslims, for the persecuted *ummah* around the world, and for the preciousness of Islam in all aspects of life.

Deeply linked with the first, the second ideological HT premise to turn the individual against the West is the idea of an everlasting 'battle between Islam and the *kuffar*' (Zallum, 2000). *Kuffar* means 'unbelievers', and on this concept the Hizb frames a dualistic vision of the world as divided between *Dar al-Islam* (Land of Islam) and *Dar al-Kufr* (Land of Unbelief). The former is where Muslims live under Islamic law (*shari'ā*), while the latter is where unbelievers rule and live according to a man-made system of regulations. Within the Land of Unbelief, there is the *Dar al-Harb* (Land of War), challenging the Islamic system and trying to colonise and oppress it. Therefore, Muslims living in those territories urgently need to be freed and to live under *shari'ā*, (HT-Australia, 2016a). HT is also strongly convinced that Western powers constantly conspire against Islam. Several times, the Hizb has pointed out the dangers to which Islam is exposed, deriving from the continuous spread of *kuffar* ideas aimed at turning Muslims away from their faith.

> The American campaign aims at turning the Muslims away from their *deen* to Capitalism by all ways and means including media misinformation, distortion of the concepts and rules of Islam, the implementation of *Kuffar* laws, as well as setting up legislation necessary for this implementation. (Hizb ut-Tahrir, 1996, p. 7, my emphasis)

This argument is not only valid for the United States, but for all Western nations. HT constantly presents Muslims in the West as endangered by institutions and private actors. Regarding institutions, besides policy-makers, the focus is usually on the educational ones (schools and universities) that sponsor a biased curriculum, 're-interpreting history as they like'.[3] For instance, the Caliphate is never presented as a viable political system in the West. Instead, it is often presented as a 'historical relic whose end has had to come in favour of democratic forms of government' (Mahmoud, HT Australia, personal communication, 3 March 2016). The propagation of these kinds of notions has fostered Muslims' acceptance of Western models as legitimate. HT works against this process, conducting informative events on the 'glorious time of the Caliphate' and the risks of conducting a non-Islamic life, which enhances Muslims' awareness on these topics.[4]

HT's strategy: shock, demolish and rebuild

The analysis of HT's theoretical and ideological premises puts in evidence the basis upon which HT's strategy is built. As NSMs do, HT frames issues in a specific way according to its worldview. For instance, HT depicts the Middle Eastern crisis as the direct consequence of Western invasion causing the end of the Caliphate, regarded as the only system granting protection to Muslims (An-Nabhani, 2007). In order to spark interest in these themes, HT uses striking images or stories that serve to cause individuals to question previous beliefs, triggering what Wiktorowicz (2005, p. 95) calls 'moral shock'. For this reason, HT Australia's Facebook Page is full of news concerning Muslim killings around the world, such as 'Footage of French crimes in Algeria' and 'Massacre in Syria' (HT-Australia 2016b, 2016c). These data shock the reader, who tends to empathise with fellow Muslims and wishes to know more about their conditions. The exposure to shocking truths can work as a catalyst to bring individuals closer to the group, to know more about a specific topic and the solutions the group presents for a certain problem. This is exactly what happened to 15 of the 20 interviewees of HT Australia. They became interested in HT after the divulgation of impacting data on Muslims, while the rest were shaken by the stories and information provided by members of their families who were already HT acolytes.

> I have always had my heart broken for Palestine and I wanted to do something to fight for my *ummah* and to be close to my brothers and sisters around the world. When my brother joined HT and he started telling me about the *Khilafah* and its glorious time, I became persuaded that it was the only solution to protect Muslims. (Amina, HT Australia, personal communication, 6 November 2015, my emphasis)

After the initial 'Shock' phase, HT aims at 'Demolishing' the individual's previous convictions which contrast with those of the group. For instance, HT stresses the relevance of the Caliphate in the modern world. As evidenced by the interviews with current HT members, the great majority of Muslims consider the Caliphate a mere historical relic:

Before HT, I never heard about the Caliphate. I thought it was a 'historical relic', as it is usually thought even within Muslim circles. That is because Colonialism changed the school curriculum, reducing the Caliphate to a mere utopia. (Mohammad, HT Australia, personal communication, 21 March 2016)

Even if I grew up in Turkey, I have never thought about the Caliphate as a viable system to be pursued in the modern world since Muslims rarely speak about it. (Atifa, HT Britain, personal communication, 5 December 2015)

After attending HT's *halaqaat* (study-circles), lectures and informative events, the individual starts questioning his previous certainties, becoming more familiar with HT's frames. Taking the Caliphate as an example, HT activists use strong intellectual and religious arguments to convince the *daris* (student) of the superiority of the Caliphate as the only effective political, social and economic system based on Islam. The *Khilafah* is presented as a *panacea* for all problems, where Muslims and non-Muslims can enjoy a better life under the protection of a just ruler (the Caliph) and a 'system based on social justice, accountability, *shari'a* and fear of God' (Fahim, HT Britain, personal communication, 20 October 2015).

Once the individual has abandoned his previous perceptions, he enters the third 'Rebuild' phase. The individual starts the process of identification with the in-group, developing at the same time, a negative view of the out-group, which pushes him toward action, and this is perceived as urgent. For instance, after accepting HT's idea of the Caliphate as the best system to protect Muslims around the world, HT's new acolyte becomes fully convinced that working for the re-establishment of the Caliphate is a religious obligation upon every Muslim.

The Caliphate is an obligation for us Muslims because it is the only system able to implement *shari'a* … Allah wants us to live our lives according to His regulations, therefore every Muslim should desire the Caliphate and work for its re-establishment. (Farah, HT Australia, personal communication, 6 March 2016, my emphasis)

The necessity for immediate action is also given by the group's vision of a suffering *ummah* around the world, to be protected by the only system able to do so: the Caliphate.

We are living in a dictatorship against Muslims, the Caliphate is the only solution … to work for our *ummah* around the world is our duty and the only way to protect them and us is to have the Caliphate back. (Hadiya, HT Australia, personal communication, 13 March 2016, my emphasis).

The *ummah* is like a human body, if one part suffers the whole body does. I always think about the sufferings of the *ummah* around the world and I see only one solution, i.e. the *Khilafah*. This is the only system about justice in every realm of life. (Khalida, HT Australia, personal communication, 6 April 2016, my emphasis).

As a result, the person will start acting according to the strategies sponsored by the group, functioning as an alternative source of learning and promoting its vision of the world through specific frames. Moreover, its religious character provides the basis for strong loyalties where the faithfulness to HT and the *ummah* are deeply intertwined with the faithfulness to God. Once the person has gone through HT's three-step strategy, he will identify the group's goals as noble and in line with God's will. Therefore, membership is usually a long-term one, as confirmed by the interviewees of HT Australia. In particular, 14 of 20 are now in their 40s, but joined HT in their early 20s, demonstrating two decades of constant commitment.

Having analysed HT's premises and strategy, focus can settle on the two main fields where HT's challenge to the West takes place: the political and the social.

HT's challenging the west in the political field

In the political field, HT has built its conceptual onslaught against the West on three main assumptions: the illegitimacy of the Western state-model, the backlashes deriving from Western foreign policy, and a Western hidden agenda for the assimilation of Muslims. Focusing on the first assumption, HT shows no hesitation in declaring Western states as illegitimate for Muslims (Ahmed & Stuart, 2009, 2010; An-Nabhani, 1998; Uthman Badar, personal communication, 12 March 2016). The main reason behind this strong conviction is the religious obligation upon every Muslim to live according to *shari'ā* law. Muslims living in the West have to obey man-made laws that sometimes oppose Islamic concepts of *haram* (forbidden) and *halal* (licit). In fact, several behaviours condemned by Islam are accepted by the West and vice versa. For example, secular laws tolerate gambling, alcohol, adultery, homosexuality and blasphemy, which are all *haram* through the lens of Islam (An-Nabhani, 2002). Simultaneously, commonly accepted behaviours in Islam, such as polygamy, are outlawed in the West. In HT's view, this problematic dichotomy is the result of Western imposition in the Middle East. Since the era of the crusades, Western states have tried to subjugate Muslims in several ways (Hizb ut-Tahrir, 2002) first with violence and then through 'new colonial means':

> New vicious forms of colonialism are based on an indirect economic, political and cultural hegemony which was represented in military accords, alliances, mutual security agreements, economic and financial aid and cultural programs. (Hizb ut-Tahrir, 1996, p. 8)

HT claims that Europeans have contributed to the decline of Muslims in a number of ways, namely through the foundation of cultural centres throughout the Middle East by Christian missionaries, by attacking the system of Islam and contaminating it with *kuffars'* thoughts (Awad, 2016), but also by pressing the Ottoman Caliphate to implement constitutional reforms to bring it in line with capitalistic states. The constitution was approved in 1908, and the *Khilafah* began its decline towards nonexistence, which came in 1924. After the abolition of the Caliphate, nation-states were created in Iraq, Jordan, Syria and Lebanon and the rest of the Muslim world was colonised (Awad, 2016). Muslims were therefore exposed to a system of laws, values, and lifestyle very different from their own, and these were coercively imposed. HT commonly highlights the glory of the Caliphate by pointing out the stability in the Middle East at the time, the flourishing economy, the good standard of living within the borders, scientific progress, and the respect for people of other faiths (Mohammad and Maryam, HT Australia, personal communication, 15 March 2016).

The second assumption used by HT to challenge Western states politically concerns the consequences of Western foreign policy. In fact, the Hizb fully endorses the idea that 'what (Western) governments call extremism is, to a large degree, a product of their own wars' (Kundani, 2014, p. 35).

> The long history of Western violent occupations around the world, the support to tyrant despots for economic reasons, the invention of arms of mass destruction and the rise of a wealthy 1st World on the blood of a massacred 3rd World' are all examples of Western misconduct, affecting Muslims' hearts and minds. (Badar, 2015)

HT links the tragic attacks in Western states to their continuous misconduct rather than to religious extremism. In fact, the official spokespersons of the group in different countries share the same view that political grievance and the continuous moral outrage of Muslims, rather than a radical vision of Islam, are the main triggers of terrorism (Badar, 2015).

More recently, HT argued that the War on Terror has worsened the situation for Muslims living in the West. Muslims have become the 'dangerous other', fostering new attitudes such as Islamophobia, which is an anxiety and fear in society towards Muslims, who can be regarded as potential terrorists. Also securitisation stands out as a consequence of the War on Terror. It is defined as 'the process of state actors transforming subjects into matters of security; an extreme version that enables extraordinary means to be used in the name of security' (Buzan, Wæver, & de Wilde, 1998, p. 25). With regard to Muslims, these extraordinary means imply a number of restricting measures, such as having imams' speeches controlled, banning religious groups presenting a more textual approach to their religion, and the demonisation of the words 'radical' and 'extreme'.

As a third assumption, HT points to a Western 'hidden agenda' aimed at forcing the assimilation of Muslims (Badar, 2015). HT claims that Western governments are using the War on Terror and the migrants crisis to induce fear among the population and encourage Muslims in the West to adopt a 'state-sponsored version of Islam' (Bsis, 2015). According to HT, Western states stand as alleged promoters of freedom of speech and religion, while setting the boundaries of these freedoms with tight controls and limitations of the activities of some mosques, Islamic groups and associations (Badar, 2015; Bsis, 2015; Mustafa, 2016). The message conveyed by Western media and governments is that Muslims should be less Islamic, more open to Western values and lifestyle, abide by Western laws without complaining, and not get involved in religious and political arguments, thus, embodying the perfect stereotype of the 'moderate Muslim', who is commonly perceived as the 'good Muslim' (Mustafa, 2016). Through HT's lens, this narrative pushes Muslims away from Islam, inducing them to lose their Islamic identity. HT works hard to challenge this Western-sponsored vision of good Muslims, presenting a number of reasons to deconstruct this narrative.

Firstly, in HT's view, the concept of 'moderate Muslims' does not exist in Islam. In fact, Islam is not just a religion, but it is a *deen,* that is, a way of life. Islam today is the same Islam revealed to Prophet Mohammed 1400 years ago and needs to be accepted as completely as it was in the beginning (Badar, 2015); those 'who pick and choose what is comfortable are not real Muslims' (Feisal, HT Australia, personal communication, 20 March 2016). According to HT, being a Muslim means going back to the sources of Islam, being educated on the system of Islam (mostly through an-Nabhani's writings), and shaping everyone's life on the Prophet's model (Hizb ut-Tahrir, 2002). For this reason, HT's members are proud to be 'radical' in the sense of being strongly linked to the roots of their religion and accepting no compromise. For instance, they support the idea that Western states are illegitimate for Muslims and therefore, do not engage in political activities, such as voting or running for an election (Hizb ut-Tahrir, 1996).

Secondly, HT strongly supports an anti-integration agenda that sees Muslim identity as a treasure rather than as a problem. Because of this, the Hizb continues to criticise Western governments and their policies; they continue to use the *Khilafah* flag (mostly associated with the violent Islamic State) regardless of any stereotype, and they hardly condemn terroristic acts (as most representatives of Muslim communities in the West do), rather, focusing on attacking Western actions over the centuries:

As a Muslim … I apologise that we failed to demolish your plots and conspiracies to destroy this great state, allowing you to install flawed Western-systems, authoritarian regimes, and Western-backed dictators in our lands who ruled with an iron fist, subjugating, persecuting and killing their people in the path of executing your plans and securing your interests, creating decades of insecurity and instability in the Muslim world … I will not apologise for the actions of a few individuals or groups whose acts of violence against innocents do not represent my *deen* or my *ummah.* (Nawaz, 2015)

This was the comment of Nazreen Nawaz, a prominent senior member of Hizb ut-Tahrir Britain (HTB) following the Paris attacks, in November 2015. It reflects HT's trend of going against the common Western-induced portrait of a Muslim community, apologising for the damage caused by terrorism. Instead, it boldly denounces the misconduct of the West in promoting a deceitful economic, social and political model, while, at the same time dissociating itself from terrorists as not associated with their *deen* or *ummah*.

As analysed above, HT's political challenge to the West consists of deconstructing the main Western narratives of the Westphalian state as an effective model, the righteousness of Western foreign policy, and the Muslim need for integration. Distilling the three arguments into a set of sub-concepts, HT aims to show the other face of the coin of political matters that are usually taken for granted. Again, the recurring argument characterising the whole process is the dichotomy between the evils of the West and the goodness of the *Khilafah*.

HT's challenge in the social field

In the social field, HT challenges the West with a rhetoric mainly built upon two main books of the adopted literature, 'Concepts of Hizb ut-Tahrir' (An-Nabhani, 2007) and the 'American Campaign to Suppress Islam' (Hizb ut-Tahrir, 1996), with both acting as an ideological base from which to attack Westerners as individuals, and members of the social-system. With regard to the individual, HT claims that a person's behaviour is dictated by their perceptions of life, their core values, and their ultimate goals:

> Life is based on the enlightened thought and man, thus, progresses in accordance with it. Enlightened thought also shows the reality of things and issues in a way enabling their correct comprehension. Thought must be deep in order to be enlightened. Deep thought is the profound view of things, whilst enlightened thought is the profound view of things, their conditions, and everything which is related to them thus, drawing conclusions from this so as to reach sound judgements. (An-Nabhani, 2007, p. 13)

In HT's opinion, *kuffars'* non-Islamic concepts lead to everything Allah dislikes, that is *sharr* (bad). HT believes that each action does not have a precise connotation *per se*, but it is the system of concepts that the individual is carrying which defines the action as *sharr* or *khair* (good). For instance, in HT's view, the act of killing can be both *sharr* and *khair*. An example of the first kind would be a thief who kills in order to steal, while killing an enemy in battle is to be considered as a noble action (An-Nabhani, 2007).

Furthermore, by citing verses from the Qur'an, HT supports the idea that man is by nature more inclined to do evil and less prone to do good. For example the group quotes: 'But it may happen that you hate something which is good for you, and it may happen that you love something which is bad for you. Allah knows and you know not' (TMQ Al-Baqara: 216). Therefore, in HT's view, only one thing could lead men towards good, and that is their submission to the *shari'ā*. HT believes that the fact that Westerners do not submit to the *shari'ā*, but rather to a man-made system of values is the driving force behind their decline as individuals and the decline of the social-system.

Based on the aforementioned premises, HT strongly criticises the concept of 'personal freedom', which is regarded as an important catalyst towards the decay of a society (Hizb ut-Tahrir, 1996): 'Freedom is bad and it is against Islam, which means submission' (Layla, HT Australia, personal communication, 6 April 2016). In HT's view, personal freedom allows every person to live his private life as he wishes, practising sexual perversion, eating and drinking whatever he wants as long as he behaves 'lawfully', the definition of which changes according to the specific historical period (Hizb ut-Tahrir, 1996). Under the flag of personal freedom, several practices considered immoral by HT have spread in the West:

> Men and women live together without any legal relationship, even establishing abnormal same sex relationships under the protection of the law. The personal and sexual perversions that prevail in the Capitalist societies result from personal freedom. Pornographic magazines and movies, sex phone lines, and nude bars are just a few examples of the abnormalities and perversions which the Capitalist societies have degenerated to as a result of personal freedom. (Hizb ut-Tahrir, 1996, p. 32)

According to HT, these tolerated libertarian *haram* behaviours are the origin of a great number of social plagues in the West. HT activists often use official data, such as those from Eurostat concerning the high rates of suicide, divorce, drug abuse, alcoholism and mental disease affecting Western countries, instilling in the minds of their interlocutors the desire to escape the imminent collapse, through the implementation of an effective counter-model based on HT's vision of the state and Islam (The Revival Production, 2013).

For these reasons, HT calls on its members to vigorously hold on to their Islamic life, their family life and their submission to *shari'a* to avoid a *kuffar* contamination, which would lead to decline. Together with daily campaigning on social media and study-circles (*halaqaat*), HT organises international events to foster an Islamic revival among the *ummah*. An example is the 2013 'International Khilafah Conference – The Great Change' in Indonesia, which called on Muslims to reject democracy and call for the re-establishment of *Khilafah*. In 2014 in Palestine, HT organised another gathering named 'Women are an honour that must be preserved', having as a subtitle 'The *Kuffar* and their tools conspire against them'. The title and subtitle of this event made clear its aim, which was to alert Muslims about Western attempts to mislead and secularise Islamic families and their social lives (The Revival Production, 2013).

As well as personal freedom, HT strongly criticises the idea of democracy. The sovereignty of people is a forbidden concept that contradicts the Islamic assumption of submission to Allah as the sole legislator. According to the Hizb, democracy lets human beings create laws that fulfil their immoral desires, leading the whole society towards moral decline. Democratic systems allow the establishment of parties that call for things that are forbidden by Islam, such as 'drug legalisation, abortion, and the use of women as sexual objects' (Hizb ut-Tahrir, 1996, p. 19). Furthermore, the very idea of a 'government of the people' is deceptive and impossible to implement. HT believes that not all people are sovereign, but only a designated elected elite, who are often inclined to corruption and the pursuance of their own interests.

Finally, HT considers the whole system of democratic values, such as equality, justice and accountability, a utopia and full of contradictions (Hizb ut-Tahrir, 1996). For instance, the United States (US) is commonly considered by the Hizb to be the greatest democratic paradox. On the one hand, the US government promotes the image of the US as a champion of freedom, fighting for human rights and equality. On the other hand, it displays significant inconsistencies inside its borders; the exclusive healthcare system (neglecting the poor), the suffering faced by minorities in the country (i.e. Blacks, Indians, Latins and Asians), capital punishment still practised in some states, and the number of wars with the US as protagonist and in which countless 'atrocities' are committed (Hizb ut-Tahrir, 2002, p. 20). When referring to democracy, HT states that 'It is obligatory upon every Muslim to reject it and to challenge all those who propagate it' (Hizb ut-Tahrir, 1996, p. 17).

Conclusion

This paper has presented the main arguments used by HT to challenge the West both politically and socially. Positioning itself as a NSM focused on post-materialistic values, HT constructs its narrative against Western states on the need to rescue a 'suffering *ummah*' all over the world. The *ummah* is mostly oppressed by *kuffar* (unbelievers) regimes, which prevent Muslims from living according to Islamic law, impeding the fulfilment of a core religious obligation.

In order to familiarise Muslims with its strongly anti-Western ideology, the Hizb has implemented a 'Shock, Demolish and Rebuild' strategy aimed at informing and then demolishing the previous perceptions individuals had about the Western system and rebuilding a new *haram* image. The author has first analysed the strategy and then explored the particular frames used by HT to challenge the West in the political and social fields. In particular, this study has highlighted three pillars on which HT's anti-Western political rhetoric is built upon: the illegitimacy of nation-states, the consequences deriving from Western foreign policy, and a Western hidden agenda against Muslims.

With regard to the social field, HT's goal is to present Western society as a wrecked one. The dissemination of figures concerning the high rates of suicide, divorce and domestic violence works as a catalyst to destroy any positive image of Western social systems. This paper has focused on two main points of HT's narrative: personal freedom as a pathway towards immorality and social decline, and democracy as a system against Islam. HT's challenge against the West aims to deconstruct the Western idea of political and social effectiveness, while emphasising all its flaws and the ontological incompatibility with the Islamic *deen*. The only system the Hizb promotes is the Caliphate, presented in contrast to the Western capitalistic-libertarian model as reliable, accountable and effective.

Disclosure statement

No potential conflict of interest was reported by the author.

Notes

1. HT's official declarations at the event '92 Years since the Caliphate', 5 March 2016, Lakemba, Sydney.
2. In respect for interviewees' privacy, all names provided are pseudonyms. The only exceptions are Uthman Badar, Ibthial Bsis and Taji Mustafa, the official spokespersons of HT Australia and Britain.
3. Ibthial Bsis, Hizb ut-Tahir Britain (HTB) senior member. Speech delivered at CAGE, during the event 'Citizens not Subjects: Empowering the Communities', 5 November 2015, London (UK).
4. An example is Hizb ut-Tahrir Australia (HTA) event '92 Years since the Caliphate: the History of the Collapse and the Global Muslim Response', articulated in two encounters (5 and 13 March 2016), in Lakemba, Sydney (Australia).

References

Adkins, S. D. (2008). *Understanding hamas through social movement theory: A dynamic approach.* (Master of Arts). Dalhousie University.

Ahmed, H., & Stuart, H. (2009). *Hizb ut-Tahrir: Ideology and strategy*. London: The Centre for Social Cohesion.

Ahmed, H., & Stuart, H. (2010). Profile: Hizb ut-Tahrir in the UK. *Current Trends In Islamist Ideology, 10*, 143–209.

An-Nabhani, T. (1998). *The Islamic state*. London: Al-Khilafah Publications.

An-Nabhani, T. (2002). *The system of Islam* (Translated from the Arabic edition). London: Al-Khilafah.

An-Nabhani, T. (2007). *Concepts of Hizb ut-Tahrir* (English Traslation). London: Khilafah.

Awad, F. (2016, March 13). *The historical lead-up: Political events leading to destruction*. Paper presented at the event '92 Years since the Caliphate: The History of the Collapse and the global Muslim Response,' Lakemba, Sydney, Australia

Badar, U. (2015). The counter-terrorism fiction *2015 Conference 'Innocent until proven Muslim.'* Retrieved from https://http://www.youtube.com/watch?v=UsmuPI6BJdI-action=share

Benford, R. D., & Snow, D. A. (2000). Framing processes and social movements: An overview and assessment. *Annual Review of Sociology, 26*, 611–639. doi:10.1146/annurev.soc.26.1.611

Baran, Z. (2005). Fighting the war of ideas. *Foreign Affairs, 84*(6), 68–78. Retrieved from http://www.jstor.org/stable/20031777

Berna, D. (2008). *A revolutionary perspective on social movements: Fundamentalism in the Islamic World*. (PhD). University of New Orleans, New Orleans.

Bsis, I. (2015, November 5). Paper presented at the citizens not subjects: Empowering the community, London.

Buzan, B., Wæver, O., & de Wilde, J. (1998). *Security: A new framework for analysis*. Boulder, CO: Lynne Rienner Publishers.

Hamid, S. (2007). Islamic political radicalism in Britain: the case of Hizb-ut-Tahrir. In T. Abbas (Ed.). *Islamic political radicalism: A European perspective* (pp. 145–159). Edinburgh: Edinburgh University Press.

Hamid, S. (2016). *Sufis, Salafis and Islamists: The contested ground of British Islamic activism*. London: I.B.Tauris & Co Ltd.

Hizb ut-Tahrir. (1996). *The American campaign to suppress Islam*. London: Al-Khilafah.

Hizb ut-Tahrir. (2002). *The inevitability of the clash of civilisations (hatmiyyat sira'a Il-hadharat)*. London: Al- Khilafah.

HT-Australia. (2016a). FAQs about the Khilafah. Retrieved from http://www.hizb-australia.org/2016/02/faqs-khilafah/

HT Australia. (2016b, July 19). Footage of French crimes in Algeria [Facebook update]. Retrieved from https://www.facebook.com/hizbaust/videos/854941941305463/

HT Australia. (2016c, July 19). Warning: Graphic photos [Facebook update]. Retrieved from https://www.facebook.com/hizbaust/posts/855164897949834

Inglehart, R. (1977). Long term trends in mass support for European unification. *Government and Opposition, 12*(2), 150–177.

Karagiannis, E., & Mccauley, C. (2006). Hizb ut-Tahrir al-Islami: Evaluating the threat posed by a radical Islamic group that remains nonviolent. *Terrorism and Political Violence, 18*, 315–334. doi:10.1080/09546550600570168

Kundani, A. (2014). *The Muslims are coming! Islamophobia, extremism and the domestic War on terror*. London: Verso.

Maber, E. J. T. (2016). Finding feminism, finding voice? Mobilising community education to build women's participation in Myanmar's political transition. *Gender and Education, 28*(3), 416–430. doi:10.1080/09540253.2016.1167175

Melucci, A., & Bimbi, F. (Eds.). (1986). *Movimenti sociali e sistema politico*. Milan, Italy: Franco Angeli.

Mustafa, T. (2016). *How should Muslims view Brussels attacks?* Retrieved from http://www.youtube.com/watch?v=EaHvSAajSaE.

Nawaz, N. (2015). [Press release]. Retrieved from https://http://www.facebook.com/nazreen.nawaz/posts/926110894142246

O'Brien, P. (2016). *The Muslim question in Europe political controversies and public philosophies*. Philadelphia, PA: Temple University Press.

Offe, C. (1985). New social movements: Challenging the boundaries of institutional politics. *Social Research, 52*(4), 817–868. Retrieved from http://www.jstor.org/stable/40970399.

Taji-Farouki, S. (1996). *A fundamental quest: Hizb al-Tahrir and the search for the Islamic Caliphate*. London: Grey Seal.

Tarrow, S. (1998). *Power in movement: Social movements and contentious politics*. Cambridge: Cambridge University Press.

The Revival Production (Producer). (2013, April 9). *A profile of the role of women in Hizb ut Tahrir* [video]. Retrieved from http://www.youtube.com/watch?v=b1vz646den4.

Roy, O. (2004). *Globalized Islam: The search for a new Ummah*. New York: Columbia University Press.

Samarov, M. V. (2008). *A social movement theory analysis of Islamist Totalitarianism*. Retrieved from http://www.dtic.mil/dtic/tr/fulltext/u2/a504756.pdf

Sutton, P., & Vertigans, S. (2006). Islamic new social movements? Radical Islam, al-Qa'ida and social movement theory. *Mobilization: An International Quarterly, 11*(1), 101–115. Retrieved from http://courses.arch.vt.edu/courses/wdunaway/gia5274/sutton.pdf

Tilly, C. (1978). *From mobilization to revolution*. New York: McGraw-Hill.

Wiktorowicz, Q. (2005). *Radical Islam rising: Muslim extremism in the west*. Lanham, MD: Rowman & Littlefield.

Zallum, A. Q. (2000). *How the Khilafah was destroyed*. London: Al Khilafah.

Zulver, J. (2016). High-risk feminism in El Salvador: Women's mobilisation in violent times. *Gender & Development, 24*(2), 171–185. doi:10.1080/13552074.2016.1200883

When actions speak louder than words: examining collective political protests in Central Asia

Dilshod Achilov

What explains the dynamics of contentious collective political action in post-Soviet Central Asia? How do post-Soviet Central Asian citizens negotiate the tensions between partaking in and abstaining from elite-challenging collective protests? By analysing cross-national attitudes in two Central Asian states, this article (1) systematically analyses the variation in collective protests by testing rival macro-, meso-, and micro-level theories; (2) reintroduces a conceptual and empirical distinction between low-risk and high-risk collective protests; and (3) examines the conditions under which individuals participate in two distinct types of elite-challenging collective actions. Three conclusions are reached. First, the evidence suggests that nuanced consideration of multi-level theoretical perspectives is necessary to explain contingencies of elite-challenging actions. Second, economic grievances and resource mobilization emerge as leading factors driving both low-risk and high-risk protests. Third, Islamic religiosity and social networking robustly predict participation in high-risk collective action.

Active citizen participation in politics has long been viewed as vital for any demo-cratization process.[1] Specifically, the question of who participates, why, and how has received a great deal of scholarly attention in social and political research. Political contestation against state power holders in the form of a collective protest is perhaps a dominant contour of democratic politics and is widely viewed as an effective check on state power. Although mass protesting has become more frequent in the public squares of the post-Soviet republics over the past decade, the literature has largely been silent on explaining the dynamics of collective political protests, particularly in the case of Central Asian Republics (CARs) – the lesser-known corner of the Muslim world. While the legacy of the Soviet-style

132

authoritarianism coupled with long-preserved clan-based clientelistic networks still prevails in the region,[2] the quest for democratization primarily driven by grass-roots mobilizations that advocate for wider civil liberties and political rights continues to emerge, evolve, and advance. Still, elite-challenging collective protests are not common in Central Asia.

Having been spared large-scale mass demonstrations during much of its post-independence period, the Central Asian socio-political landscape has begun to shift unpredictably in recent years. Specifically, there have been significant mass mobilizations in the region that potently have challenged the authoritarian status quo. Examples include two mass uprisings in Kyrgyzstan, which toppled two authoritarian regimes in 2005 and 2010: the Andijan uprising in Uzbekistan, which caught many by surprise in 2005, and the Zhanaozen riots in Kazakhstan, which lasted over six months in 2011.

In 2010, the Kyrgyz Republic experienced its second wave of mass protests (the first being the Tulip Revolution), which ultimately ousted the incumbent Kyrgyz president from office, who had come to power following the Tulip Revolution in 2005. On 16 December 2011, Kazakhstan's security forces in riot gear used indiscriminate force to suppress a protest by oil workers, who were on strike in the western Kazakh city of Zhanaozen, leaving at least a dozen protesters dead and dozens more wounded.[3] Although the Kazakh government continued to apply heavy-handed repressive measures to silence the opposition, collective protests did not cease. To many, these events were surprising given the rarity of collective protests in the country. Although limited in scale and frequency, these developments signify the growing tension and increased citizen engagement in politics in the region. Situated within contentious politics literature, this study examines the conditions under which individuals pursue "collective political struggle".[4] In defining elite-challenging collective action, I rely on Tarrow's conceptualization that frames collective action as activities in which "ordinary people, often in league with more influential citizens, join forces in confrontations with elites, authorities, and opponents" via "coordinated efforts on behalf of shared interests" and make a collective claim.[5]

Collective political protesting has not only played a key role in shaping political history but has also been considered a "potent tool of public influence" over government policies.[6] Particularly, research on the dynamics of contention suggests that "civic pay-off" is significantly higher when citizens manifest self-assertive, elite-challenging collective behaviour vis-à-vis more passive forms of participation.[7] Although collective protests are commonly linked with wide-scale public uprisings or revolutions that bring about massive political changes, a majority of collective upheavals rarely reach the point of major revolutions. The prime objective of collective actions is not to overthrow incumbent regimes; most of the time, the goal is to obtain substantive changes, reforms, or implementation of new policies, which in turn contribute to a democratization of the political system.[8] In this view, even though the streets of Central Asia have not yet become free and safe spaces for citizens to collectively protest, the dynamics of collective contention are increasingly shaping the discourse of demo-cratization in the region.[9]

What explains the dynamics of contentious collective political protests in post-Soviet Central Asia? How do Central Asian citizens negotiate the tensions between partaking in or abstaining from elite-challenging collective actions? By analysing cross-national attitudes in two Muslim-majority CARs – Kazakhstan and the Kyrgyz Republic – this article (1) systematically analyses the variation in collec-tive protests by testing rival macro-, meso-, and micro-level theories, (2) reintro-duces a conceptual and empirical distinction between low-risk and high-risk collective protests, and (3) examines the conditions under which Central Asian citi-zens participate in two distinct types of elite-challenging collective actions.

The analysis is organized into six parts. The first section takes stock of recent collective protest activities in both CARs. Next, theoretical linkages that explain collective action are discussed. The third section proceeds with a conceptual clar-ification and empirical operationalization of low-risk and high-risk collective pro-tests. The fourth section presents the hypotheses that guide the empirical analysis. Next, data and methods are explained followed by a discussion of the results and findings. Lastly, the article presents concluding remarks.

Emerging dynamics of collective protests

Kazakhstan

Protests are not common in Kazakhstan. However, the social and political dynamics of the Republic began to shift as significant elite-challenging mobiliz-ations took place over the past decade. In December 2011, unarmed oil workers in the western Kazakh town of Zhanaozen clashed with government security forces. The oil workers had been collectively protesting for six months, demanding better pay. On 17 December, a day after clashes between protestors and police that left at least 11 dead, a state of emergency was declared in Zhanaozen; main roads and the local airport were closed, the internet was shut down, and cellular phone coverage was blocked. While the government claimed that the police were forced to defend themselves, eyewitnesses reportedly observed the security forces opening fire indiscriminately at unarmed protestors.[10]

In 2012, Kazakhstan's opposition activists continued to hold protests in Almaty, Astana, and other cities to voice grievances over human rights abuses. The main protest themes revolved around an alleged fraud during the 15 January parliamentary elections, the use of lethal force in Zhanaozen, arbitrary police arrests, intimidation, and harassment of opposition activists and journalists.[11] To facilitate public mobilization, opposition activists effectively utilized online social media to coordinate the public meeting places.

On 15 February 2014, approximately a dozen protesters, including two journal-ists, were arrested in Almaty following the protests that had erupted as a result of public anger towards the Kazakh government's decision to devalue the national currency, Tenge, by approximately one-fifth against the United States (US) dollar. In a country where public protests are rare, 15 February marked the seventh collective protest in Almaty within a 10-day period.[12] Reportedly, the crowd of ~200 protesters marched towards City Hall shouting *"Alga! Kazakhstan"* [Forward! Kazakhstan], *'we have nothing to fear in our own country!'*.[13] Riot police reacted decisively to disperse the crowd.

In May 2014, a highly unusual trade ban on the import, production, or sale of synthetic lace underwear caused another public outrage in Kazakhstan. Women activists protested the ban by wearing panties on their heads.[14] This bizarre ban, if not reversed, makes all laced, synthetic underwear illegal in the Eurasian Union consisting of Russia, Kazakhstan, and Belarus. While it is premature to claim that public contestation of state elites has become a common activity in Kazakhstan, an increased collective spirit and the public's willingness to collectively mobilize are clearly on the rise. Whether or not this trend will contribute to the development of a more vibrant civil society through which citizens can freely mobilize to challenge the elites, studying the protest activity in a systematic fashion remains a priority.

Kyrgyzstan

The Kyrgyz Republic is arguably the most dynamic in terms of the frequency of collective protests among all CARs. According to the Kyrgyz Prime Minister Zhantoro Satybaldiev, nearly 1286 protests took place across Kyrgyzstan in 2012 alone, meaning that there were roughly three protests a day on average.[15] The politics in the Kyrgyz Republic are largely shaped by clan-based loyalties, weak institutions, fragmented independent elites, and regional differences. With its sizable Uzbek minority, the south is less homogeneous and is generally more conservative compared with the north. In terms of political attitudes, for instance, "the northern and southern Kyrgyz tend to have opposite views on the state, its institutions and politicians".[16]

The Tulip Revolution was the first uprising in Central Asia since the collapse of the USSR that toppled an incumbent president. It began with a public protest over the hotly contested parliamentary elections in 2005, growing public discontent towards rampant corruption and failed economic policies. As a result, President Askar Akayev fled the country. In April 2010, massive public protests erupted again in Bishkek that eventually overthrew the government of Kurmanbek Bakiyev, who had become the nation's second president following the Tulip Revolution of 2005. The events turned into a bloody ethnic clash between the ethnic Kyrgyz and minority Uzbeks in the south. At least 400 people, mostly Uzbeks, were killed and about half a million people were displaced.[17]

More recently, in March 2013, several hundred protesters rallied in Osh, the largest city in the south, demanding the immediate release of three opposition members of parliament and the leaders of the Ata-Jurt (Fatherland) political party. The protests quickly diffused to other cities: Jalal-Abad and Karakol. The activist leaders of Ata-Jurt were charged with provoking public unrest during the October 2012 protests in which about 1000 demonstrators had collectively staged an anti-government rally in Bishkek.

In May 2013, several hundred protesters besieged a Canadian-owned gold mine and clashed with riot police. The protestors demanded higher pay, benefits, and the gold mine to be nationalized. The clash turned bloody as protests quickly spread to a major southern city of Jalal-Abad; as many as 50 people were wounded and 80 protestors were arrested.[18] The scale of the incident prompted the government to declare a state of emergency in the region.

To an extent, solving problems through protesting has become an effective tool that has a higher chance of pay-off in the Kyrgyz Republic. People from all facets of society – merchants, farmers, truck drivers, casino owners, and policemen – are increasingly taking their grievances to the streets. Ironically, several hundred people tired of public protests held a demonstration against demonstrating in the capital city of Bishkek in 2013.[19] Overall, the collective protest culture appears to have gained a sustained momentum in the Kyrgyz Republic.

Conceptualizing low-risk and high-risk collective action

In this article, I examine the conditions under which Central Asians negotiate the tensions between participating in and abstaining from collective political actions by conceptualizing two distinct types of collective protesting: *low-risk* and *high-risk* collective action.[20] In this framework, the level of risk is associated with "the anticipated dangers – whether legal, social, physical, financial, and so forth – often engaging in a particular type of activity".[21] *Low-risk collective action* (LRCA) is conceptualized as less confrontational collective protests that bear a low risk of prosecution, arrest, or intimidation by contested elites. For instance, signing a collective petition that challenges a particular policy is a relatively low risk action that does not attract large-scale punitive reactions from contested elites. On the other hand, *high-risk collective action* (HRCA) is conceptualized as a more confrontational collective protest that bears a high risk of prosecution, arrest, or intimidation.

This conceptualization is grounded on the dimensionality of collective action via the principal component analysis of six variables of interest derived from the 2012 World Values Survey: (1) signing collective petitions, (2) joining in boycotts, (3) attending peaceful demonstrations, (4) joining strikes, and (5) participating in other acts of collective protests.[22] For details of variable measurement and coding see the appendix.

Derived from theoretically relevant variables (Table 1), the loadings support the conceptualization of low-risk and high-risk collective protest behaviour in Central Asia: while only "signing collective petitions" loads above 0.9 on factor 2 (that is, LRCA), all the remaining variables load distinctively higher than 0.48 on factor 1 (that is, HRCA). Although signing collective petitions is a significantly less risky way to express one's demands compared with taking part in mass

Table 1. Dimensionality of collective protest activity.

Item	Indicator	High-risk collective action	Low-risk collective action
V85	Signing collective petitions	0.287	0.958
V86	Joining in boycotts	0.603	0.363
V87	Attending peaceful demonstrations	0.489	0.297
V88	Joining strikes	0.818	0.143
V89	Attending other acts of protest	0.568	0.224
	% of variance	34.0	24.0

Note: Principal Component Analysis via maximum likelihood with Varimax rotation.

demonstrations, participating in street protests, boycotts, or strikes carry higher risks that largely attract counter reactions, mostly punitive, from repressive regimes. HRCA is more likely to turn into violent clashes, while LRCA often does not. A conceptual distinction with respect to risks involved in "joining" or "abstaining" from collective action is particularly important for the post-Soviet regimes in which heavy-handed, indiscriminate, and arbitrary state prosecution still remain a grave threat to free, peaceful, democratic contestation.

Macro-, meso-, and micro-level theories of collective action

Multiple theories at macro-, meso-, and micro-levels compete to explain collective actions in politics. At the macro-level, the political opportunity structure (POS) explanations focus on institutional structures and political processes that promote or impede political activism. Goldstone and Tilly define political opportunities as "the probability that social protest actions will lead to success in achieving a desired outcome".[23] In part, one assumption of a POS relies on the rational choice theory in which protestors evaluate their political environment and calculate the likely impact of their collective action. For instance, Tilly argues that closely divided, competitive political situations create venues or windows of opportunity for collective protests.[24] In this view, regime characteristics, an electoral system type, and varying degrees of political institutional arrangements present or impede opportunities for mobilization.[25] In societies with high civil liberties, individuals are more likely to engage in peaceful political actions without fear of reprisal.[26]

According to an alternative macro-level theory that emphasizes the lack of available political channels (POS) for citizens to express their preferences via mass demonstrations due to the closed nature of a political system (for example, repression), grieving citizens are more likely to seek elite-challenging protests.[27] The proponents of this approach also cite the degree of socio-economic development, financial well-being, and behaviour of the state to prompt collective action. Scholars also highlight that social and economic inequality, poverty, oppression, regime exploitation, and other negative living conditions that trigger mass protests.[28] By and large, major social revolutions are also largely attributed to political repression and violence.[29] In this perspective, nations that offer no or limited platforms for citizens to express their political interests through legal state institutions increase the levels of public dissatisfaction which, in turn, stimulate unauthorized protests.

A theory of modular diffusion, introduced by Beissinger, is another macro-level context that has shaped the dynamics of contestation in the post-Soviet space.[30] Modular diffusion relates to previous successful mobilizations having an effect on other regional or contextually similar states.[31] Previous research suggests that diffusion can occur in many ways through which "ideas, models and the like can spread across boundaries, simply because they provide precedents that are unusually appealing to actors in other states and that influence their thinking, goals and behavior".[32] Social networks that operate at the meso-level are often instrumental in importing transnational experience and adopting critical lessons from other successful mobilizations.[33]

At the meso-level, the resource mobilization is another leading theory in the literature. In this view, the extent of available resources of various social networks is central in mobilizing collective protests.[34] For instance, from 1995–2005, non-governmental organizations (NGOs) led by students played a game-changing role in facilitating colour revolutions in the post-Soviet space. To identify a few, youth-led social networks, such as *Otpor* in Serbia, *Pora* in Ukraine, *Kmara* in Georgia, and *Kelkel* in the Kyrgyz Republic, staged highly influential non-violent protests and achieved monumental political gains in the Bulldozer, Orange, Rose, and Tulip Revolutions respectively. Beissinger argues that a modular diffusion played a central role in successful mobilization of these student organizations who worked in close cooperation by constantly learning from one another.[35] Recent studies have shown that resources, particularly the level of education and network memberships, are robustly associated with collective protests.[36] For instance, involvement in a dense relational social context (for example, social networks) enables activists to remain in constant contact with the protest movement and the contentious issues at stake on a daily basis.[37]

It is equally important to account for meso-level centre-periphery relations in a Central Asian context.[38] Shedding light onto collective mobilization in the authoritarian setting of Central Asia, Radnitz formulates the subversive clientelism explanation that centres on how independent elites can manipulate the unexpressed grievances of society to serve their own interests and argues that wealthy independent elites "may choose to ally with (or co-opted by) the regime to ensure the maintenance of their privileges" or "may harness the power of the masses to mobilize against the regime".[39] Rather than seeing the protest dynamics in a two-way interaction between the state and society, the subversive clientelism approach adds an important third dimension into the equation – independent elites who can strategically (and resourcefully) orchestrate collective mobilization. This is more pronounced in Kyrgyzstan given its comparably high local autonomy than Kazakhstan.

On similar ground, McGlinchey finds that the state's inability or failure to meet the society's basic economic needs may have propelled the masses to seek assistance from independent elites, Islamic charities, or other resourceful networks, which ultimately reduced their dependence on the regime and increased the anti-regime sentiments.[40] These informal patronage networks, run mostly by charity and business elites, often emerge "as alternatives to the state as economic and cultural focal points in local communities" that can at times seek national power and be mobilized "against the central state when local populations feel aggrieved".[41] For instance, widespread elite defection is viewed as a leading factor that ultimately accelerated the state's demise (for example, Tulip Revolution) in Kyrgyzstan.[42] In contrast, the larger number of elites and their close integration into the authoritarian structure (thus higher elite turnover rates) might have substantially prevented the emergence of a large-scale anti-regime mobilization in Kazakhstan.

The variation of patronage politics in Central Asia, according to McGlinchey, can be explained by the interaction of (1) the legacy of perestroika-era institutions; (2) economic opportunities; and (3) the varying degrees of Islamic revivalism. Particularly, weak state institutions and a relatively fragmented ruling elite are associated with increased likelihood of an anti-regime collective mobilization.[43] While this path-dependent explanation of the enduring authoritarianism in CARs is insightful, the dynamics of incremental and unpredictable change in popular mobilization should be analysed in a more *dynamic* perspective (and in multi-level context) in parallel to historical institutionalism.

The level of educational attainment is widely viewed as a stimulating factor for partaking in protests.[44] Many theorists agree that education fosters a "culture of democracy" and commitment to civil liberties among various political actors.[45] In addition, people with a higher degree of schooling are inclined to be more tolerant of others' actions and less supportive of violent protests.[46] Although the level of educational attainment is a micro-level, individual characteristic, it is an integral component of social networking – a meso-level structure. The level of education is often associated with higher social status; "More status means a greater stake in the outcomes of the political system, a greater incentive to participate, and a louder voice in elected officials' ears. This is where social networks come in."[47] Campbell demonstrates that individual-level and meso-level social explanations complement one another and argues that, "instead of schism, there ought to be synthesis".[48] In this respect, the following hypotheses are put to the test.

Hypotheses 1a–b: Membership in social networks is associated with higher levels of collective protest. Individuals with higher educational attainment are more likely to participate in collective protests.

The rise of the internet has also had an immense impact on stimulating collective protest behaviour. In recent years, using Facebook, Twitter, and other social networking sites has been effective in quickly disseminating information, inciting inspirations, and ultimately calling for mass demonstrations in a systematic and unparalleled fashion.[49] The age of fast telecommunications and online social media has been a game-changer in facilitating rapid transfer of translational experience (that is, diffusion) of successful elite-challenging protest mobilizations. With this in mind, it is important to consider the mediating influence of the internet.

> Hypothesis 2: Individuals with a higher level of access to computers are more likely to participate in collective protests.

At the micro-level, individual economic *grievances* that originate from mainly financial difficulties often influence protest behaviour.[50] The emergence of the rational choice (RC) school reinforced the notion that the individual is a central unit of analysis for an understanding of who participates. The RC is largely grounded in economics, wherein individuals seek to maximize utility by calculating costs and benefits. At a glance, given the lack of fair and transparent judicial due process and the presence of state repression, it may not be rational for many Central Asian citizens to risk their lives or their livelihoods unless the stakes are unusually high. Given the substantial increase in worker mobilization in both countries (for example, Zhanaozen events, gold mine riots) signifies the prominence of economic deprivation in motivating individuals to challenge the elites. To this end, individuals whose livelihoods are at risk may be better positioned to join in higher risk collective protests compared with those who are more financially secure.[51]

> Hypothesis 3: Individuals with high economic grievances are more likely to participate in collective protests.

How does the level of religiosity account for the variation in collective political behaviour? In terms of predictive power, frequency of attending religious services is widely cited as a potent addition to any model of who participates in the literature; that is, ceteris paribus, religious individuals who frequently attend houses of worship are more likely to engage in virtually every form of civic and political participation than non-attenders.[52]

Though religiosity is another micro-level phenomenon, it is too closely enmeshed in the meso-level context. Relying on a detailed panel survey, Putnam and Campbell argue that *social networks* are the secret ingredients to explain why churchgoers are more prone to get involved in both religious and secular civic activities.[53] When controlling for the effects of different religions, "[s]ynagogue friends or mosque friends appear to provide the same civic boost as friendship networks in Catholic parishes or Protestant congregations".[54] In part, religious affiliation is also viewed as a resource mobilized to connect individuals sharing the same faith and help nurture a fertile ground for collective action.

The findings from Muslim "attitudes in the Arab world",[55] Africa,[56] Central Asia,[57] and non-Arab Muslim states[58] show that (a) popular support for democracy is remarkably high in the Muslim world, (b) Islam and democracy are not inherently incompatible, (c) Islam neither fosters antidemocratic attitudes nor diminishes support for democracy.[59] In this respect, it is theoretically plausible to expect that Islam may be positively positioned to motivate citizens to participate in elite-challenging actions.

> Hypothesis 4: Islamic religiosity is positively associated with higher levels of collective protest.

Next, are globally-connected youth of Central Asia more prone to embark on collective political contestation? In 2011, a majority of the Arab Spring protesters were under the age of 30. Today, the internet generation is more globally connected than ever before through their smartphones and tablets. Youth civic engagement in the non-governmental sector has been on the rise, including "increases in community volunteer work, high levels of consumer activism, and impressive involvement in social causes from the environment to economic injustice in local and global arenas".[60] To this end, testing the age factor in protest behaviour is imperative.

> Hypothesis 5: The youth are more likely to engage in collective protests.

Data and methods

To probe the propositions introduced above, an individual-level survey data from the sixth Wave of the World Values Survey (2012) is utilized for Kazakhstan (n=1500) and the Kyrgyz Republic (n=1500).

Dependent variables

My first dependent variable is a LRCA, measured dichotomously by respondent's participation in signing any elite-challenging collective petition in the past year (2010–2011). The second dichotomous dependent variable is a HRCA measured by a respondent's participation in any of the following elite-challenging collective protests: joining in boycotts, attending peaceful demonstrations, joining strikes, any other act of protest. A scale reliability analysis was conducted for HRCA (the Cronbach's alpha – 0.741).

Independent variables

Economic deprivation is captured by a four-point scale of cash income shortage. *Religiosity (Islam)* is measured using a 2–15 scale that captures the frequency of daily prayers and attendance at religious services apart from funerals and weddings. *Age (30 or older)* is a dummy variable that categorizes respondents by a

30-year-old age threshold. *Education* is a nine-point scale of the survey respondents' education level. *Social networking* is measured on a 0–10 scale based on membership status of various civil society organizations. *Secular values* measures the overall attachments to secular values dichotomously. *Computer/internet* indicates the level of access to a computer/internet. *Government employee* is an employment status at government or public institutions. CARs traditionally have a significantly high percentage of public sector employees. Given that government employees are generally more likely to fear losing their jobs or face state repression upon joining anti-regime protests, it is deemed important to control for this effect. Details of measurement and coding are listed in the appendix.

Macro-level analysis

Overall, collective protest activity has been on the rise in Central Asia. As of 2012, approximately one out of every three Kazakh and Kyrgyz nationals participated in at least one high-risk collective action. Since 2004, the rate of participation in high-risk actions in Kazakhstan increased from 3.5% to 27%. This is an astounding 671% increase in high-risk protest activity in eight years. For low-risk collective action, Kazakh citizens' participation doubled. Comparatively, in the Kyrgyz Republic, participation in high-risk protests increased by 18%, whereas the level of low-risk involvement decreased by almost half (48%) in the same period (Table 2).

To compare the mean protests in both countries, an analysis of variance (ANOVA) was conducted.[61] On average, Kazakh citizens appear more likely to participate in low-risk protests compared with their Kyrgyz counterparts

Table 2. Macro-level indicators and participation in collective action in Central Asia.

	Kazakhstan			Kyrgyz Republic		
	2004	2012	% change	2004	2012	% change
High-risk collective action (%)	3.5	27	+671	28	33	+18
Low-risk collective action (%)	8.1	16	+98	23	12	−48
GINI index	36	29	−19	32	34	+6
Human Development Index (HDI)	0.71	0.74	+4	0.61	0.62	+2
Political rights (1–7, lower is freer)	6	6	0	5	5	0
Civil liberties (1–7, lower is freer)	5	5	0	5	4	−20
Freedom of expression and belief (0–16; higher is freer)	7	6	−14	10	9	−10
Rule of law (percentile)	16	32	+100	24	9	−63
Control of corruption (percentile)	11	17	+55	13	12	−8
Voice and accountability (percentile)	18	15	−17	20	26	+30

Source: WVS 6th Wave 2010–2012; The World Bank Governance Indicators, 2004–2010); Freedomhouse (2004–2011); UN Data (2004–2011).

($p<0.01$). In terms of high-risk actions, the mean protest in the Kyrgyz Republic is significantly higher than in Kazakhstan ($p<0.01$). Perhaps not surprisingly, given the two major mass uprisings in the Kyrgyz Republic, the proportion of high-risk collective action increased while low-risk protests scaled down since 2004.

Although authoritarian structures largely dominate post-Soviet Central Asia, appreciable difference in civil liberties and political rights exist. Figure 1 illustrates the patterns of change, over time, in the levels of individual freedoms in five CARs. Comparatively, the Kyrgyz Republic stands out as the only "partly free" republic in the region. In contrast, Kazakhstan has firmly remained "not free" with virtually no appreciable improvement for the last 10 years.

While opportunity structures for collective protests are significantly amenable in the Kyrgyz Republic, Kazakh officials have been systematically restricting and preempting all venues for collective demonstrations through strict security measures. From 2004 through 2012, the Kazakh government's voice and account- ability declined to the 15th percentile in the global governance indicator ranking. Even though Kazakhstan is a signatory to the International Covenant on Civil and Political Rights (ICCPR) since 2006, which grants rights to peaceful assembly as stated in Article 21, public assembly is tightly controlled by the regime. In 2005, to stave off possible protest diffusion in the country, Kazakhstan banned street

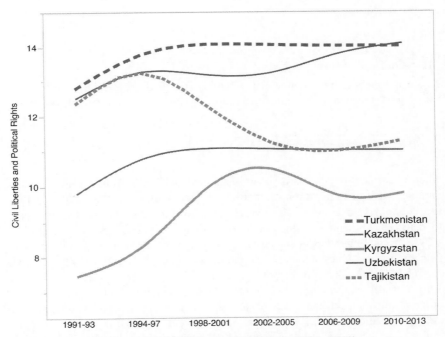

Figure 1. Civil liberties and political rights in Central Asia (1991–2013).
Source: *Freedom in the World* reports 2013; combined score 2–14 (lower score is freer), Freedomhouse, http://www.freedomhouse.org.

protests during national elections following the fall of the Kyrgyz President, Askar Akayev, in the Tulip Revolution. On legal grounds, potential protestors must register with the mayor's office at least 10 days in advance in Kazakhstan. Although these strict rules did give the Kazakh authorities a better tool to regulate public gatherings, they have not been fully successful in keeping people off the streets.

In contrast, collective protest culture appears to have gained momentum in the Kyrgyz Republic. The Kyrgyz government's voice and accountability has improved by 30% since 2004 (Table 2). Although Kyrgyz officials have been reluctant to employ a heavy-handed approach to squelch collective protests, state security agencies continue to monitor all potential protest activities. From this view, political opportunity structures accorded by the regimes may seem to have played an instrumental role in stimulating protest behaviour in the Kyrgyz Republic. However, the POS fails to explain why Kazakhstan has experienced an unprecedented surge in collective protests (a six-fold increase in HRCA from 2004–2012) given the grave structural constraints imposed by the government. Unlike the POS, a structural political repression thesis better explains the situation in Kazakhstan. Since no single macro-level theory can fully account for the variations in both republics, viewing macro-structures in rigid dichotomy may lead to an incomplete account of the complex nature of collective protest behaviour. Therefore, a more nuanced analysis of meso-level structures and micro-level social interactions is necessary.

Meso- and micro-level analyses

Given the dichotomous dependent variables, a logistic regression is estimated, $y=p(y=1)$, for parameter values β_k via the maximum likelihood method:

$$\text{Logit}(p) = \log\left(\frac{p}{1-p}\right) = \beta_0 + \beta_1 x_1 + \ldots + \beta_k x_k$$

where the effects of the x_k variables are estimated on y_1 (LRCA) and y_2 (HRCA). To facilitate easier interpretation of coefficients, odds-ratios and predicted probabilities are closely examined. The Variance Inflator Factor (VIF) method was used to detect the potential multicollinearity among all independent variables. The VIF scores among independent variables ranged from 1.0 through 1.2. No VIF statistic for the variables under investigation was higher than 1.48 (VIF < 1.5), suggesting that multicollinearity is not present.

It is hardly surprising that, given the Kyrgyz Republic's poor economic conditions and Kazakhstan's financial mismanagement, economic deprivation strongly predicts the level of both low-risk and high-risk collective actions (Table 3: models 1–2 and 4–6); individuals with relatively higher economic satisfaction appear less likely, whereas those who are less financially secure are more likely to participate in collective protests ($p<0.01$). Substantively speaking,

Table 3. Logistic estimates predicting low-risk and high-risk collective protests.

	Low-risk collective protest			High-risk collective protest		
	Pooled (1)	Kazakhstan (2)	Kyrgyz Republic (3)	Pooled (4)	Kazakhstan (5)	Kyrgyz Republic (6)
Economic deprivation	1.130** (0.057)	1.260*** (0.074)	1.017 (0.092)	1.369*** (0.024)	1.270*** (0.060)	1.369*** (0.024)
Education level	1.038 (0.032)	1.001 (0.042)	1.122** (0.054)	1.005 (0.024)	0.994 (0.034)	1.005 (0.024)
Networking and volunteerism	1.193*** (0.043)	1.035 (0.087)	1.345*** (0.053)	1.411*** (0.038)	1.192*** (0.068)	1.411*** (0.038)
Computer/internet usage	1.331*** (0.074)	1.412*** (0.094)	1.058*** (0.129)	1.237*** (0.058)	1.420*** (0.078)	1.237*** (0.058)
Islam (religiosity)	0.993 (0.015)	1.031 (0.021)	0.986 (0.025)	1.044*** (0.011)	1.040*** (0.017)	1.044*** (0.011)
Secular values	4.622*** (0.429)	4.329*** (0.544)	5.497*** (0.719)	1.021 (0.331)	0.965 (0.447)	1.021 (0.331)
Age (30 or older)	1.411*** (0.127)	1.374*** (0.165)	1.357 (0.204)	1.205** (0.097)	1.173 (0.134)	1.205** (0.097)
Gender (female)	0.892 (0.115)	0.936 (0.152)	0.708* (0.186)	0.886 (0.088)	0.842 (0.125)	0.886 (0.088)
Government employee	0.625*** (0.129)	0.573*** (0.173)	0.729 (0.200)	0.837* (0.094)	0.883 (0.134)	0.837* (0.094)
Constant	0.052*** (0.380)	0.024*** (0.485)	0.022*** (0.640)	0.370*** (0.286)	0.086*** (0.387)	0.370*** (0.286)
Log-likelihood	2135.71	1231.57	869.29	3187.99	1660.83	3187.99
Pseudo R^2	0.050	0.057	0.074	0.097	0.053	0.097
Percentage correctly predicted	87	89	84	72	70	72
N	2804	1478	1326	2800	1478	2800

Note: Odds ratios shown. Standard errors are in parentheses. Stars indicate levels of statistical significance: ***$p < 0.01$. **$p < 0.05$. *$p < 0.10$.

for every additional level of economic deprivation, individuals are 13% more likely to participate in low-risk and 37% more likely to partake in high-risk elite challenging actions, on average. This finding is in sync with the recent uprisings emanating from public discontent towards economic policies (for example, currency devaluation in Kazakhstan) and low wage compensation (for example, gold mine riots in Kyrgyzstan), which lends support for Hypothesis 3: as financial satisfaction decreases, citizens are more likely to seek action by petitioning to state authorities or taking their grievances to the streets.

All other factors being equal, memberships in NGOs and civil society networks are associated with higher rates of participation in both LRCA and HRCA. In perspective, those who belong to a civil society network are 19% and 40% more likely to join in LRCA and HRCA, respectively. In line with Hypothesis 1a, social networking strongly predicts protest behaviour in Central Asia. Contrary to Hypothesis 1b, the impact of education is not significant.

The predictive strength of secular values for low-risk actions stands out. While a secular lifestyle is not statistically relevant to explain high-stake collective action, more secular individuals are impressively 4.6 times more likely to participate in low-risk actions ($p < 0.01$). While the effects of religiosity (Islam) on participation are positive ($p < 0.01$) for high-risk collective action (models 4–6), there is no evidence for Islam's influence on low-risk collective action. Although the substantive effect of Islam is relatively small, this finding suggests that more religious citizens are more likely to engage in high-risk collective actions, on average, which partly lends support for Hypothesis 4. In sharp contrast, the effects of overall secular values are overwhelmingly large on low-risk protest participation.

The impact of computer/internet usage also stands out, ceteris paribus, with a statistically significant net-effect ($p < 0.01$). As expected by Hypothesis 2, increased computer/internet usage appears to promote collective political actions: for every additional opportunity in computer usage (for example, from "never" to using "occasionally"), citizens are 24–40% more likely to mobilize, on average. This finding highlights the importance of increasingly influential online social networking.[62]

In regard to age, the evidence contradicts Hypothesis 5; older citizens appear more likely to be a part of collective protests compared to younger citizens ($p < 0.05$). The proposition that the younger generation may be driving the collective protests similar to that of the Arab Middle East (for example, Arab Spring) in recent years is not supported. Substantively, citizens older than 30 years of age are 20–40% more likely than those under 30 to participate in either LRCA or HRCA.

Across all six models, the evidence for gender to explain the propensity towards engaging in low or high-risk collective actions is insufficient. While Kyrgyz women appear less likely to be part of collective protests than men, the impact of gender is insignificant in Kazakhstan. Nevertheless, more research is necessary to further scrutinize the effects of women's unequal rights/opportunities of women in the region. Further, government employment status is negatively related to both types of collective action (model 1 and 4). Those who work in

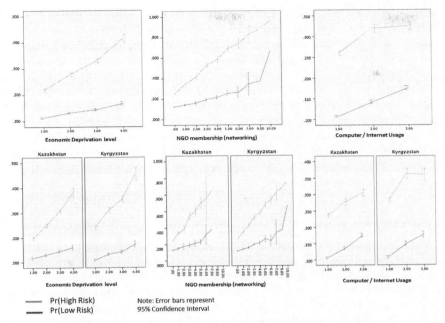

Figure 2. Predicted probabilities for low-risk and high-risk collective action.

the public sector may be more fearful of losing their jobs or face state repression upon joining anti-regime demonstrations.

As the predicted probabilities in Figure 2 indicate, the propensity to participate in elite-challenging actions appears to systematically increase as the level of economic deprivation, NGO membership/networking, age, and computer/internet usage increases. Government employment status, on the other hand, decreases the probability of participation. Strikingly, the likelihood for high-risk collective

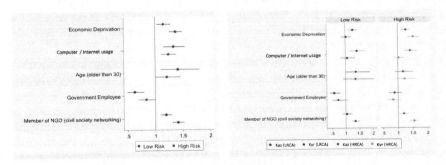

Figure 3. Marginal effects for low-risk and high-risk collective protests.
Note: Units are in odds ratios.

action is significantly higher than low-risk action for each explanatory factor. When the probabilities are collapsed for each republic, the general patterns for LRCA and HRCA still hold. In other words, there is inappreciable difference in the predicted probabilities for both kinds of collective action in Kazakhstan and the Kyrgyz Republic.

To put the influences of the explanatory variables in a comparative perspective, Figure 3 shows the marginal effects (in odds ratios) of the statistically significant variables. Accordingly, the substantive effects of NGO membership and economic grievances stand out with the highest impact on *high-risk* collective protesting. The effects of computer usage and age, on the other hand, are more pronounced in participating in low-risk protests. At the state level, the marginal effects are hardly discernible from general patterns.

Concluding remarks

This study has attempted to analyse the variation in collective protests and empirically examine the extent to which rival theories explain the propensity towards partaking in low-risk and high-risk collective protests in the context of a relatively understudied corner of the Muslim world – Central Asia. This study does not assert to have accounted for all complexities of contentious politics, nor does it claim to have considered all potential confounding factors that explain collective protests. Despite these limitations, the study makes several theoretical and empirical contributions and offers new clues on the emerging patterns of collective protest behaviour.

Four conclusions are drawn. First, the conditions that enable collective protests are causally complex and demand nuanced consideration of multi-level theoretical perspectives to explain contingencies of elite-challenging actions. Specifically, macro-, meso-, and micro-level indicators are embedded in dynamic social, political, and economic interactions that produce conditions of possibility for diverse repertoires of collective action. Put otherwise, no single level appears to fully account for collective protest behaviour and, thus, multi-level theorizations remain central to systematically analyse protest behaviour.

Second, economic grievances strongly predict the level of collective political protests in Central Asia. The tendency towards collective protest increases as the economic deprivation rises. This finding is hardly surprising given the increased tensions involving economic mismanagement in both republics in recent years.

Third, the level of religiosity as well as secular values reveals insightful patterns. While religious Muslims seem more likely to participate in high-risk collective protests, secular values appear to translate into actions that bear lower risks of state reprisal. The findings lend support for micro-level religious preferences that shape the protest behaviour in Central Asia, that is, more conservative individuals with deeper religiosity appear more prone to join riskier protests.[63] Both republics predominantly pursue assertive secularist policies. Given that support for greater visibility of Islam in public life is largely present among people in Central Asia, the oppositional forces tend to favour higher religious freedoms, which may partly explain this outcome. Furthermore, assertive and somewhat repressive policies may also increase the risk for radicalizing various Islamist actors.

Fourth, consistent with more recent scholarship, being part of an official group, network, or organization appears to play an instrumental role in strengthening activists' commitment for action.[64] Membership in various civil society associations provides individuals with onnections to a sustained flow of information and guidance to partake in forthcoming organized protests. At the same time, this finding partly highlights the centrality of informal patronage networks that often operate through various organizational structures (for example, charities) to mobilize the public by capitalizing on certain grievances. In this process, the internet has become an inseparable component in the cross-national diffusion of collective action (for example, the diffusion of tactics and strategies) and strong social networking; using Twitter, Facebook, or other online social networking sites is becoming increasingly effective in systematically coordinating mass demonstrations.

The question of under what conditions Central Asian citizens participate in collection action can hardly be fully answered by the findings situated in linear modelling. The complexity of contentious politics needs to be understood in a wider context and in the light of numerous causally complex, combinatorial compositions of explanatory factors. In addition, statistical models, and the assumptions thereof, are limited to explicate the intricate mechanisms at play that explain why citizens protest. The focus of this article is not to reduce the causality of LRCA and HRCA to mere statistically significant variables but, rather, to examine the emerging patterns that shed light on the evolving dynamics of collective protest behaviour. The findings are particularly helpful for taking stock of individual-level protest inclinations and, thereby, evaluating the extent to which the contextual conditions help shape the level of collective contestation.

One of the specific implications offered by this study deals with its explicit challenge of the conceptualization of collective action as a monolithic, one-size-fits-all framing often employed without appreciation to an underlying variation with respect to *risks* involved in collective protesting. Nevertheless, much remains to be explored in future research to further investigate the causally complex and multifaceted mechanisms at play that explain elite-challenging collective behaviour.

Whereas large-scale uprisings generally attract the world's attention and are often more likely to yield higher pay-offs, small-scale protests should not be underestimated. Rising up to challenge powerful incumbent authoritarian structures for the first time is never easy; the absence of a protest culture precedence often poses uneasy concerns for "early risers".[65] However, these early actions become instrumental for establishing an important precedence for subsequent elite-challenging collective actions in the long term. The early signs of collective protest behaviour have a potential to break the ice in perceived conformities to authoritarian regimes, and facilitate a possible *diffusion* of change in the region.

From this vantage, an increasing number of protests, though limited in scale and frequency, continue to play a key role in the democratization process of post-Soviet Central Asia. Yet, probing the impact of elite-challenging collective actions on the substantive democratization process (for example, pay-off in civil/political liberties) is another important avenue for future research. While this study examined the conditions conducive for citizens to collectively challenge the political status quo, it has also sought to advance the debate by bringing into the picture an empirical nexus between macro-level contexts, meso-level structures, and micro-level social interactions that, often jointly, contribute to democratization.

Disclosure statement

No potential conflict of interest was reported by the author(s).

Notes

1. Almond and Verba, *The Civic Culture*; Putnam, Leonardi, and Nanetti, *Making Democracy Work*; Putnam, *Bowling Alone.*
2. Shaykhutdinov, "Accommodation of Islamic Religious Practices."
3. Schenkkan, "Kazakhstan."
4. McAdam, Tarrow, and Tilly, *Dynamics of Contention*, 5.
5. Tarrow, *Power in Movement*, 2; Tilly and Tarrow, *Contentious Politics*, 4.
6. Dalton, Van Sickle, and Weldon, "The Individual–Institutional Nexus of Protest Behaviour," 1.
7. See, for instance, Welzel, Inglehart, and Deutsch, "Social Capital, Voluntary Associations."
8. Vairel, "Protesting in Authoritarian Situations."
9. Shaykhutdinov and Achilov, "Islam, Islamism and Collective Action in Central Asia."
10. BBC, "Kazakh Oil Strike."
11. Human Rights Watch, *Kazakhstan: Allow Peaceful Protests*; Human Rights Watch, "World Report 2012: Kazakhstan."
12. Lillis, "Kazakhstan: Almaty Police Arrest Anti-Devaluation Protesters."
13. The public outrage was particularly pronounced as the National Bank chairman had previously denied any possibility of currency devaluation.
14. Al-Shibeeb, "Lace Underwear Ban Irks Kazakh Women."
15. Abdurasulov, "What Is Driving Kyrgyzstan's Protest Culture?"
16. Ryabkov, "The North–South Cleavage and Political Support in Kyrgyzstan."
17. Hanks, "Crisis in Kyrgyzstan."
18. Saralayeva, "Hundreds Storm Office of Canadian Centerra Mine in Kyrgyzstan, 55 Wounded in Clashes."
19. Ibid.
20. In conceptualizing the level of risk in collective protests, I draw from McAdam's ("Recruitment to High-Risk Activism") prominent study on Freedom Summer events.
21. McAdam, "Recruitment to High-Risk Activism," 67.
22. The WVS database does not clearly specify the boycott type utilized in the survey. My framing focuses on the political dimension of boycotting. Although the rate of boycotts is extremely rare, a few examples exist. In Kazakhstan, for instance, the

opposition called for boycotting the national elections in 2011. Similarly, Kyrgyz activists in Osh boycotted the parliamentary elections following Ruziyev's arrest in 2005.

23. Goldstone and Tilly, "Treat (and Opportunity)," 128.
24. Tilly, *From Mobilization to Revolution*.
25. Achilov and Shaykhutdinov, "State Regulation of Religion and Radicalism in the Post-Communist Muslim Republics"; Fetzer and Soper, *Muslims and the State in Britain, France, and Germany*, 10–11.
26. Foweraker and Landman, *Citizenship Rights and Social Movements*; Rootes, *Environmental Protest in Western Europe*; Tarrow, *Power in Movement*; Shaykhutdinov, "Accommodation of Islamic Religious Practices and Democracy in the Post-Communist Muslim Republics."
27. Brockett, "The Structure of Political Opportunities and Peasant Mobilization in Central America"; Hafez, *Why Muslims Rebel*; Kitschelt, "Political Opportunity Structures and Political Protests."
28. Gurr, "A Causal Model of Civil Strife'; Gurr, *Why Men Rebel*.
29. Goodwin, *No Other Way Out*.
30. Beissinger, "Structure and Example in Modular Political Phenomena."
31. Although data limitation inhibits testing for possible effects of regional diffusion in this study, modular diffusion is an important factor to be considered in future research.
32. Bunce and Wolchik, "International Diffusion and Postcommunist Electoral Revolutions," 287.
33. Radnitz, Wheatley, and Zurcher, "The Origins of Social Capital."
34. McCarthy and Zald, "Resource Mobilization and Social Movements."
35. Beissinger, "Structure and Example in Modular Political Phenomena."
36. Dalton, Van Sickle, and Weldon, "The Individual–Institutional Nexus of Protest Behaviour."
37. Passy and Giugni, "Life-Spheres, Networks, and Sustained Participation in Social Movements."
38. Radnitz, *Weapons of the Wealthy*; McGlinchey, *Chaos, Violence, Dynasty*.
39. Radnitz, *Weapons of the Wealthy*, 21; Radnitz substantiates "subversive clientelism" by illustrating how independent elites in Kyrgyzstan extend "investments" or donations targeted to fix infrastructure or fund construction projects in communities or by supporting public demonstrations.
40. McGlinchey, *Chaos, Violence, Dynasty*.
41. Ibid., 38.
42. Ibid.
43. Ibid.
44. Campbell, "Social Networks and Political Participation"; Dalton, Van Sickle, and Weldon, "The Individual–Institutional Nexus of Protest Behaviour."
45. Hyman and Wright, *Education's Lasting Influence on Values*; Kohn, *Class and Conformity*; Lipset, "Some Social Requisites of Democracy"; McCloskey and Brill, *Dimensions of Tolerance*.
46. Hall, Rodeghier, and Useem, "Effects of Education on Attitude to Protest," 565.
47. Campbell, "Social Networks and Political Participation," 37.
48. Ibid., 36.
49. Breuer, Landman, and Farquhar, "Social Media and Protest Mobilization."
50. Ibid.
51. Shaykhutdinov and Bragg, "Do Grievances Matter in Ethnic Conflict?"
52. Putnam and Campbell, *American Grace*.
53. Ibid.
54. Campbell, "Social Networks and Political Participation," 39.
55. Jamal and Tessler, "Attitudes in the Arab World."

56. Bratton, "Briefing."
57. Rose, "How Muslims View Democracy."
58. Hofmann, "Islam and Democracy."
59. Norris and Inglehart, *Sacred and Secular*; Esposito and Mogahed, *Who Speaks for Islam?*; Achilov, "Social Capital, Islam, and the Arab Spring in the Middle East."
60. Bennett, "Civic Life Online," 2.
61. A one-way ANOVA was conducted to compare the mean scores of LRCP and HRCP for both countries ($n=3000$).
62. For robustness, I analysed the same model with two additional *internet* variables: reading news from (1) email and (2) a mobile phone. The findings revealed indistinguishable results and thus, have been omitted.
63. It is important to emphasize that it is personal religiosity – and not support for Islamist political ambitions – which appears to have an effect on collective protests.
64. Passy and Monsch, "Do Social Networks Really Matter in Contentious Politics?"
65. Beissinger, *Nationalist Mobilization and the Collapse of the Soviet State*, 159.

Bibliography

Abdurasulov, Abdujalil. "What Is Driving Kyrgyzstan's Protest Culture?" *BBC Asia*, June 11, 2013.
Achilov, Dilshod. "Social Capital, Islam, and the Arab Spring in the Middle East." *Journal of Civil Society* 9, no. 3 (2013): 268–286.
Achilov, Dilshod, and Renat Shaykhutdinov. "State Regulation of Religion and Radicalism in the Post-Communist Muslim Republics." *Problems of Post Communism* 60, no. 5 (2012): 17–33.
Almond, Gabriel A., and Sidney Verba. *The Civic Culture: Political Attitudes and Democracy in Five Nations*. Newbury Park, CA: Sage Publications, 1989.
Al-Shibeeb, Dina. "Lace Underwear Ban Irks Kazakh Women." *Al-Arabiya*, February 17, 2014.
BBC. "Kazakh Oil Strike: 10 Dead in Zhanaozen Clashes." *BBC Asia*, December 16, 2011.
Beissinger, Mark R. *Nationalist Mobilization and the Collapse of the Soviet State, Cambridge Studies in Comparative Politics*. Cambridge, UK: Cambridge University Press, 2002.
Beissinger, Mark R. "Structure and Example in Modular Political Phenomena: The Diffusion of Bulldozer/Rose/Orange/Tulip Revolutions." *Perspectives on Politics* 5, no. 2 (2007): 259–276.
Bennett, W. Lance. *Civic Life Online: Learning How Digital Media Can Engage Youth*, The John D and Catherine T Macarthur Foundation Series on Digital Media and Learning. Cambridge, MA: MIT Press, 2008.
Bratton, Michael. "Briefing: Islam, Democracy and Public Opinion in Africa." *African Affairs* 102, no. 408 (2003): 493–501.
Breuer, Anita, Todd Landman, and Dorothea Farquhar. "Social Media and Protest Mobilization: Evidence from the Tunisian Revolution." *Democratization* (2014): 1–29.

Brockett, Charles. "The Structure of Political Opportunities and Peasant Mobilization in Central America." *Comparative Politics* 23 (1991): 253–274.

Bunce, Valerie J., and Sharon L. Wolchik. "International Diffusion and Postcommunist Electoral Revolutions." *Communist and Post-Communist Studies* 39, no. 3 (2006): 283–304.

Campbell, David E. "Social Networks and Political Participation." *Annual Review of Political Science* 16, no. 1 (2013): 33–48.

Dalton, Russell, Alix Van Sickle, and Steven Weldon. "The Individual–Institutional Nexus of Protest Behaviour." *British Journal of Political Science* 40, no. 1 (2010): 51.

Esposito, John L., and Dalia Mogahed. *Who Speaks for Islam?: What a Billion Muslims Really Think*. New York: Gallup Press, 2008.

Fetzer, Joel S., and J. Christopher Soper. *Muslims and the State in Britain, France, and Germany*. Cambridge: Cambridge University Press, 2005.

Foweraker, Joe, and Todd Landman. *Citizenship Rights and Social Movements: A Comparative and Statistical Analysis*. Oxford: Oxford University Press, 1997.

Goldstone, Jack A., and Charles, Tilly. "Threat (and Opportunity): Popular Action and State Response in the Dynamics of Contentious Action." In *Silence and Voice in the Study of Contentious Politics*, edited by R. Aminzade, Jack Goldstone, Doug McAdam, Elizabeth Perry, William Hamilton Sewell, Sidney Tarrow and Charles Tilly, 179–194. Cambridge: Cambridge University Press, 2001.

Goodwin, Jeff. *No Other Way Out: States and Revolutionary Movements, 1945–1991*. Cambridge: Cambridge University Press, 2001.

Gurr, Ted. "A Causal Model of Civil Strife: A Comparative Analysis Using New Indices." *The American Political Science Review* 62, no. 4 (1968): 1104–1124.

Gurr, Ted. R. *Why Men Rebel*. Princeton, NJ: Princeton University Press, 1970.

Hafez, Mohammed M. *Why Muslims Rebel: Repression and Resistance in the Islamic World*. Boulder; London: Lynne Reinner, 2003.

Hall, Robert L., Mark Rodeghier, and Bert Useem. "Effects of Education on Attitude to Protest." *American Sociological Review* (1986): 564–573.

Hanks, Reuel R. "Crisis in Kyrgyzstan: Conundrums of Ethnic Conflict, National Identity and State Cohesion." *Journal of Balkan and Near Eastern Studies* 13, no. 2 (2011): 177–187.

Hofmann, Steven R. "Islam and Democracy: Micro-Level Indications of Compatibility." *Comparative Political Studies* 37 (2004): 652–676.

Human Rights Watch. *Kazakhstan: Allow Peaceful Protests*. New York: HRW, 2012a.

Human Rights Watch. "World Report 2012: Kazakhstan." *World Report*. New York: HRW, 2012b.

Hyman, H. H., and C. R. Wright. *Education's Lasting Influence on Values*. Chicago, IL: University of Chicago Press, 1979.

Jamal, Amaney A., and Mark A. Tessler. "Attitudes in the Arab World." *Journal of Democracy* 19, no. 1 (2008): 97–110.

Kitschelt, Herbert. "Political Opportunity Structures and Political Protests: Anti-Nuclear Movements in Four Democracies." *British Journal of Political Science* 16 (1986): 57–85.

Kohn, M. Class and Conformity: A Study in Values. Homewood, IL: Dorsey, 1969.

Lillis, Joanna. "Kazakhstan: Almaty Police Arrest Anti-Devaluation Protesters." *Euroasianet*, February 15, 2014.

Lipset, S. M. "Some Social Requisites of Democracy: Economic Development and Political Legitimacy." 69–105, 1959.

McAdam, Doug. "Recruitment to High-Risk Activism: The Case of Freedom Summer." *American Journal of Sociology* 92, no. 1 (1986): 64–90.

McAdam, Doug, Sidney G. Tarrow, and Charles Tilly. *Dynamics of Contention, Cambridge Studies in Contentious Politics*. Cambridge, NY: Cambridge University Press, 2001.

THE PEOPLE AND THE STATE

McCarthy, John D., and Mayer N. Zald. "Resource Mobilization and Social Movements: A Partial Theory." *American Journal of Sociology* (1977): 1212–1241.

McCloskey, H., and A. Brill. *Dimensions of Tolerance: What Americans Believe About Civil Liberties*. New York: Russell Sage, 1983.

McGlinchey, Eric Max. *Chaos, Violence, Dynasty: Politics and Islam in Central Asia*. Pittsburgh, PA: University of Pittsburgh Press, 2011.

Norris, Pippa, and Ronald Inglehart. *Sacred and Secular: Religion and Politics Worldwide*. New York: Cambridge University Press, 2011.

Passy, Florence, and Marco Giugni. "Life-Spheres, Networks, and Sustained Participation in Social Movements: A Phenomenological Approach to Political Commitment." *Sociological Forum* 15, no. 1 (2000): 117–144.

Passy, Florence, and Gian-Andrea Monsch. "Do Social Networks Really Matter in Contentious Politics?" *Social Movement Studies* 13, no. 1 (2014): 22–47.

Putnam, Robert D. *Bowling Alone: The Collapse and Revival of American Community*. New York: Simon & Schuster, 2000.

Putnam, Robert D., and David E. Campbell. *American Grace: How Religion Divides and Unites Us*. 1st ed. New York: Simon & Schuster, 2010.

Putnam, Robert D., Robert Leonardi, and Raffaella Nanetti. *Making Democracy Work: Civic Traditions in Modern Italy*. Princeton, NJ: Princeton University Press, 1993.

Radnitz, Scott. *Weapons of the Wealthy: Predatory Regimes and Elite-Led Protests in Central Asia*. Ithaca, NY: Cornell University Press, 2010.

Radnitz, Scott, Jonathan Wheatley, and Christoph Zurcher. "The Origins of Social Capital: Evidence from a Survey of Post-Soviet Central Asia." *Comparative Political Studies* 42, no. 6 (2009): 707–732.

Rootes, Christopher. *Environmental Protest in Western Europe*. Oxford: Oxford University Press, 2003.

Rose, Richard. "How Muslims View Democracy: Evidence from Central Asia." *Journal of Democracy* 13, no. 4 (2002): 102.

Ryabkov, Maxim. "The North–South Cleavage and Political Support in Kyrgyzstan." *Central Asian Survey* 27, no. 3–4 (2008): 301–316.

Saralayeva, Leila. "Hundreds Storm Office of Canadian Centerra Mine in Kyrgyzstan, 55 Wounded in Clashes." *Financial Post*, May 31, 2013.

Schenkkan, Nate. "Kazakhstan: One Year after Zhanaozen." New York: Freedomhouse, 2011.

Shaykhutdinov, Renat. "Accommodation of Islamic Religious Practices and Democracy in the Post-Communist Muslim Republics." *Politics and Religion* 6, no. 3 (2013): 646–670.

Shaykhutdinov, Renat, and Dilshod Achilov. "Islam, Islamism, and Collective Action in Central Asia." *TRAMES Journal of the Humanities and Social Sciences* 18, no. 4 (2014).

Shaykhutdinov, Renat, and Belinda Bragg. "Do Grievances Matter in Ethnic Conflict? An Experimental Approach." *Analyses of Social Issues and Public Policy* 11, no. 1 (2011): 141–153.

Tarrow, Sidney G. *Power in Movement: Social Movements and Contentious Politics*. Cambridge: Cambridge University Press, 1998.

Tilly, Charles. *From Mobilization to Revolution*. New York: McGraw-Hill, 1978.

Tilly, Charles, and Sidney G. Tarrow. *Contentious Politics*. Boulder, CO: Paradigm Publishers, 2007.

Vairel, Frederic. "Protesting in Authoritarian Situations: Egypt and Morocco in Comparative Perspective." In *Social Movements, Mobilization, and Contestation in the Middle East and North Africa*, edited by Joel Beinin and Frederic Vairel. Stanford, CA: Stanford University Press, 2011.

Welzel, Christian, Ronald Inglehart, and Franziska Deutsch. "Social Capital, Voluntary Associations and Collective Action: Which Aspects of Social Capital Have the Greatest 'Civic' Payoff?" *Journal of Civil Society* 1, no. 2 (2005): 121–146.

Appendix

Variable coding, source, and description statistics

Variable	Measurement and coding
Low-risk collective protest (LRCP)	*V90: Tell me for each of these activities how often you have done it in the last year. [Signing a petition]* (At least once in the last year =1, none= 0)
High-risk collective protest (HRCP)	A dichotomous measure based on participating in any of the following protests: *Tell me for each of these activities how often you have done it in the last year.* *V91. Joining in boycotts; V92. Attending peaceful demonstrations; V93. Joining strikes; V94. Any other act of protest?* (At least once in the last year =1, none= 0) [Scale reliability: the Cronbach's alpha = 0.742]
Economic deprivation	*V191. In the last 12 months, how often have you or your family [gone without cash income]* ("Never" = 1; "Often" =4)
Educational attainment	*V248. What is the highest educational level that you have attained?* ("No formal education" = 1, "University-level education, with degree" = 9)
Islam (religiosity)	An aggregate scale of 1–15 of survey respondents' responses to how often they pray and attend religious services: *V146. Apart from weddings and funerals, about how often do you pray?* ("Several times a day" = 8, "Never" = 1); *V145. Apart from weddings and funerals, about how often do you attend religious services these days?* ("More than once a week" = 7, "Never" = 1).
Overall Secular Values	*SACSECVAL* ("High secular values" = 1; "Low secular values" = 0)
NGO membership (networking)	An aggregate 0–10 scale based on: *For each organization, could you tell me whether you are an active member, an inactive member or not a member of that type of organization?* (Active member = 2, non-member = 0 for each item) *V25. Church or religious organization; V28. Labour Union; V30. Environmental organization; V31. Professional association; V32. Humanitarian or charitable organization*
Computer/internet usage	A 1–3 scale based on the interaction of these variables: *V225. How often, if ever, do you use a personal computer?* *("Never" = 1, "Frequently" = 3); V223: Use Internet to obtain news information in this country and the world.* *("Weekly or daily" = 1, else = 0)*
Government employee	*V230. Are you working for a government or public institution, for private business or industry, or for a private non-profit organization?* ("Government or public institution" = 1, else = 0)
Age (older than 30)	*V242. Actual age.* (Age older than 30 = 1, Age 30 or less = 0)
Female	*V240: "Female" = 1, "Male" = 0*

Source: 2010–2012 World Values Survey (Kazakhstan and the Kyrgyz Republic).

Political religion and the rise of transnational right and left-wing social movements since 9/11

David Martin Jones

The Austrian philosopher, Eric Voegelin, argued that the ideological fanaticism of the Nazis was a spiritual perversion. More precisely, so far, as the political religions of the twentieth century, Fascism, Stalinism, Maoism and Islamism, are concerned, the meaning or substance of religious phenomena moved from a spiritual concern with transcending the mundane world towards the realisation of imaginary fantasies of immanent apocalypse and the fashioning of this worldly utopias. These fantasies are not always recognised for what they are because the image of an earthly condition of perfected humanity was often expressed in scientific language. This was not the case with revolutionary Islamic thought, but it remains so with other ideological social movements of both left and right that have evolved since 9/11. This is the case with both race-based and anti-capitalist social movements that pursue national or global purificationism. In this essay, we shall discuss the commonalities between these evolving political religions before examining the Western state response and its implications for the future of secular, liberal democracy.

Eric Voegelin, the Austrian philosopher who fled the Third Reich in the wake of the *Anschluss* in 1938, argued that the ideological fanaticism of the Nazis was not only a moral and political mistake, but also a spiritual perversion. More precisely, so far as the political religions of the twentieth century, Fascism, Stalinism, Maoism and Islamism are concerned, the meaning or substance of religious phenomena moved from a spiritual concern with transcending the mundane world towards the realisation of imaginary fantasies of immanent apocalypse. These fantasies, as Barry Cooper observes, are not 'always recognized for what they are because the image of an earthly condition of perfected humanity' was, in Europe before 1990, expressed in scientific, or more accurately, 'scientistic' language (Cooper, 1999, p. 4).

This was not the case with revolutionary Islamic thought, but it remains so with other ideological social movements of both left and right that have evolved since 9/11, whose animating political religions focus, paradoxically, upon the renunciation of God. This is the case with both race-based and anti-capitalist social movements that pursue what Ernest Sternberg terms, 'world purificationism' (Sternberg, 2010, p. 64). In this essay, we shall discuss the commonalities between these evolving political religions before examining the Western state response and its implications for the future of secular, liberal democracy.

The extremist right after 9/11: cultural nationalism and political activism

As Emilio Gentile argues, totalitarian ideologies, of a Marxist-Leninist, or a national socialist provenance, attribute 'sacred status to an earthly concept' whether that concept is the race, the nation, the proletariat or, in more recent green left thought, the planet itself (Gentile & Mallett, 2000, pp. 18–19). This sacralisation of the political provides the space for an apocalyptic clash between the world waiting to be born and the doomed quotidian order that resists it. Such an ideological perspective, as Hannah Arendt classically explained, reveals a decadent past about to perish, a present that reveals the opportunity for radical change and the potential for realising an ideal future (Arendt, 1951, pp. 472–479). Those who possess the ideological key to history, moreover, accept the necessity of violence to bring it about. In fact, the politically religious mind considers violence purgative. Since the nineteenth century, all modern revolutionary creeds have shared this perspective.

The concept of three ages that informs such thinking – a corrupt past, the divided present and the purified third age waiting to be born – ultimately revives, in a modern guise, a tradition of gnostic speculation that dates from the speculations of Cistercian monks like Joachim of Fiora (1145–1202) and subsequently elaborated in the chiliastic practice of millenarian sects in sixteenth- and seventeenth-century Europe who sought to realise the *teleion* of the age of perfection (Cohn, 1969; Voegelin, 1974, p. 268).

In contrast to religiously focused ideologies, race-based ones emphasise the *palingenesis* or rebirth of the nation or race through a purgative process of ethnic cleansing. Exemplified in Third Reich ideology and practice, fascist ideology shares the sense of living at an imminent turning point in history when the dominance of the bankrupt forces of liberal democracy gives way to a new era where an activist nationalism triumphantly reasserts itself (Griffin, 1991, p. 32).

From this perspective, violence is necessary to overcome national degeneracy and eliminate parasitic elites who have betrayed the nation. This apocalyptic nationalist vision informs the white supremacist thought that has exercised an extremist, minority, but growing presence in Western democracies since the early days of the Cold War, the era of European decolonisation and the US fear of international communism. Post-9/11, racist or fascist ideology has proved increasingly attractive to an alienated, working-class, white demographic in both Europe and the US. This has been particularly evident as the period of post-war social democratic consensus in the West gave way to an era of speculative, millennial capital. Its socio-economic consequence was the emergence of a new class, the 'precariat', in low-paid, semi-skilled work on short-term contracts subject to the vagaries of finance capital, immigration and the global marketplace. This somewhat amorphous 'class', if it can be classified as such, emerged with the decline of traditional, blue-collar industries as multinational corporations moved offshore and reshaped the global economy after 1990. This new precariat in developed Western democracies became more evident as the Western financial crisis deepened after 2008. As unemployment levels, especially amongst young, male workers in Europe and the US, reached historic highs, the alienated, white former blue collar, precariat offered a fertile breeding ground for right-wing extremism (RWE) (Standing, 2011, pp. 3–5). Networks, movements and parties committed to this white nationalist or white supremacist ideology hold that the cosmopolitan, liberal, ruling elites have abandoned their national cultures and the white race in favour of international or regional arrangements like the United Nations or the EU. At the same time, a transnational business and political elite, the 'Davoisie', exploit bureaucracies, constitutions and courts to exercise a tyranny over once free peoples.

In the US, this alienation took the form of movements like the Ku Klux Klan (KKK), whose origins date from the era of Reconstruction in the Southern US after 1865, but whose clan organisational structure revived in the 1960s to oppose the movement for civil rights. KKK members often shared links with the Aryan Nations Church of Jesus Christ-Christian that felt that the government 'no longer represents the White Race in this Nation' (Church of Jesus Christ, Christian Aryan Nations Converse, 2016, p. 1). The RAND Corporation described the Aryan Nations churches of the 1990s as 'the first truly nationwide terrorist organization' in the US (Hoffman, 1988, p. 48). The 1960s also witnessed the foundation of Lincoln Rockwell's American Nazi Party. After Rockwell's assassination in 1967, the party mutated into the National Socialist White People's Party, before settling on its current title, the National Alliance in 1974.

Alongside such clearly racist groups, there emerged in the 1980s various state-based militia movements associated with the right-wing *Posse Comitatus* that treated attempts to restrict gun ownership and the imposition of federal law at the expense of state rights as part of an international conspiracy against the values of the American revolution. Prior to 9/11, anti-Semitism characterised these movements. Indeed, they termed the tyranny they confronted the Zionist Occupied Government (ZOG). It was the role of the various state militias to resist this federally imposed, Zionist tyranny. Militias adopted both a libertarian and a Christian, white, fundamentalist rhetoric and were prepared to organise and train for the prospect of an imminent racial Armageddon.

National Alliance leader William Luther Pierce outlined the terms of a future apocalyptic race war in *The turner diaries* (Macdonald, 1978). Set in 2099, the diaries recount Earl Turner's guerrilla insurgency to overthrow the US federal government and exterminate inferior races first in America and subsequently globally. In 1993, the Southern Poverty Law Center described it as 'the bible of the racist right' (Southern Poverty Law Center, 2004).

The work inspired Robert Jay Mathews to form The Order or Silent Brotherhood, which undertook a series of robberies and bombings between 1983 and 1984, culminating in the murder of talk show host Alan Berg. Mathews died in a shoot-out with the FBI in December 1984. Somewhat later, Pierce wrote *Hunter* (1989) that provided a fictional account of a developing terrorist character, the lone wolf, Oscar Yeager (Macdonald, 1989).

The paranoia that informed US RWE ensured that white supremacist groups interpreted the FBI's siege of Christian Identity survivalist Randy Weaver's farm at Ruby Ridge, North Idaho in 1992, followed by David Koresh's Branch Davidians compound in Waco, Texas between February and April 1993, which culminated in the death of 76 sect members, as further proof of ZOG's tyranny. To counter it, white supremacy activists maintained, demanded a strategy of leaderless resistance and lone wolf attacks on federal agencies.

By the mid-1980s, Louis Beam, a former Vietnam veteran, had emerged as the leading strategic thinker of the extreme right in the US. He served as both a state leader of David Duke's Knights of the KKK and as the Aryan Nations' Ambassador at Large. It was Beam who linked lone wolf white right actors to a wider strategy. Beam considered his concept of leaderless resistance 'a fundamental departure in theories of organization' (Beam, 1992, p. 1; Michael, 1995, pp. 5–15).

This thinking inspired Timothy McVeigh to bomb the Alfred P. Murrah Federal Building in Oklahoma City in 1995. McVeigh's action claimed 165 lives. It was the most serious terrorist attack on US soil prior to 9/11. McVeigh and his accomplices sympathised with the militia and patriot movements but acted outside any formal structure.

In the course of the 1990s, websites like *stormfront.org* promulgated the racist mythology and the strategic thinking of the US white right to an international audience. Started by Klan leader David Duke in 1990, by 2000, it was the most visited hate site on the Internet. Significantly, the Internet has come to serve as the critical organising and propaganda medium for promulgating the post-9/11 proliferation of white supremacist ideas and Beam's phantom cell structure of leaderless resistance both in the US and across Europe and Australia.

European disunion and 'patriotic' extremism

Although identity and race-based nationalism never died out in Western Europe after 1945, right-wing nationalist and neo-fascist social movements have attracted growing popular support in both the UK and Western Europe since the mid-1990s. Thus Germany, Austria and Italy, states that experienced fascist regimes between the 1920s and 1940s, have, since the 1990s, witnessed the re-emergence of extreme nationalist political parties informed by racist myths of Aryan supremacy. Whilst the German *Strafgesetzbuch* (criminal code) forbids neo-Nazi material and the 'use of symbol of unconstitutional organisations', this has not prevented the emergence of the extreme right Nationalist Party (NPD), which captured 9.2% of the vote in the Saxony state elections in 2004. Attempts to ban the party have thus far failed (Spiegel, July 2016). Meanwhile, Germany has also witnessed the emergence of an illegal neo-Nazi movement, the National Socialist Underground (NSU), allegedly responsible for a number of unsolved murders of migrant workers and gay men since the mid-1990s (Spiegel, 2016).

Since 2014, the rise of Islamic State in the Middle East and the civil war in Syria that dramatically increased migrant flows into Europe, and Islamic State-inspired jihadist attacks in Paris in January and November 2015 and in Brussels in 2016, together with the confused German and European response to the migrant crisis, gave a powerful boost to far-right nationalist and anti-migration social movements across Europe and notably in Germany. By 2016, the populist, nationalist anti-European, Alliance fur Deutschland (AfD) Party founded in 2013 had established a significant electoral presence in Landtag elections in Saxony Anhalt (where it polled 24.2% of the vote), Baden Wurtemberg and Rhineland Palatinate. The AfD also established links with the Austrian Freedom Party (FPO) and the anti-European UK Independence Party (UKIP). At the same time, the foundation in Dresden in 2014 of the ethno-nationalist and anti-Moslem, social movement *Patriotische Europaear Gegen die Islamisierung des Abendlandes* (PEGIDA – Patriotic Europeans against the Islamization of the West) constituted a more disturbing movement prepared to engage in violent street demonstrations to promulgate its anti-migrant and anti-Moslem stance (Hugler, 2015). Its appeal grew in the wake of assaults on German women perpetrated, it appeared, by North African migrants, in Cologne on New Year's Eve 2015. By 2016, PEGIDA had established a presence in the Netherlands, Belgium, Denmark and the UK.

The period from the end of the Cold War also saw growing electoral support for ethno-nationalist political parties in Austria. In the 1999 general election, the FPO captured 27% of the vote and briefly shared government with the Conservative People's Party. Like anti-Islamic and anti-EU 'patriotic' parties elsewhere in Europe, the FPO benefited from the incoherent EU response to the Syrian refugee crisis. The FPO polled 20.5% of the legislative vote in 2013, and in the Presidential election of 2016, the FPO candidate Norbert Hofer led the first round of polling with 30.5% of the vote (Breitbart, July 2016).

Meanwhile, in Italy, far-right parties have never been absent from the political scene since the fall of Benito Mussolini's Fascist regime in 1944. The neo-fascist Italian Social Movement (MSI) dates from 1946. Constitutional changes after 1995 saw the formation of parties canvassing a return to Mussolini-era activist politics. These included the Northern Alliance (*Lega Nord per l'independenzia di Padania*) formed in 1991, the National Alliance formed in 1995 and the *Forca Nuova* or New Force Party founded in 1997. These faction-prone parties have periodically formed alliances, and participated in coalition governments of the right with Silvio Berlusconi's *Forza Italia* and, after 2008, with Berlusconi's People of Freedom Party (*Il Popolo della Liberta*) (PdL). Mussolini's granddaughter, Alessandra, sits in the Italian parliament as a PdL representative, whilst Northern Alliance leader Gianfranco Fini served as President of the Chamber of Deputies between 2008 and 2011. The migration crisis in Europe since 2015 has, as elsewhere in Europe, significantly boosted extreme right social movements and the rehabilitation of Benito Mussolini's reputation and ideas on national rebirth promoted by his granddaughter Alessandra, 'the mouth from the South' (Adokoyo, 2014).

Elsewhere in Europe, Jean Marie Le Pen's *Front National* (National Front) (FN) dates from 1972 and emerged from a number of militant right-wing groups opposed to the decolonisation of Algeria and the inauguration of the Fifth Republic (1958). Le Pen's party initially attracted former Poujadists, the Ordre Nouveau (ON), and alienated former servicemen with links to the right-wing terror group 'the OAS' (*Organisation de l'Armée Secrète*) that attempted to assassinate President Charles De Gaulle in 1965. Over time, however, Le Pen's anti-immigration and anti-EU policies proved popular electorally. By the 1990s, the FN emerged as the third force in French politics, and under the leadership of daughter Marine le Pen since 2012, the FN has enjoyed more popular support than the two mainstream French political parties (Carswell, 2013). Islamist attacks on the satire magazine *Charlie Hebdo* in January 2015 and the Islamic State-inspired attack of November 2015 boosted the appeal of the FN. In regional elections in 2015, it polled over 27% of the vote and is now the official third party in French politics.

Similarly, in Greece, the anti-immigration, national socialist Golden Dawn party has achieved growing political prominence as the Eurozone financial crisis unravelled the Greek economy. Led by Greek nationalist Nikolaos Michaloliakos Golden Dawn registered as a political party in 1993. In 2012 national elections, it gained 7% of the popular vote and 21 parliamentary seats. By 2015 in the wake of the Greek immigration and financial crises, it had established itself as the country's third largest party. The party has a violent paramilitary wing, the *stormarbeitung*, responsible for attacks on migrants and synagogues. It also has links with the FN, the Italian *Forca Nuova*, the German NDP and the ethno-nationalist Hungarian *Jobbik* Party which in 2015 polled 20% of the popular vote in a country where the ruling *Fideisz* Party already embraces an ideology of illiberal democracy.

Elsewhere in Europe by 2016, extreme nationalist and anti-immigrant parties had achieved an electoral presence in Sweden, the Netherlands, Norway, Denmark and Finland. In the Netherlands, anti-immigration parties such as Pim Fortuyn's *List* briefly shared government in 2002, whilst Geert Wilder's anti-Islamic and anti-immigration *Freedom Party* commands 17% of the popular vote and, since elections in 2012, holds 18 parliamentary seats. In Finland, the *True Finn* Party, like the FN in France, had, by 2013, more popular support than traditional mainstream centre right and centre left parties.

In the UK, the British National Party (BNP), a party with links to the US National Alliance, also saw its electoral appeal improve during the 1990s. Formed in 1982 as the white extremist National Front Party factionalised and declined, the BNP attracted alienated, young, white, working-class voters, especially in areas of high Asian migration in London and in Northern cities like Rochdale and Bradford. The aftermath of 9/11 and the London bombings of 2005 saw a further surge in support amongst the white precariat. Under the leadership of Nick Griffin, the BNP won 6.2% of the vote and two seats in the European parliament elections in 2009. Although it formally eschews violence, the party's stance attracts a violent fringe. The neo-Nazi lone wolf David Copeland, who carried out three nail bomb attacks in London in 1999, belonged to both the BNP and the National Socialist Movement. In 2009, the BNP joined the French NF and the Hungarian *Jobbik* Party to form an Alliance of European National Movements.

All these parties share an ideology of ethnic nationalism and promote a political message of protectionism and hostility to mass migration and open borders. They all seek the dissolution of the EU and oppose the political elitism and Euro federalism that characterise the mainstream

European conservative and social democrat political parties. Extreme right parties support pro-grammes of either repatriation or coercive integration for legal migrants from non-European or Muslim backgrounds. The political credibility of these movements received a powerful boost from the European financial crisis after 2009 and the austerity measures unelected European Commissioners imposed upon national economies that created very high levels of unemployment across the Eurozone apart from Germany. The emergence of Islamic State in 2014 and the migration crisis that followed from the Syrian Civil War only further fuelled their already potent appeal and have further exacerbated the precariat class' consciousness of its political and economic marginalisation.

Historically, as with the US white supremacist movements, these right-wing parties initially asserted an anti-Semitism that reflected their national socialist origins. Jean Marie Le Pen, for example, is a Holocaust denier, and Zionism constituted the focus of both right-wing conspiracy theories and political violence prior to 9/11. These movements also share a race mythology that assumes, in its more extreme manifestations, that only violence and an apocalyptic race war can abate national decline.

After 9/11, however, this racial ideology increasingly substituted Islam for Zionism as the main protagonist in a Manichaean struggle for supremacy. In some versions of these race-based political religions, both Zionism and Islam represent the cancer incubated within the decaying national body politic that requires surgical removal. Significantly, the electoral appeal of right-wing nationalist parties correlates directly with the emergence of leaderless jihadist resistance across Europe. Indeed, it was only as this threat became increasingly home-grown after 9/11 that these extremist groups opportunistically targeted Islam, rather than Zionism, as the root of national decline.

After 9/11, the appeal of leaderless resistance and defence against leaderless jihadism directly affected the ideology of European RWE. It also facilitated the development within white RWE of a European Counter Jihad Movement (ECJM) comprised of English, Dutch, Norwegian, Danish and Swedish Defence Leagues. After 2009, the leagues shared a commitment to an over-arching ethno-nationalism combined with a willingness for street combat. Thus, the ECJM 'is a loosely organized, decentralized network of sympathetic groups' (Meleagrou-Hitchens & Brun, 2013, p. 3). The Internet plays a crucial role in maintaining this structure and facilitating a pan-Western network to Stop the Islamization of Nations (SION), with similarly minded groups in the US, Australia and New Zealand.

In this context, the English Defence League (EDL) has no formal membership, but evolved out of white football supporters opposed to the recruitment activities of *al-Muhajiroun* in Luton. The EDL founder, Tommy Robinson (a.k.a. Stephen Yaxley-Lennon), had belonged to the BNP and now leads Pegida's UK branch. At various street protests organised between 2009 and 2013, Robinson argued, 'I am a hundred per cent certain that there will be civil wars within Europe between Muslims and non-Muslims' (Lowe, 2016). This is a position Robinson shared with supporters from Islamophobic websites such as Robert Spencer's *Jihad Watch* and Pamela Geller's *Atlas Shrugged*. As Alexander Meleagrou-Hitchens and Hans Brun explain:

> The ECJM's activism is inspired by an ideology which presents the current jihadist terrorist threat to the West as part of a centuries-long effort by Muslims to dominate Western civilization. The ideology also insists on the existence of a conspiracy to 'Islamize' Europe through the stealthy implementation of Islamic Sharia, and holds that many of Europe's Muslims are actively engaged in this conspiracy in various ways ... The other main protagonists in this conspiracy ... are found within a European liberal elite that refuses to resist the attack. (Meleagrou-Hitchens & Brun, 2013, p. 5)

From this totalising perspective, all European Muslims are engaged in an assault on European cultural identity. Thus, Niccolai Sennels' influential blog, *The Gates of Vienna*, contends that

'Islamization is a phenomenon that has existed since the Muslim prophet Mohammed lived 1400 years ago' (Sennels, 2012, p. 240). The website continues, 'We are now in a phase of a very old war' (Sennels, 2012, p. 240). In a similar vein, Bat Ye'or in *Eurabia* (2005) promoted an influential conspiracy theory that demonstrated how European political elites accommodated Middle Eastern states after the 1973 oil crisis, facilitating both the Arab world's desire to eliminate Israel and mount a cultural conquest of Europe (Ye'or, 2005). Contemporary Muslim migrants to Europe, Bat Ye'or explains, represent the latest phase in a historical mission dating from the seventh century to eliminate Europe and subsume it into the greater caliphate (Ye'or, 2005, p. 67). On the basis of such reasoning, the ECJM believes that Europe is on the brink of a civil war to be fought between indigenous Europeans and Muslim migrants. This is, the ECJM contends, the only logical outcome of the EU and the European political class' betrayal of national interests, witnessed in the increase in the Muslim population of Europe and the fact that Islam is a religion immune to reform and secularisation.

In March 2012, the various defence leagues from Norway, Denmark, Sweden, Finland, Germany and the UK met in Copenhagen, where Mimosa Koiranen of the Finnish Defence League condemned the creeping Islamisation of Europe. The EDL similarly considers Islam an existential threat and responds with violent demonstrations against jihad inspired attacks. Thus, when Michael Adebolajo and Michael Adebowale murdered off-duty soldier Lee Rigby in Southeast London in May 2013, the EDL and BNP organised protest marches in Woolwich and Whitehall. Elements connected with these groups were also responsible for a dramatic increase in attacks on mosques and culture centres in the weeks following the murder (Daily Telegraph, 23 May 2013; The Independent, 28 May 2013).

The case of Norwegian white supremacist and Norwegian Defence League member Anders Breivik demonstrates the growing attraction of ideologically motivated lone wolves to leaderless asymmetric violence. Breivik's July 2011 attack on Oslo and a youth league camp on the island of Utøya resulted in 77 deaths. Breivik stated that the purpose of his killing spree was to draw attention to his 500-page compendium, *2083: A European Declaration of Independence*. The work alludes to the EDL and was published online under the pseudonym Andrew Berwick, Justiciar Knight Commander for Knights Templar Europe and the pan-European Patriotic Resistance. The Knights Templar, of course, were a medieval, European crusading order (1129–1312). Breivik, like the ECJM more generally, presents his modern crusade in terms of a historic civilisational clash (Berwick, 2013).

Extreme right leaderless resistance represents an emerging threat to European liberal democracy. Such 'patriotic' extremism finds mainstream, secular, democratic politics corrupt, hypocritical and tyrannical. The EU's failure to deliver higher living standards, the economic recession caused by locking different European economies into a single currency, together with its open border policy, has fuelled the xenophobia upon which ethno-nationalist identity politics thrives. In the context of marginalisation and European resistance, in June 2016, Thomas Mair assassinated Labour MP Jo Cox, shouting 'Britain First', the slogan of the BNP breakaway faction National Action. Mair had long established links to the US National Alliance (Southern Poverty Law Center, May 2016). In the same month a Royal United Services Institute report claimed that right-wing, neo-Nazi extremists like Mair and Breivik had conducted more lone actor attacks than their 'religiously motivated' equivalents in Europe (Pantucci & Ellis, 2016, p. 3).

By a curious irony, a similarly apocalyptic political religion informs the anti-capitalist movement of post-democratic radicals like *Anonymous* and Internet-linked anarchist groups. It also informs the worldview of social movements for global peace, justice and emancipation. We shall, therefore, next consider what Bernard-Henri Levy termed the 'new barbarism' of the anti-capitalist transnational left (Levy, 2008), before finally turning to consider why Western democracies have struggled to contain these anti-political threats to secular political order.

The Zombie left and world purificationism post-9/11

An anti-anti-Islamism characterises new left transnational thinking about post-9/11 jihadism. Since the 1990s, leading European university departments promulgated a critical theory about world politics that afforded ideological support to non-governmental organisations (NGOs), and legal elites that questioned the politics of fear that, they alleged, Western democratic governments and their security agencies promoted. These opinion-forming elites share a common suspicion of Western government responses to al-Qaeda and more recently Islamic State, both at home and abroad. They prefer instead transnational structures and global forums that, whilst deploring the violence of non-state actors such as Islamic State, empathise with their alienation and condemn capitalism and Western liberal democratic states for perpetuating the global injustices that induce 'resistance'.

This critique informs an emerging global movement against a Western-imposed security order. This 'transnational progressive movement' also assumes the character of a political religion (Fonte, 2002, p. 14). Like the rise of ethno-nationalism, transnational progressivism emerged from the end of the Cold War as a radical rejection of liberal market states, advocating instead cosmopolitan 'post-national constellations' like the United Nations and the EU (Jones, 2005, p. 63). Since 2001, this ideology considers redemptive social movements and transnational NGOs locked in combat with global capitalism and the US-inspired neo-liberal 'Empire' that sustains it (Sternberg, 2010, p. 61). Just as Marxist-Leninist thought recognised in the international proletariat a revolutionary class that exposed the contradictions in industrial capitalism, so new social movements, such as the World Social Forum, play an analogous role exposing the current contradictions of global capitalism (Chomsky, 2004; Hardt & Negri, 2001; Valle, 2010).

Critics of this transnational progressivism, like Bernard-Henri Levy, argue that it replaced the post-1968 libertarian left's commitment to personal freedoms, with the assumption that we are living in dark times, where a world controlling state–military–corporate complex enforces an unjust global order (Levy, 2008, p. 24; Sternberg, 2010, p. 63). In this context, the US and its allies function as the concrete imperial enemy, whilst Israel plays a special role as its demonic accomplice (Levy, 2008, pp. 23–30). Nick Cohen argues that this new Left movement experienced a 'dark liberation' after the Iraq war of 2003, inspiring its adherents to 'spread the theories of Jewish-Zionist world conspiracy … and excuse even the most brutal theocratic-fascist regime, as long as they opposed the United States and the capitalist status quo' (Cohen, 2007, pp. 4–14). Its world 'purificationism' contrasts a degenerate present with a utopian future. As Ernst Sternberg explains:

> The world system that perpetuates oppression is known as Empire. It exercises domination through corporate tentacles, media manipulation, state power and military prowess. It is selfish, greedy, ruthless, racist and exploitative and heedlessly pollutes the earth. (74)

By contrast, the *alter* globalisation movements comprising transnational networks of NGOs, sympathetic academics, radical pacifists, indigenous peoples and environmental activists seek to overthrow this western capitalist *imperium* (Levy, 2008, pp. 137–145). By 2011, those committed to this anti-capitalist worldview

> lead hundreds of activist groups and NGOs, conduct seminars and hold marches at international conferences, receive support from governments and eleemosynary institutions, enjoy various despots as

their cheerleaders, are woven into the workings of the UN and the EU ... and subscribe to a coherent though not uniform doctrine. (Sternberg, 2010, p. 66)

To overthrow the global neo-liberal order, activists form 'bunds' or affinities with like-minded groups networking across communities, borders and cultures (world social forum, 2011). This transnational network of purified victims seeks to instantiate an environmentally clean, culturally harmonious, politically just and sustainable world, liberated from both capitalism and carbon (Sternberg, 2010, p. 76). As the nation state order weakens, a trans-national cadre of NGOs will replace it and serve as the globe's humanitarian enforcers and equalisers.

The movement's ideology is post-democratic. It dismisses mainstream political parties and representative democratic institutions as oppressive. It favours instead a form of direct, participa-tory democracy where grassroots activists in local forums create conditions for the rectification of false consciousness, and the enforcement of local and global justice.

Moreover, although these loosely structured network of local groups embraces pacifism, it nevertheless empathises with the grievances that motivate the global resistance of the al-Qaeda-inspired leaderless variety. 'Resistance', as opposed to the more pejorative term, 'terror', explains, for example, the insurgency in Iraq since 2003 (Cohen, 2007, p. 301). This demonisation of Western influence, whether it is actively engaged in Afghanistan or Iraq or pas-sively indifferent to inter-tribal and sectarian civil war in Syria and North Africa, fuels a relativist culture of grievance settlement.

Yet, at the same time as the new radicals denounce Western hypocrisy, they minimise the crimes that occur in regimes that their ideology considers 'subaltern' and non-western. Such rela-tivism annihilates 'whole chapters of contemporary history, killing one more time, millions of men and women, whose whole crime was being born and whose second was in dying the wrong way' (Levy, 2008, p. 137). Exposing hypocrisy in liberal democracies, somewhat per-versely entails 'excus(ing) the pervasive crimes of despots' (Sternberg, 2010, p. 83).

Since 2008, the global financial crisis, which exposed major flaws in the Western financial system, boosted this radical critique of liberal democracy. At the end of the Cold War, Western elites assumed that the liberal market state order would reshape the globe through its soft cultural and commercial power. Twenty-five years on, a liberal end of history appears increasingly unli-kely. Government bailouts of banks too big to fail revealed the limitations of the rational market as well as the hubris of investment bankers. The crisis legitimated loose congeries of anarchist-inspired, direct action groups to promote the non-violent, but highly visible Occupy movement that disrupted Wall Street in September 2011.

Since 2003, Anonymous, the international collective of anarchist-inspired activist entities that spread this leaderless, anti-capitalist resistance, conducts denial of service attacks on government, religious and corporate websites it deems antithetical. In particular, Anonymous has conducted cyber-attacks in support of whistle blowers such as Edward Snowden, Bradley Manning and Julian Assange (Anonymous, 2014a). Its You Tube videos declare, 'We are Anonymous. We are legion. We do not forgive. We do not forget. We are coming. Expect us' (Anonymous, 2014a). In its 2014 apocalyptic challenge to the so-called global capitalist elite, Anonymous informed its fellow 'citizens of the world' that they spread the message of 'true love, peace and compassion' against the 'unsustainable' order based on 'murder, hate, oppression and dis-order' that was 'killing the surface of the planet ... We are the new world order' they declared (Anonymous, 2014b).

There is an evolving, if loose, symmetry between the new transnational left, and extreme right social movements, the anti-political paths they follow and the politically religious certitudes they embrace and promote. Interestingly, they share a common belief in a decadent and corrupt past, a failed present Western political order and the necessity for resistance, and in some cases purifica-tory violence to engender a harmonious new order or third age. How, we might finally consider has secular, political, democracy responded?

Pluralism, democracy and deracination

Since the end of the Cold War, the pursuit of political and spiritual purification and an apocalyptic transformation of a corrupt world order is by no means confined to Islamism. Al-Qaeda, and now Islamic State, only represents the most obvious manifestation of this ideological style. The chal-lenge posed by the world purificationist and ethno-nationalist versions of political redemption is the latest in a line of revolutionary assaults on the political systems of modern Europe since the nineteenth century. Those attracted to this style and the utopian and apocalyptic solutions they provide to local and global problems pose a complex challenge for political rule and the secular order. At the core of the West's current difficulty is a need both to take utopian ideologies seriously, whatever their provenance, whilst reaffirming the idea of politics as a distinct form of activity practised within a territorial unit of rule.

Problematically, however, Western governments have underestimated the role that political religion plays in both recruitment and the passage to the violent act. Instead, a secular and pro-gressive commentariat disregards the ideological commitment, re-describing it instead as a response to social and economic grievance.

Yet, during the Cold War the Western understanding of political democracy 'sustained a common world in which we may talk to each other' that contrasted dramatically with a variety of ideological alternatives (Arendt, 1954/1993; Arendt, 2005; Crick, 1962/2005; Minogue, 1995; Oakeshott, 1962; Strauss & Cropsey, 1963/1986). Central to the political rule was a limited government that separated the public from the private realm (Strauss & Cropsey, 1963/1986, p. 3). Recognising this separation 'distinguishes politics, which we may loosely identify with freedom and democracy, from despotism' (Strauss & Cropsey, 1963/1986, p. 5). The over-arching public world of the state further maintains a structure of law appropriate to a self-determining association in order to sustain civil life. Against this, despotism considers everything in society its property (Minogue, 1995, p. 4). The politically religious postmodern versions of despotism see everything in society, and on the planet, ripe for intervention and regulation.

It further assumes, as we have seen, the achievement of a post-democratic state of perfection via resistance, regulation and purification. Politics, by contrast, accepts the human condition for what it is, and imperfectible. As Bernard Crick observed, politics is 'not religion, ethics, law, science history, or economics. It neither solves everything nor is present everywhere' (Crick, 1962/2005, p. 23). Crucially, it is about the acceptance of difference rather than the despotic impo-sition of unity. 'There is a point', as Aristotle first recognised,

> at which a polis by advancing in unity will cease to be a polis: there is another point short of that at which it may still remain a polis, but will none the less come close to losing its essence and will become a worse polis. It is as if you were to turn a harmony into mere unison or reduce a theme to a single beat, the truth is that the polis is an aggregate of many members. (1946, p. 200)

Ultimately, politics can only occur in organised units of rule whose members, or citizens, accept themselves to be an aggregate of many members and not a single tribe, religion, interest or tra-dition. It necessarily recognises a plurality of contending interests at its foundation. Political freedom is a result of this recognition. Politics becomes the public activity of free citizens, and freedom is the privacy of citizens from public action. Consequently, politics became a plausible response to the problem of governing a complex, modern state. Yet it offers only one solution to the problem of order. Despotism, oligarchy and even democracy in its majoritarian tyranny, or direct activist version, are alternative and anti-political forms of rule.

A particular order thus sustains the practice of political freedom and political rights. The authority to make a common law through representative institutions and apply it equally to all citizens requires, as Thomas Hobbes first observed, a Leviathan state. As Steven Pinker subsequently demonstrated 'a state and a judiciary with a monopoly on the legitimate use of force can ... inhibit the impulse for revenge, and circumvent the self-serving biases that make all parties believe they are on the side of the angels' (Pinker, 2011, pp. 682–683).

'We can also trace', Eric Voeglin contended, 'the attempts to rationalize the shelter-function of the *cosmion*, the little world of order, by what are commonly called political ideas' (cited in Cooper, 1999, p. 39). In other words, political thinking from Aristotle to Pinker rationalizes the territorially bounded shelter that gives meaning to human life against the external forces of 'disintegration and chaos, a shelter in the end that is maintained by force'. (Cooper, 1999, p. 39)

Ultimately, the order that enables political activity and commerce to thrive confined within a limited territorial unit or state that exercises a monopoly on the legitimate use of violence to sustain itself. It is not transnational or international. Politics thus requires the constitutionally limited authority of the state for its practice. Maintaining borders and the terms of membership are matters of prudence rather than abstract global justice. As early modern theorists of the state from Machiavelli to John Milton acknowledged, the *res publica* (the public thing) has the right to maintain itself. This right, moreover, may be expressed in terms of both the right of the state's survival as well as the conditions for, in the language of Miltonic republicanism, maintaining liberty and virtue.

Somewhat problematically, however, the political classes in the West have abandoned politics, properly understood, together with a prudential statecraft in pursuit of post-national projects of rational modernisation and globalisation. More particularly, catch-all political parties, that, during the first wave of modern representative political democracy, served as the political vehicle for marshalling a collocation of social and political interests and organising citizens for political engagement, have given way to cartel parties. Indeed, since the end of the Cold War, mainstream political parties 'adopt themselves to declining levels of participation and involvement in party activities by not only turning to resources provided by the state but by doing so in a collusive manner' (Katz & Mair, 1995, pp. 5–31). Significantly, in the post-Cold War era, democratically elected governments increasingly function like 'a large media corporation' (Barnett, 2000, p. 3). This fusion of the media and political domains has produced a new system of government, where 'techniques of manipulation, deception, smear and constitutional capture have taken power away from the ordinary voter and placed it in the hands of the (new) political class' (Oborne, 2007, p. xvii). Such manipulative corporatism has fractured the relationship between political elites and the people and led to a hollowing out of mainstream parties and the democratic political process. Peter Mair even declared that:

> The age of democracy has passed. Although the parties themselves remain, they have become so disconnected from the wider society, and pursue a form of competition that is so lacking in meaning, that they no longer seem capable of sustaining democracy in its present form. (2013, p. 1)

The changing character of modern Western political parties has affected their standing, legitimacy and effectiveness and, as a consequence, the legitimacy and effectiveness of political democracy. Problematically, political leaders and the parties they serve no longer represent ordinary people but function as emissaries of a centralised bureaucracy. This is particularly the case in Europe, where mainstream party elites have turned the EU into a 'protected sphere, safe from the demands of voters and their representatives'. Accordingly, a technocratic directorate has progressively taken decision-making away from national parliaments. From the currency and the economy, to counter-terrorism and immigration, decisions are made elsewhere. Somewhat disturbingly, politicians encouraged this process, as they sought 'to divest themselves of responsibility for potentially unpopular policy decisions and so cushion themselves against possible voter discontent' (Mair, 2013, pp. 125–130).

Consequently, mainstream political parties are failing because 'the zone of engagement – the traditional world of party democracy where citizens interacted with and felt a sense of attachment to their political leaders – is being evacuated' (Mair, 2013, p. 16). This abandonment has led to a burgeoning popular indifference to politics and created a climate conducive to extremist and anti-political enthusiasms. Politics and politicians appear increasingly remote to the quotidian concerns of citizens they ostensibly represent. The rhetoric of manipulative populism reinforces this perception. Leaders such as Tony Blair in the UK, Barack Obama and Donald Trump in the US, and Kevin Rudd and Malcolm Turnbull in Australia presented themselves as above politics (Mair, 2013, p. 3). As a result, Mair noted:

> Citizens withdraw from parties and a conventional politics that no longer seem to be part of their own world … There is a world of the citizens – or a host of particular worlds of the citizens – and the world of the politicians and the parties and the interaction between them steadily diminishes. (2013, p. 98)

Arising out of this new alignment, European political and business elites have come very close to the abolition of 'what we have been brought up to regard as politics and have replaced it with rule by bureaucrats, bankers and various kinds of unelected expert' (Osborne, 2014, p. 12).

Nor are things much better on the other side of the Atlantic. As David Runciman argues, during the financial crisis that overwhelmed the US economy after September 2008, 'no one could doubt that democracy was deeply implicated' (Runciman, 2013, p. 265). The fact that Obama presented himself as a post-partisan and post-political redeemer only heightened the sense of political malaise. At the same time, the failure of the long wars in Iraq and Afghanistan seemed to confirm the fact that democracies have not learned how 'to avoid unwinnable wars' (Strachan, 2014, p. 3).

It is no surprise that the period after 1990 that witnessed the rise of manipulative populism coincided with the rise of political religions that sought solutions to the disenchantment and hollowing out of political democracy in Islamist, right-wing populist, or transnationally progressive post-political soteriologies. These versions of Salvationism offer refuge from the disintegration of political practice properly understood in ways that the Western political classes failed to appreciate. As former Liberal Democrat leader, Lord Ashdown, observed, 'if this is the age of the collapse of [democratic] beliefs, the dissolution of institutions, then what you are going to find is people who find an appeal in answers that are simplistic' (cited in Coates, 2014, p. 1). These simplistic answers range from a recourse to jihadism and the white supremacist reaction, to communities in the UK, 'born under other skies [and] … from other cultures who would prefer to police themselves' (*The Guardian*, 19 January 2014). When minority communities 'take the law into their own hands', the rule of law, integral to a political self-understanding, 'dissolves' (*The Guardian*, 19 January 2014).

Yet, although a crisis of politics now threatens Western democracy, it has survived similarly severe crises in the course of the twentieth century. As David Runciman shows, the history of democracy in the modern age is both cumulative and cyclical: 'The experience of crisis builds up over time, no crisis is quite like the one before, because the one before is always there to serve as a warning and a temptation.' Yet, the 'repeated sequence of democratic crises over the past hundred years also describes a single over-arching narrative', namely that twentieth-century democracy was a success story. At the end of that short century (1914–1990), liberal democracies emerged as the richest and most powerful states the world has ever seen. 'They had defeated their enemies and enabled their citizens to prosper. But success on that scale comes at a price' (Runciman, 2013, p. 296). Ironically, it 'blinded democracies to the enduring threats they face'. Indeed, 'the cumulative success of democracy … created the conditions for systemic failure (Runciman, 2013). The elite abandonment of the idea of politics and the failure of established representative political parties contributes to the potential for failure. Democracies, however, have a way of stumbling through crises, and it is perhaps this capacity over time that gives it an edge, over its politically religious rivals.

Acknowledgements

I would like to thank my two reviewers for their suggestions to improve this paper.

Disclosure statement

No potential conflict of interest was reported by the authors.

References

Adokoyo, R. (2014, May 26). Meet the new faces in the European parliament. *The Guardian*. Retrieved from https://www.theguardian.com/world/2014/may/26/meet-the-new-faces-in-the-european-parliament
Arendt, H. (1951). *The origins of totalitarianism*. New York, NY: Houghton, Mifflin Harcourt.
Arendt, H. (1954/1993). *Between past and future*. London: Penguin.
Arendt, H. (2005). *The promise of politics*. New York, NY: Random House.
Aristotle. (1946). *The politics*. Oxford: Clarendon Press.
Barnett, A. (2000, May–June). Corporate populism and partyless democracy. *New Left Review*, 3, 80–89.
Beam, L. (1992, February). Leaderless resistance. *The Seditionist*, 12, 1–3.
Berwick, A. (2013). *2083: A European declaration of independence*. Retrieved from https://publicintelligence. net/anders-behring-breiviks-complete-manifesto-2083-a-european-declaration-of-independence/
Breitbart. (2016, July 31). *Nationalists set to win Austrian rerun presidential race*. Retrieved from http://www.breitbart.com/london/2016/07/31/right-wing-nationalist-set-win-rerun-austrian-presidential-race/
Carswell, C. (2013, October). *Why is the Front National is the most popular party in France*. Retrieved from http://boscoredmondworld.blogspot.co.uk/2013/10/why-is-front-national-most-popular.html
Chomsky, N. (2004). *Hegemony and survival: America's quest for global dominance*. London: Penguin.
Church of Jesus Christ, Christian Aryan Nations Converse, Louisiana. (2016). Retrieved from https//:www.aryan-nations.org
Coates, S. (2014, January 4). Voters trust in society is collapsing, says Ashdown. *The Times*, p. 1.
Cohen, N. (2007). *What's left? How the left lost its way*. London: Harper.
Cohn, N. (1969). *The pursuit of the millennium*. London: Palladin.
Cooper, B. (1999). *Eric Voegelin and the foundations of modern political science*. Columbia: University of Missouri Press.
Crick, B. (1962/2005). *In defence of politics*. London: Continuum.
Fonte, J. (2002, Summer). Liberal democracy versus transnational progressivism: The future of the ideological Civil War within the West. *Orbis*, *46*(3), 1–14.
Gentile, E., & Mallett, R. (2000). The sacralization of politics: Definitions, interpretations and reflections on the question of secular religion and totalitarianism. *Totalitarian Movements and Political Religions*, *1*(1), 18–55.
Griffin, R. (1991). *The nature of fascism*. London: Pinter.
Hardt, M., & Negri, A. (2001). *Empire*. Cambridge, MA: Harvard University Press.

Hoffman, B. (1988). *Recent trends and future prospects of terrorism*. Santa Monica, CA: Rand.

Hugler, H. (2015, October 22). Warnings over resurgence of German far right movement Pegida. *The Daily Telegraph*.

Jones, D. M. (2005). Peace through conversation. *The National Interest*, *79*(1), 53–57.

Katz, R. S., & Mair, P. (1995). Changing models of party organization and party democracy: The emergence of the cartel party. *Party Politics*, *1*(1), 5–28.

Levy, B.-H. (2008). *Left in dark times: A stand against the new barbarism*. New York, NY: Random House.

Lord Paddy Ashdown cited in Sam Coates, 'Voters' trust in society is collapsing, says Ashdown. (2014, January 4). *The Times*.

Lowe, J. (2016, February 5). Pegida UK: What does Tommy Robinson want? *Newsweek*. Retrieved from http://europe.newsweek.com/tommy-robinson-edl-pegida-uk-423623

Macdonald, A. (a.k.a. William Luther Pierce). (1978). *The turner diaries*. Hillsboro, WV: National Vanguard Books.

Macdonald, A. (1989). *Hunter*. Hillsboro, WV: National Vanguard Books.

Mair, P. (2013). *Ruling the void: The hollowing out of Western democracy*. London: Verso.

Meleagrou-Hitchens, A., & Brun, H. (2013). *A neo-nationalist network: The English Defence League and the European Counter Jihad Movement*. London: International Centre for the Study of Radicalization and Political Violence.

Michael, G. (1995). *Lone Wolf terror and the rise of leaderless resistance*. Nashville, TN: Vanderbilt University Press.

Minogue, K. R. (1995). *Politics: A very short introduction*. Oxford: Oxford University Press.

Oakeshott, M. (1962). *Rationalism in politics and other essays*. London: Methuen.

Osborne, P. (2007). *The triumph of the political class*. London: Pocket Books.

Osborne, P. (2014, January 1). Europe is slowly strangling the life out of national democracy. *The Daily Telegraph*.

Pantucci, R., & Ellis, C. (2016). *Lone actor terrorism*. London: RUSI.

Pinker, S. (2011). *The better angels of our nature: Why violence has declined*. London: Penguin.

Runciman, D. (2013). *The confidence trap: A history of democracy in crisis from World War I to the present*. Princeton, NJ: Princeton University Press.

Sennels, N. (2012). *Gates of Vienna*. Retrieved from gatesofvienna.blogspot.co.uk/p/nicolai-sennels.html

Southern Poverty Law Center. (2004). Retrieved from https://www.splcenter.org/ … /turner-diaries-other-racist-novels-inspire-extremist-violence

Southern Poverty Law Center's Hatewatch site. (2016, May). Retrieved from https://www.splcenter.org/hatewatch/2016/06/16/alleged-killer-british-mp-was-longtime-supporter-neo-nazi-national-alliance

Speigel. (2016). *Right wing extremism*. Retrieved from http://www.spiegel.de/international/topic/right_wing_extremism/

Standing, G. (2011). *The precariat: The new dangerous class*. London: Bloomsbury.

Sternberg, E. (2010, Winter). Purifying the world: What the new radical ideology stands for. *Orbis*, *54*(1), 61–86.

Strachan, H. (2014). *The direction of war contemporary strategy in historical perspective*. Cambridge: Cambridge University Press.

Strauss, L., & Cropsey, J. (1963/1986). *History of political philosophy*. Chicago, IL: Chicago University Press.

Valle, A. (2010). *I Rossi Neri, Verdi: la convergenza degli Estremi opposti. Islamismo, comunismo, neonazismo*. Torino: Lindau.

Voegelin, E. (1974). *Political religions and the Ecumenic Age, vol. 4 in order and history 5 Vols*. Baton Rouge: Louisiana University Press.

Ye'or, B. (a.k.a. Giselle Litman). (2005). *Eurabia the Euro-Arab axis*. Teaneck, NJ: Fairleigh Dickinson University Press.

Newspaper Articles and Websites

Anonymous. (2014a). http://www.youtube.com/watch?v=AcDnjFemPuc.

Anonymous. (2014b). http://www.youtube.com/watch?v=o74sMCU_kPQ. (b)

Communities 'taking law into their own hands', says police chief inspector. (2014, January 19). *The Guardian*.

Murder of Lee Rigby provokes anti-Muslim attacks. (2013, May 23). *The Daily Telegraph*.

Islamophobia attacks rise dramatically after the murder of Lee Rigby. (2013, May 28). *The Independent*.

Worldsocialforum. http://www.forumsocialmundial.org.br/noticias_1.php?cd_news=2556&cd_language=2

Index

Page numbers in italics refer to figures. Page numbers in bold refer to tables. Page numbers with "n" refer to notes.

INDEX